To Andy —

With Best Wishes, from

Mervyn Spencer Doe (Ted).

and Auntie.

A ROUGH PASSAGE

A Rough Passage

by

Mervyn Spencer Doe

The Pentland Press Limited
Edinburgh · Cambridge · Durham · USA

First published in 1999 by
The Pentland Press Ltd.
1 Hutton Close
South Church
Bishop Auckland
Durham

British Library Cataloguing in Publication Data.
A catalogue record for this book is available
from the British Library.

ISBN 1 85821 728 8

Typeset by George Wishart & Associates, Whitley Bay.
Printed and bound by Bookcraft Ltd., Bath.

In memory of my Father
Spencer Alfred Doe,
who died, three months before I was born,
and also in memory of three of my four brothers,
Spencer Farel, Lewis William and Phillip Sidney,
who experienced the National Children's Home
and Orphanage, in those hard days
of the 1920s to 1930, with me.

Douglas Harold Doe, my fourth brother, who was
two years older than me, was the baby at the
time of our father's death, was taken and brought
up by our Uncle Harry, who lived in
Haverhill, Suffolk.

Acknowledgements

My grateful thanks are due to the following for allowing their photographs of aircraft to be used in this book:

Fleet Air Arm Museum,
RNAS, Yeovilton, Somerset.

The Imperial War Museum,
Lambeth Road, London.

Finally, I would like to take this opportunity of thanking my daughter, Sandra Jane Doe, whose sterling work made this book possible.

And for the help and patience of my wife, Cynthia Rosamund Doe, who encouraged me during the last five years.

Illustrations

The orphanage with John Fowler House on the left 5
Group photograph, John Fowler House, 1923 19
Tea in the Dell, 1925 35
The Author on Overton Hill 37
The Author with Eddie, 1926 43
My first uniform – the Author in 1938 134
HMS *Cumberland*, County Class cruiser, Portland, June 1939 ... 146
The *Graf Spee* shortly after being scuttled 162
HMS *Hood* – a beautiful lady 166
The Author on leave after the Dakar operation, 1941 174
Blackburn Skua 183
The Author in Clacton-on-Sea, 1951 194
Armistice Day, 1996 – after my stroke 197
The Author at York Minster 198

Chapter I

I found myself on a train, going from Winchester to Chester, for one week's holiday in Chester with my wife Cynthia. We had looked forward to it: the area had memories for me, memories of a bygone age.

The train rumbled over an iron bridge. I knew instinctively we were entering Leamington Spa station, the place where I was born. Slowly the train came to a halt; while we sat there, my mind went back to the summer of 1922. Then, my brother shared the compartment of a train at this spot; his name was Phillip and he was eight years of age. I was only barely four years of age – *where* we were off to, I did not know!

The train was about to move off, when suddenly a lady, dressed all in black, carrying a baby all in white, came rushing up to our compartment. She said in a hurry, 'Are you both alright – there will be someone to meet you at Chester!' Then she was gone! With that, the train moved off, Phillip managed a wave from the window – that was my mother.

We had lived at 30 Grove Street, Leamington. My father used to travel to Coventry each day on his 'Sunbeam' motorcycle. We had only lived in Leamington since about 1915; originally, we were of Suffolk stock, living in Haverhill and Ipswich, for hundreds of years, since 1188.

The Does were all blacksmiths, grandfather was a journeyman blacksmith, who had a smithy in Lavenham, but usually travelled all over Suffolk on his horse, 'Black Bess', who, in the end, crushed him to death in the stables at forty-nine years of age.

My father, Spencer Alfred Doe, had died in 1918 of enteric fever, at the age of twenty-nine. He had broken away from the family, and eventually became an aeronautical engineer, very much ahead of his time, fifty years ahead, so the family reckoned. He worked at the then known 'Standard Motors', Coventry, and the 'C' Class submarines, Chatham, Kent. At Coventry, he worked on the Sopwith Pup, which was the equivalent fighter as the Spitfire was in the last war. As an aeronautical engineer, he was in great demand everywhere.

I was born in July 1918, the last son – the unwanted baby! I never saw my father! The eldest brother was Spencer, followed by Lewis, Phillip and Douglas. Spencer, Lewis and Phillip were born in Suffolk; Douglas and I were born in Leamington Spa. In 1918 Douglas was the baby of the family, so Uncle Harry took Douglas and brought him up in Haverhill.

Upon arriving in Chester, we were met by a lady who wore a uniform, like that of a Nun, only more so. In the centre of her collar at the front was a large badge in the form of a lifebelt, all in silver, above it read, 'To Seek and To Save!' with the letters, 'N.C.H. & O., Frodsham', below it.

She said, 'Are you Phillip and Mervyn?' Phillip replied, 'Yes.' She took my hand and walked us round to the adjoining platform, where there was a train waiting. I thought, It's not so big as the one we just left, this is a tiny little engine with a tall funnel, drawing three little coaches, and I said so. 'A tiny little engine?' I said. No answer! Tugging at my brother, I said, 'A tiny little engine?' 'Oh! shut up,' he said, Phillip had other things on his mind.

We eagerly climbed aboard the train; the guard walked quickly past the door waving a green flag and a whistle which seemed to be permanently in his mouth. 'Oh look – whistle!' I said. The train gave a jolt and we were off – to heaven knows where. The lady sat opposite me, she seemed to have a kind face, I stared at her. She quickly turned to me, smiled and said, 'You are only four years of age, aren't you?' Feeling a little shy, I nodded. Phillip said, 'Yes, he is!' 'Well,' she said, 'this is going to be a big occasion – you will be the youngest boy we have ever had at the home!' A home? What kind of a home? What we didn't know was that Spencer and Lewis had been there a year already!

After what seemed like an age, the train stopped and the lady said, 'This is Frodsham! We get out here!' As the door opened, I looked up to a great big hill, it looked as big as a mountain; at the top, there stood a great big tower. I pointed at it. The lady saw me staring upwards and pointing, and said, 'That is a Helter-Skelter!' I was none the wiser. 'Hurry! the train will move off!' 'What is a Helter-Skelter?' I asked, 'You will know one day, when we go up there!' she replied. We hurried down some steps at the side of the station and came out by some shops and what seemed a busy road. Over we walked to a car that seemed to be waiting for us; the driver was old and seemed to have a stern look on his face. Perhaps we had kept him waiting. What caught my eye was a huge moustache he was wearing, pointed at each end, and he kept twisting it with his thumb and forefinger. 'Right Ho! Let's go, let's get in then!' he said. I had a lovely seat in the back, between the lady and Phillip; then we waited for the car to start!

Mr Moustache, as I named him, because he couldn't leave it alone for five minutes, was busy with what was the starting handle. His head was down, facing the bonnet of the car, rattling the starting handle, trying to get it in. His face looked a bit flushed, then he started turning the handle, round and round it went! Nothing happened, so he stopped, gave each side of his moustache a twist or two, then taking a deep breath or two, started yanking it round and round, round and round – well, he gave up the starting handle, lifted the bonnet and started fiddling inside for a few minutes. He then closed the bonnet and returned to the starting handle with fresh gusto – it's going to start now! You could feel it, the way he returned to the job in hand! Yank, Yank, Yank, over and over he went, nothing seemed to happen! He stopped for a minute to get his breath back, his face was crimson! He gave a quick glance at his passengers in the back, but we quickly glanced anywhere. A deep sigh came from inside the car, I don't know who it was! 'Bad tempered, isn't he?' somebody said.

He began mumbling to himself, his breathing became more difficult, and after what seemed like an age, he had another go, putting all his effort into it this time. We could hear loud murmurings coming from the front of the car. Yank, Yank, Yank, it went, when suddenly, there was an almighty, BANG!! followed by a second BANG!! The air was full of smoke and the car jolted from side to side – it had started!

The man stood up, his face beetroot red through his efforts, black as thunder! We daren't look at him. I looked up at the lady, who whispered, 'He is the Governor of the Orphanage, Mr Schofield.' Oh dear!

Greatly relieved, he returned the starting handle to the rear of the car and got in the front. Before he drove off he gave his moustache the inevitable two strokes with his thumb and forefinger and we were off up the hill. After a long climb, we slowed down and turned right through some large iron gates. These were the 'Main Gates', and there before me lay a large round field, with a very high wall around it. The road, which went around it, was known as the 'Circle' came out at the Main Gates.

We turned left; there were four very large houses, on the other side of the Circle; there were another four houses, all identical, in between, at the top of the Circle stood a very large building; it dominated the whole place, which I took to be a church, or a school. I was soon to learn it was both; there was a high tower at the far end, where the Governor had his office, three floors up. He had an uninterrupted view of the orphanage, of the boys and girls. There were two entrances to the building, one for the girls at the far end, and one for the boys at the near end; this was strictly enforced. It was known as the Main Hall, which had a staff dining hall, kitchen and bakery, to the rear of the building. There was one other building on the right side, just inside and laid back from the Main Gate; this was the Governor's House.

We stopped at the fourth house on the left, just before you came to the Main Hall; this house was known as 'John Fowler House'. The lady thanked the Governor who had brought us from the station, then beckoned Phillip and I up a flight of steps to the front door, which was to the side of the house. The door opened, and there stood a middle-aged lady, who appeared rather stout, in a uniform, similar to the first lady, but with darker material. She was smarter, her white starched collar and cuffs were immaculate and her badge was gold, on a gold chain. *She* was the senior sister!

'Come along in!' she said, leading us across a red-tiled floor of the hall into a small room, which was nicely furnished and which, I learnt later, was the staff room. 'I'm Sister Florence, this is Sister Thomas. We are pleased to have you here in John Fowler House. Your two brothers are here, Spencer and Lewis! And who do we have here?' Looking down at me, she nearly made me squirm. I mumbled, 'Mervyn!' 'That's a nice name, isn't it? And how old are you?' she asked. 'Four!' said Phillip. 'And you are Phillip!' 'Yes!' said Phil. 'It will be nice, altogether in the same house! You will be the youngest boy we have ever had – you will be my baby!!' 'Who me?' Pointing to myself, I thought, Where is my mummy, I want my mummy!

I never cried, not the whole time I was in the orphanage – I grew bitter instead!

The orphanage was known as the National Children's Home and

The orphanage with John Fowler House on the left.

Orphanage. There are two hundred orphanages all over England and Wales, which are not to be confused with the Barnados Homes. Originally, it was known as Newton Hall. The house still exists and lies to the south of the orphanage, in its own grounds, and large gardens which supply the orphanage with regular supplies of fruit and vegetables. The house is now used for sick boys and girls, but serious cases go to Chester Infirmary; a small number of children live there.

Looking at her watch, Sister Florence said, 'It won't be long for tea, I think it best to go and have a wash and freshen up after your long journey and then we can go around and look at the house!' With that, we left the Staff Room, never to see it again, across the red-tiled hall, through double swing doors to the washplace, where we gave our hands and face a rinse and wiped ourselves on a towel that the Junior Sister provided. On thanking her, we returned through the swing doors, making our way opposite to the left of the Staff Room. We opened the door and were informed this was the Day Room. All the main walls were covered by lockers, one for every boy in the house. Just inside, on the left, stood an upright piano; the first thing which caught my eye, was a large picture above it. Phillip saw it too because he said, 'The Boyhood of Raleigh!' It was a picture of two young boys sitting on a beach, with an old sailor pointing out to sea, and was the first thing which had an effect on me. There was one remaining item in the room, an enormous square table in the centre of the room, with lots of chairs all the way round, one for each boy.

We turned left out of the Day Room, passing the Staff Room on our left, and opened the next door. This was the Dining Room; what I noticed were two long wooden tables, one situated on the left-hand side, the other, at right-angles to the first, down the right-hand side. In the far corner, diagonal to us, was a smart gate-legged table, seating for three – it didn't take long to work out whose table that was!

There was a large window opposite, which looked out on the Circle, giving a good view of everything and everybody in the orphanage.

The tables looked as though they were scrubbed every day and the forms too; at one end of each table there were two piles of enamel plates, and mugs, a large tea urn and a roll of American cloth.

I walked over to the large window and looked out – many another boy of four years would have burst into tears, but I didn't! I never ever shed a tear! Where's my mother? What are we doing here, the four of us, so far away from home? Perhaps we have done something so terribly wrong? Where was my Dad? I didn't know he was dead! Nobody said anything to me! Phillip picked up a book from the table. 'What's that?' I said. He replied, 'a Bible!' I remember that day at the orphanage in 1922, and the years I spent there, as though it was yesterday!

Suddenly, there was a banging of doors! The doors at each end of the Main Hall opened, out rushed the boys and girls from their respective areas, the boys rushed to the houses on this side of the Circle and the girls disappeared to theirs on the far side of the Circle; the Junior Sister stood at the front doors to greet them. 'Hurry now! wash your hands and faces, tea will be ready in five minutes,' she shouted, above the din of the boys being let out of school.

There was a hive of activity in the kitchen behind us; two of the older boys came in and started laying the tables; the roll of American cloth was flung out on each table till each reached the far end. It was not wide enough to cover both sides, and so it remained, just a cloth for the centre of the table. It always had that smell about it, alright when it was rolled up, but, boy! did it stink when unrolled. The enamel plates followed, then the large enamel mugs, one of each for each boy. Every place had a Bible and a hymn book alongside each plate, 'Oh! I wonder what they are for?' I said to Phillip. 'I don't know!' he replied.

The kitchen door opened, and a tea trolley was pushed by a Junior

Sister over to the gate-legged table; a beautiful white embroidered cloth was placed over it, followed by china and cutlery. Under the trolley she produced a silver teapot and silver milk jug, followed by carefully cut sandwiches and cakes; alongside their plates was a serviette with a silver serviette ring around it!

The boys came in, quietly taking their places at each table, standing behind the forms, quite still, waiting till everyone was at his place, including the Sisters, who took their places at the gate-legged table, over in the far corner of the room. Sister Florence said, 'You may all sit!' then she said The Grace! 'For what we are about to receive, May the Lord make us truly thankful, Amen!' 'Amen,' said every boy.

Sister Florence, then went on to say, 'There are two new boys with us today, brothers of Spencer and Lewis Doe, Phillip and Mervyn. They will be excused this week's Bible reading and hymn. The remainder of you will turn to the Book of Matthew, chapter so and so, read verses, so and so'. Having read out the verses, which seemed to go on and on and on, she turned to the Methodist hymn book and read out a hymn. 'Learn the first five verses only. They will be the lesson for this week. I will expect you to know it by Friday evening. One of you will be called on, at random, to stand up and say the passage from St Matthew and the hymn. Failure to do so will mean punishment!' There was total silence! She turned to Phil and myself and said, 'You may find room on the smaller table for the time being. They will be your regular places until I tell you otherwise!' There continued to be a hushed silence. I looked about me, everyone seemed engrossed with the lesson for the week. Phil and I looked at each other in total disbelief – a lesson you had to learn, every week; failure to do so, would mean punishment! What sort of home was this?

Then, suddenly, there was a mad scramble, the head boy at the end of the tables was handing out great slices of bread, two each, one inch thick, down to the next boy, the next, and so on, until two of these slices reached me. They were like doorsteps, and so they became 'Doorsteps'. They were covered with a white grease; it certainly wasn't a margarine and it didn't taste like dripping. The Sisters seemed to be enjoying their sandwiches and cakes from the stand! I returned to my plate, a mug of tea had just arrived from the other end, no sugar in the tea! It tasted foul, everyone seemed to be tucking in to their slices of cart grease. I noticed that fingers were going into a large white jar situated in the centre of the table, 'What's in that jar?' Phil said. Someone said, 'Salt!' I made a dive for it as it was right next to me, my little fingers nearly turned the jar over in my desperation. Every day there would be a large jar of salt on the table, which would be our only means of condiments we would see on the table. Anyway, the salt would give plenty of taste to the bread. Everyone ate as though they were starving. I reluctantly ate mine too, there was nothing else – eat, or you starved! Besides there were plenty of others who would soon take it!

All the boys were eating with one hand, and turning over pages of the Bible, or hymn book with the other, everyone engrossed with the week's lesson, swatting up, for Friday was not far away. The sooner you learnt it the better, some seemed to learn the lesson easier than others. Heaven help you if you happened to be one of the others. It must have been a nightmare facing this every week of one's life! Every week, for fifty-two weeks of the year!

When everyone was finished eating, we all sat still, waiting for the Sisters to finish. I wonder how many times I saw the nearest Sister raise her best china to her mouth to drink sweet tea, or put her serviette folded perfectly into her silver serviette ring. I wonder how many times, spring; summer; autumn; winter; over the years I saw that, it was like a ritual!

We made our way into the Day Room, the boys carrying their hymn books and Bibles; certain boys cleared the tables and washed up; every boy had a job to do, either first thing in the morning, or at meal times. No one was excused. I took a place round the very large table, and was given paper and some crayons. The Sister said I could do what I liked. I remembered the train that had brought us to Frodsham, so I started to draw the engine, all red; it had several large wheels and a tall chimney coming out of the engine at the front. I remembered it had the letters, L.M.S. painted on the side of the tender, which I learned later was, London, Midland & Scottish.

I was admiring my drawing, when the Sister said, 'It is time for bed!' It was 6.30 p.m. 'Time for bed?' I exclaimed. 'Yes, time for bed, you must be tired!' the Sister said. Other little boys and myself, we made our way upstairs, the foot of which was situated in the hall. Next to the swing doors, up two flights of stairs which led to a landing, on the left, was a toilet, then there was a recess in which there were three doors, two for the Junior Sisters, and for Sister Florence. Nearest to the small dormitory, which was on our left, she had a small window in that dormitory, so that she was able to keep an eye on us young ones. On the right was the large dormitory which contained at least twenty beds, with a door at the far end which I learnt later was a fire door, which remained locked and bolted. This led down an iron staircase on the outside to the yard below. The older boys said it was a way out to the gardens – we would find out as time went by.

I got undressed, put on a large nightshirt that came down to my ankles and jumped into bed, which was right underneath the window of Sister Florence's bedroom, which I would find out would open quite regularly. 'Now, come on, you little ones, hurry up, settle down and get to sleep!'

I didn't see Phillip for a day or two, in fact, it was several days. He was eight years of age and mixed with boys his own age group. I didn't see my brothers very often during the whole time I was in the orphanage. My friends would be my age. All four of us would grow up together, in all sorts of scrapes we would get into. My brothers I would see, from time to time. I had to be content with that. That was the way we grew up together as a family – distant! Never remembering one's birthday, never sending the others a card at Christmas, that's how it was in the orphanage; that's how we started life; that's how we grew up – distant!

It had been a full day, full of travelling, no longer would I be put into a crèche for the day; I was no longer a baby, every day at Dale Road, Leamington, I would remember one of the songs the nurse would sing:

Show me the way to go home,
I'm tired and I want to go to bed,
I had a little dream about an hour ago,
And it's gone right through my head.
No matter where I roam,
On land, or sea, or foam,
You will always hear me singing, that song,
Show me the way to go home.

Then, I thought, Why have we all been sent here? What have we done? We have left our home in Leamington! Left our mother! I couldn't find the answer, so with that, I fell asleep!

I had a rude awakening, being woken by the clanging of a bell! 'Come along now, get up you boys, come on, get up!' Sister was standing at the door of the dormitory, with a large brass bell, swinging it as though the house was on fire, as if her life depended upon it. When she was satisfied that we had all got out of bed, she turned and disappeared into the large dormitory; so did the noise. 'Good Heavens! What a rude awakening!'

I started getting dressed, and looked around, managing to sort some routine out of the chaos. We had to make our beds with the top sheet folded back to the bottom of the bed – it would show a wet stain in the middle of the bed. How many times during the years, my bed would reveal a WET BED? So did several other boys, including my eldest brother Spencer; sometimes he wet the bed, sometimes he didn't. How many times was the top sheet stretched under the bottom of the mattress, or the sheet pulled up under the pillow. We tried every scheme, but the Sisters always found out in the end, and we were punished for not owning up to it; it often meant going without your tea, standing for an hour outside the Staff Room.

Satisfied my bed was alright, I ran and slithered on the red polished linoleum floor, passing the toilet door on my right. A boy was piling up enamel potties, then emptying them down the toilet, putting a lot of urgency into it, putting them into three piles, for thirty boys – thirty potties! Suddenly, one pile came off balance, they fell in all directions, and rolled along the landing, spreading the contents in all directions, causing chaos to all the boys who were making their way from the dormitories to go downstairs to the washplaces. One or two of the potties rolled along the landing and before anyone could catch them, they emptied their contents down the staircase!

Now the staircase was always looked upon as a plumb job, only Sister Florence's favourites got it. In this case, Lewis, my brother, had got himself in her good books and had become her favourite boy. He could do no wrong, butter wouldn't melt in his mouth! He had made his bed and was starting to do his job before breakfast, coming upstairs with a dustpan and brush, and was just rounding the well of the stairs, when Whoosh! he was met by a deluge! He caught the contents of what happened to be two potties stuck together, until they hit the first step, when they separated – not just one, but two potties!

I did not wait to see how much he was soaked, or what the outcome was. I dashed past 'Lew' on the stairs, and down through the swing doors of the washplace. There, the Junior Sister was waiting for us little ones to come down to be washed. 'Come now, Mervyn, let's have a good wash!' she said. I waited over the basin for the Sister to plaster me with soap, which was horrible. I tasted it. I learnt later, very much later, that we used carbolic soap. I dried myself, with the help of the Sister, when into the washplace came Sister Florence, looking a little put out! She dashed straight into the large linen cupboard on the left, passing unsavoury remarks to the Junior Sister as she passed, retrieved a clean shirt for Lewis, who by now was washing his head and right down for the second time that morning. He looked at me, but never spoke, so I ignored him, he seemed pre-occupied with the mess that had gone all over himself. Little did I know then, he would hardly ever speak to me the whole time I was in the orphanage; he spoke to Phillip, never to me. I suppose it was because of his status in the family. He was the second eldest, six years older than I was, and so the 'die was cast', as far as Lewis and I were concerned. We grew up poles apart, although we were both the same, mechanically minded, and remained that way all our lives.

After my wash, I was rolling down my sleeves, when suddenly I was attracted by what all the boys were doing over by the shoe rack. There seemed to be a mad scramble over some shoe brushes; when I looked closer, there was only one brush. What were they putting on their shoes? Horrible black muck which wasn't shoe polish – it wouldn't shine! It was Dubbin! I learnt much later – 'A Preparation of Grease, for Preserving and Softening Leather.' These shoes would never shine again, ever! The Junior Sister saw me watching the boys and said, 'It's alright, Mervyn, you don't have to do your shoes!' With that I went through the swing doors and across the tiled hall into the Dining Room. I took my place at the top of the table, where I had sat the evening before, near the window. I had time to look around the room. The table I was sitting at was for the junior boys; on the larger table, at the other side of the room, next to the kitchen, sat Spencer, Lewis, and the older boys; Phillip sat at the far end of my table; the boys around me would be my mates as time went by.

The door opened, older boys came in, two or three of them carried thirty 'doorsteps' each, the others carried two very large 'dixies' of porridge, with two ladles, followed by the Junior Sisters with their breakfast of bacon and eggs, toast and coffee, served on the best silverware and crockery. Then, when Sister Florence came in, silence reigned, the Senior Sister, who, by now we had come to recognise, stood at her place at the gate-legged table and waited; when everyone was quiet, and not until, and only then, she said, 'You may all sit!' When everyone was seated and heads bowed, she said 'The Grace! For what we are about to receive, may The Lord make us truly grateful. Amen!' I looked across at their table! The plates started rattling down to my end; I sat and looked.

We had a plateful of lumpy porridge as big as golf balls, on the other plate I had a large 'doorstep', bigger than ever before, an inch and a half thick, with no margarine on it, just jam. Sometimes it was treacle, I don't know which tasted the best. By now, I was hungry; I tucked in, finishing off with a large mug of tea with no sugar; bread with no margarine on it, just jam, ugh!

With breakfast over, we young ones retired to the Day Room, while the older boys had to clear the breakfast things and wash up; by then it was time to go to the Main Hall for prayers.

A Junior Sister came in and said, 'Phillip and Mervyn, will you come with me, please!' Through the swing doors we went, stopping outside the large linen cupboard; we waited, seeing it for the first time, close up. The linen cupboard turned out to be a large store, with shelves for clothes and bedding; the Sister went foraging inside, and appeared with a pile of clothes. She said, 'Will you both take your pullovers, trousers and shirts off, please!' and on went the clothes that I would wear for the next two or three years. Because they were too big, the shirt was like a nightshirt; the trousers came right over my knees, held up by a pair of braces, which had to be adjusted and adjusted, until they wouldn't go up any more. 'They will be alright, you will soon grow into them, we haven't got things for a boy as small as you. How old do you say you are?' 'Four years old!' said Phillip. 'That is young, isn't it?' said the Sister. 'We don't usually have children at that age!' Perhaps I should have said, 'What's wrong with the clothes we came in?' but, in those days you never questioned anyone or anything, you just did what you were told, or you got the big stick! The big stick, that was the deterrent in those days. The shoes were too large, they came right up the calves of my legs. Phillip said, 'They are girls' boots!' because they had eyelets right up the front. The Sister said, 'I'm afraid they are the only boots we have of that size!' They were definitely girls' boots. Underneath, on the soles, were long bars of iron, that went from the toes to the instep, and on the heels, it was nearly all metal. These would never wear out, what with a regular dose of Dubbin overnight. Finally, I was given another jumper, navy blue, more in keeping with the orphanage; last, but not least, a handkerchief! 'Where do I put this?' The trouser pocket was stitched up, there were no pockets for anything. The Sister came forward with a safety pin, reached for my braces and pinned the corner of my handkerchief to it, saying, 'You will keep the handkerchief there at all times, the only time it will come off is on Friday nights, when I shall come round before tea and collect the dirty ones and give you a fresh one, to pin it to your braces!' So there was going to be nothing to put into your pockets, nothing, ever! Nobody, not any boy, would have pockets, they were all stitched up, work-day clothes and Sunday clothes too – what a state of affairs!

I laced up my big girls' boots, uncomfortable though they were, but as time wore on, they would stand me in good stead; in cold weather or wet, they would be a handy pair of boots. I kept on feeling for my pockets. I wasn't used to this, it was like a punishment; I didn't realise at that tender age what she meant. As the years went by, I realised only too well – we would never, ever have anything, from Mother, from anybody! The one possession we had – a handkerchief! That was pinned to your braces, morning, noon and night, and stayed there every week. Woe betide anyone who lost his handkerchief!

Later that morning we were marched over to the Main Hall, where after prayers were held every morning at 7.45 a.m., the hall was quickly converted to three classes – six, seven and eight – by heavy curtains that used to be drawn across between each class; thereby, there was privacy for each class. At the right end of the building, stood the tower, the ground floor of which was a room for the Kindergarten. Two other classrooms, in wooden buildings, were at the rear of the Main Hall, opposite the Boiler House, for four and five classes, while two other wooden-type buildings, further up the rear drive near the frog pond, were for two and three classes. Number two classroom was used in the evenings for choir practise. Phillip was taken to class six in the Main Hall; I was taken to the Kindergarten and there I stayed till lunchtime.

There was a flagpole situated on the edge of the lawn at the front of the Main Hall, exactly halfway between the boys' entrance and the girls' entrance; it was used as a halfway mark between the boys and the girls. Nobody dared cross it, only us little ones going to the Kindergarten which was where the tower came in – it was constantly under observation from there during daylight hours, because the girls side was strictly out of bounds to the boys and vice versa. The mast was painted white, and there was quite a ceremony when they hoisted the Union Jack on the King's birthday, the Queen's birthday, Empire Day and St George's Day, and of course, on Founders' Day!

At John Fowler there were approximately thirty boys, with four houses on our side of the Circle and four houses on the girls' side, large houses, built in the 1800s, identical, and all named after old beneficiaries to the orphanage. There were 240 children in the eight houses. Newton Hall, had another thirty girls and boys, most of them crippled or with some ailment or other; those numbers remained constant while I was there.

At twelve o'clock the doors of the Main Hall opened, the boys and girls rushed out and went to their houses for dinner, as I approached John Fowler, Sister Florence, I noticed, came out of the house and walked in the direction of the Staff Dining Room, situated at the rear of the Main Hall, where there was a kitchen and a bakery. The teachers had their midday meal at the Staff Dining Room and were able to liaise with the Sisters as to how the children were progressing. The two Junior Sisters remained behind to attend to the boys' dinner; when Sister Florence returned, they would go and have their dinners.

We went to dinner – a plateful of hot stew with vegetables thrown in; for afters, we had sago, or frogspawn as we always called it. The younger boys, of which there were four of us, were excused the clearing away and the washing up, but no doubt, we would be pulled into doing the chores as we grew older. With nothing to do, we made our way out to the yard, via, the swing doors, the washplaces, the toilets and, of course, the back door. It was a large area, both sides of the house and round the back; the one thing which caught my eye was the iron staircase which came out of the door belonging to the large dormitory; we'll see more of the iron staircase later on.

Some boys played Hopscotch. Squares were drawn on the tarmac with chalk, and one boy went hopping from one square to another, kicking a flat stone as he went. Tit-tat was another popular game: six inches of wood, sharpened at each end, placed on the ground; with a good strong piece of wood, as long as a walking stick, you hit the pointed end, which would spin upwards, then hit it as hard as you could; the one who knocked it the farthest, round a given square, won. Several boys had tops! These were made out of cotton reels, with one end shaved off to a point, a stud knocked into the pointed end, painted with rings of different colours, and there you had a super top, with a whip made of a piece of wood and string. Then, there was the hoop, an old bicycle wheel with the spokes knocked out, with an old stick – many an hour was spent pushing the wheel around the yard.

With that the school bell rang and we returned to the Kindergarten. I can't remember what we did all day, but I do remember the girl who sat next to me, while I was there, was the sister of one of my mates; her name was Nora. I remember the hymn we always sang at the end of each day.

> Now the day is over, night is drawing nigh,
> Shadows of the evening, steal across the sky.

Each day was the same with slight variations, although Friday night was never looked forward to. We all sat at our wooden tables, waiting for the Sister to arrive carrying two linen bags, one for the dirty handkerchiefs, the other one with the clean ones in. 'Now boys, dirty handkerchiefs, please!' she would bellow, and tick us off in a long book as we handed one in. There was a bit of a scuffle along the table as one boy had lost his, so in front of all the boys he had to stand up, his name was taken, then he left the room, only to stand outside the Staff Room in the hall for an hour, without any tea. If he kept losing his hanky he would be reported to the Governor and that would mean so many strokes of the 'Stick'.

After the Sister had collected the dirty hankies and given us fresh ones, there were the prayers to be said, after we had had our tea, which consisted of two doorsteps spread with treacle, no margarine on the bread first, just treacle! I used to think it was awful, but one was hungry, and down it went, washed down with a mug of tea, no sugar!

Tonight was prayers night! Sister Florence was sitting waiting for the boys to settle down. Now everyone would have learnt the prayers that she had given out at tea on Monday night; any boy could be called upon, to get up when his name was called out, and say either the passage from the Bible, or the hymn, or both. It depended what she asked for and woe betide anyone who couldn't say either. Sometimes the passage from the Bible was long and difficult; the hymn was easier, the lines used to rhyme more often than not. Even today, seventy years later, I don't need to look at the hymn book at a service, I had to learn them by heart. If a boy didn't know it, he was punished, if he said it well, he would be congratulated by the Sister, if he said it the best, he might be asked to say it at Prayers in the Main Hall the following morning.

At 7.45 a.m. on Saturday morning, we all marched over to the Main Hall, John Fowler House took its place in the front two rows on the left, the Sisters sitting on the end of each row in the centre, the other houses took their places behind us, the girls on the right, boys on the left. When everyone was seated, in marched the Governor and took his place at the pulpit. His eyes used to narrow through his glasses, as if he were looking for somebody in particular. He looked left then right – you could feel people squirm – then he used to start on his moustache, left, then right; it used to come to a sharp point at each end. When he was satisfied and not until, he would say, 'We shall sing hymn number so and so.' After the hymn, a prayer, and then he would say, 'It gives me great pleasure this morning to ask John Fowler House to say the prayers for this week!' Up would get the boy who had been chosen to say the prayers! It was the only time I felt a sudden pride in John Fowler House! We all felt like clapping as our boy sat down, but the feeling was broken by the voice of the Governor, who said, 'We shall hear the prayer from Annie Fowler House, please!' And so a girl got up and said her piece – no doubt, they felt a sudden pride in her also.

I looked at Sister Florence, she looked as though butter would not melt in her mouth, looking several sizes bigger than she normally looks, and she was a large woman too.

The prayers ended with another hymn and a prayer, then the Governor came down from the pulpit, looked first at Sister Florence, which, no doubt put another feather in her hat, followed by a look at Annie Fowler House; then he walked out without a trace of a smile – he never did smile ever.

The rest of Saturday was more relaxed, and we were allowed to go up to the play area at the rear of the boys' houses; we went up a path that took you up a steep bank and there were lots of trees, which eventually brought you to the gardens and to Newton Hall, which went right round the building. It was a beautiful place, so peaceful, ideal as a small hospital for convalescence; the gardens grew every fruit and vegetable which supported the orphanage, even the cherry apple, which we liked to get hold of, and did, on our nightly raids on the garden when everything was in season, by way of the fire-escape, at dead of night.

The gardens were well fenced off by high privet hedges, and wire fencing, secured by a large gate which was padlocked. It was controlled by a Farmer John, a giant of a man who wore gaiters and boots, the largest boots I've ever seen. You could hear him coming to work every morning at 7.00 a.m., passing the rear of the house on his way to the gardens. There was no chance of any free apples, so I left the gardens and walked back to the play area where there was a vacant swing. Two or three older boys came over and said, 'Do you want a swing?' I said, 'Yes, please!' The oldest boy said, 'I will give you a leg up!' It was the first time I had been on a swing, and I felt elated. Here I was, going higher and higher, the boys were pushing me for all they were worth. They said, 'Hang on, we're going to push you higher!' so I gripped the ropes tighter, as I went higher and higher. I felt as though I was nearly upside down, and started slipping on the seat. 'Stop now!' I yelled, but the big boys were enjoying seeing a youngster of four years of age, frightened out of his wits. I could hear them laughing, but suddenly, I slipped, nearly off the seat, still swinging upwards amongst the branches. I was hanging on for dear life, every swing upwards seemed my last! I'll come off, I thought, then I will hit the ground with a bang. 'Stop that!' I heard somebody shouting, the swing eased, and the boys dashed off. I felt someone's strong hands bringing the swing to a stop – it was Spencer, my eldest brother, who had come in the nick of time. I thanked him and stayed in his company till dinner time; every time he tried to move off, I gripped his arm! I knew he would get fed up with me holding his arm, but there wasn't anyone else, no Dad! No Mother! There was only 'Spen'.

On Saturdays, we apparently went for a long walk, out of the orphanage. After dinner we all got ready, and I said, 'Where are we going then?' 'Down to the River Weaver!' said one of the boys. I hadn't heard of the River Weaver. 'Where is it?' I asked. 'Not far away!' said another. The Sister said, 'Quickly now, boys, in the hall in twos. We dashed into the hall, small boys at the front, big boys to the rear. The

Sister having counted us, satisfied that we were all there, marched out of the front door, passing the Main Hall to our right and the Staff Dining Room and the kitchens, up the cinder roadway, passing the wooden classrooms to our right. The boiler house and washplaces were to our left, then the choir hut, and four and five classrooms just before we came to the Frog Pond and the rear entrance of the orphanage.

The Frog Pond looked dark and deep, with hedges hanging low over the sides. Every spring it used to come alive, with thousands of tadpoles, then later the cinder road would be covered with minute little frogs making for the other side of the road and beyond. We were never short of a few frogs.

After passing through the rear entrance, we turned sharp right, down another cinder road, passed a farm on the left, then turned left into the main Kingsley to Frodsham Road, taking up a position on the right side of the road because there was only a footpath for about a mile, and the Sisters walked on the footpath. We always walked in the road, and that was the position we took on Sundays when we went to outside church, or for a walk when the whole house was together.

We came to another farm on the right and turned off right down another country lane, passing a spring coming out of a bank on the corner, the second spring we had seen while we were walking. The Frog Pond was also a spring, the water just gushing out of the ground. The area seemed to be inundated with springs.

We went down the lane for quite a while until we came to the river, where there were several brightly coloured barges all being pulled by a horse on the bank, turning right in the direction of Northwich, which was several miles upstream. First we would come to Delamere Forest, but that would be too far to walk that afternoon. So we kept on walking in single file along the river bank; there were several bushes we had to get round and the grass was thick and high; in fact, there were times when we sank in the thick grass, which seemed very wet in places, because my girls' boots were getting very wet, when suddenly a Sister let out a yell. 'Help!' she shouted. We at the front turned round to see her sinking in a bog. She had been walking over to the right of us, and was in a black slimy sort of a pond; but there was no water, just very thick grass, up to her waist. She was sinking, so the boys had to move fast; they all joined hands and pulled, but it was no good; other boys

Group photograph, John Fowler House, 1923.
Author in white at 5 years.

tore down branches from a tree and stuffed them down close to her legs and laid them down into the bog. At the same time the big boys in the chain continued to pull; in the end, boys pulled bushes apart and stuffed them down; the situation was desperate, but the combined effort had its effect, the Sister managed to get one leg up and the boys got branches underneath. Then she got one leg on to a branch and with the heaving she managed to get free and clear of the bog. What a mess she was in, black from the waist down, black slimy mud. She was very relieved, and so were we. We turned up a lane that led to Pear Lane, then turned right on the Kingsley Road, eventually turning left at the Main Gates of the orphanage. We never went down to the River Weaver again, not in all the years I was there.

Sunday was definitely a quieter, if not a different sort of a day. After we had washed, and had had breakfast of the lumpy porridge and two doorsteps, with just jam on them, no margarine, we all had to go to the large linen cupboard and get fitted out for outside church. It didn't take much changing for me and my other little mates; we were issued with white pullovers, trousers and white socks, so that we were presentable. The Junior Sister was so pleased that she told Sister Florence, who went to the Staff Room and produced her prehistoric Kodak folding camera and took photos of two of us on the lawn, outside the front of the house.

For the older boys, it wasn't so easy: they put on jackets which they called 'Norfolk Jackets', something out of the last century, with straps which came over the shoulders and fitted to a belt round the waist; there were buttons on the cuffs and on the trousers; the collar consisted of a high, stiff, white collar with a bow attached to the front. Last but not least, the older boys were given a navy blue cap; it had a badge on the front, with the letters 'N.C.H. & O.' on it.

The same procedure was going on in the other houses, no doubt. We left the house at 10.00 a.m., along with the girls and boys of the other houses, and soon could be heard the sound of marching feet, all going one way round the Circle towards the Main Gates, about 150 all told – the orphanage was going to church!

As I was one of the small boys, I was near the front and could see clearly ahead. The Main 'Centre' Gates were open, and the side gates were closed. It was the first day I would be going through the gates, which were huge iron gates, open only to vehicles, except on Sundays. The only thing was, there were no vehicles, only the Governor's 'Bull Nosed' Morris Cowley; there were no cars on the road in 1922–3. As we turned left, I could see and hear the orphanage marching to church. Right ahead and in the distance I could see the different houses of boys and girls making their way to Five Crosses Church and beyond they were forking off to the right to go to Holy Trinity Church, further down on the Warrington Road.

After what seemed like hours of marching we came to Five Crosses Church, a yellow-bricked building with five crosses on the apex of each gable. As we entered the church every boy who was wearing a cap took it off; down the right-hand side went the boys, down the left went the girls, turned into a recess, then turned about facing the pulpit and each other. The service started with a hymn, then a prayer; first we knelt, then stood up, and sat, then we went through it all over again. I felt half asleep, so much so, that I was standing when I should have been kneeling, and sitting when I should have been standing. I was constantly getting a dig in the ribs, or a knock on the shoulder, either from a Sister or one of the older boys; when we finally sat down I got frowns galore from the Sisters. I was glad when the sermon came, then I could really nod off. I got my final dig in the ribs when we all had to stand and it was the final hymn!

I was glad it was all over and we started to file out of church. The Minister was at the door shaking everybody by the hand. I would give him a kick on the shins, accidentally of course, at the same time as I would smile and shake his hand, but no! when it came for me to shake his hand, there was a sudden commotion back down the line of boys! One of the older boys had thrown a fit; all I could hear were people saying, 'Have you got a key, that will do the trick. No! a large key!' What on earth did they want with a key? The boy lay on his back, quite motionless;; he looked ill. Perhaps he would go to hospital. With that, it seemed as though the whole congregation was involved, including the Minister, so the Sister ushered the remainder of us outside the church and there we waited. What happened to the boy I never did know, as we were all assembled and marched off back to the orphanage. We went back with a sort of gusto, perhaps it was due to hunger, but we need not have worried what was for dinner because there was no cooking on a Sunday. That was a golden rule: we had cold fat meat and cold potatoes; there was always a jar of salt on the table; it took plenty of salt to hide the white fat, which nearly made me retch, but, there was nothing else to eat, no bread, or a drink of tea, nothing! What's for 'Afters,' I wondered; we soon found out, because the Junior Sister came round with a pear for each of us.

After dinner we retired to the Day Room, a large bookcase was opened in the Dining Room and books were brought through to the Day Room. The older boys had first preference, we, the young ones had to wait until the last. I had the choice of a boys' annual but soon got tired of it because it was nearly all print and no pictures. I found it tedious, as I couldn't read yet, so I went to my locker and took out some paper and crayons. I was happy drawing, and could pass many an hour, completely absorbed. I would draw engines, carriages, royal mail vans, a church on a hill with a steeple, cows grazing in a field, and so on. Later, there was a rose in a vase on the table, I copied that, and went on to draw roses of different colours, becoming interested in how the rose was formed with its many petals. As I grew older, I became quite an expert on painting the 'rose' in watercolours; it came naturally to me. My eldest brother became quite an artist. I used to spend a lot of time watching him paint the 'rose'; they used to be absolutely perfect; he would have become an artist if he had lived.

After what seemed like an age, the Sister called out, 'Tea-time, bring your books with you!' I took my boys' annual, to see if I could change it, and Sister gave me a book of trains, all trains in different colours.

Sister Florence said, 'Put your books aside, we are going to have tea!' The grace was said by Sister Florence, and round came the plates, and two 'doorsteps' with jam on and a slice of seed cake, which tasted delicious – cake once a week! After tea, we were allowed to remain in our places and read our books; only on a Sunday we were allowed to do this.

Sunday evening, and the prayers seemed to be longer, the service being taken by a lay preacher. I remember Farmer Reed who used to own the land above the rear of the orphanage, and used to take Sunday evening service. He had a loud voice, which used to wake up those who had nodded off, including me. 'Praise Be!' he used to shout!

We sat on the left as usual, facing the pulpit. Sister Ida, the choir mistress, was playing quietly on the piano; the choir sat right in the front right-hand corner, made up of boys and girls, Lewis and Phillip amongst them.

The hall quickly filled up, then the Governor and Farmer Reed came in, and the Governor took his place at the pulpit, Farmer Reed sitting farther back. The Governor gave his moustache, the one, two, three, treatment, and also gave a good look round at everybody, then he put a few slips of paper down on the pulpit. I thought they must be notes, but soon found out I was wrong. The service took its usual course, started with a hymn, followed by a prayer, then another hymn, followed by the first lesson, followed by a third hymn, and then Farmer Reed came forward and took the pulpit; the Governor retired to a back chair. Farmer Reed was going to give the sermon. With a voice like thunder, he started; everyone's eyes were upon him; you just couldn't let your mind wander; he was like a human thunderstorm; just when you felt like nodding off, he'd bellow forth. He had a habit of looking towards a large window of the hall so often that I had to turn half right to see what he was looking at, I couldn't see anything. It was only after two or three visits to the sermon on Sunday evenings that I realised it was an irritating habit that he had. After about fifteen minutes he finished the sermon. I wonder how many other boys and girls got an ache in the neck, turning round to see what he was looking at!

The Governor came forward and said, 'As you know from time to time we get reports of our old boys, who have emigrated to Australia,

New Zealand, Canada and South Africa! I have here,' handling the small sheets which laid on the pulpit, 'reports from the sheep farms in Australia, two from the wheat farms in Canada!' and so on, and so on. Some boys were settling down alright, others were not! Apparently, boys who had no parents were automatically drafted to the colonies when they reached the age of fifteen – they had no choice, they just went. One day you would see them, the next day, they were gone. From Frodsham, just a few miles to Liverpool, they left on a boat to heaven knows where, like ships in the night. This was going on continually, year after year, never to be seen again!

The Governor finished the service with a prayer for all the boys and girls who had emigrated, then a hymn, followed by a final prayer. It had seemed a long, drawn-out service. He finally came down with Farmer Reed from the pulpit. He stopped to have a few words with Sister Florence and passed a crafty look at me, as I was next to the Sister, being the baby of the house. He looked at me hard, as if to say, 'I'll soon knock him into shape!' I had to look away from him as I couldn't match his penetrating eyes. Every now and then, he would give his moustache the treatment, one, two, three; the other side got the same treatment, until they came to a sharp point.

We made our way back to John Fowler; we young ones were told to take off our shoes and go on up to bed; it was long after seven o'clock, way past our bedtime. It would be some time before the older boys would come up to bed. The Junior Sister saw us into bed and said, 'Goodnight!' As soon as she had gone downstairs, one boy jumped out of his bed, stripped the top blanket off it and laid it on the floor, then said, 'Come on, two on the blanket, and two to pull!' I saw for the first time how smooth and highly polished the floors were: all the floors upstairs were covered with a red linoleum, polished to death, which made a good skating rink. 'Go on, you two first!' We zoomed down the middle of the small dormitory, across the landing, turned to the left, through the door of the large dormitory, and gathered speed down the centre; we had quite a job to stop as it was a very long room. We turned round, changed places, we were pulling this time; down the centre of the large dormitory, across the landing, down the small dormitory. 'Good fun this!' we all said, and did a second run, going faster and faster each time, a supreme effort to go faster still. On the return from the large dormitory, we would get a hell of a speed by the time we reached the landing. Off we went, heads down in concentration, going like bats out of hell! Faster and faster we went, there was no stopping us, through the door, on to the landing, when, Bang!! a figure stepped into us from nowhere, collided with us, and went down with the two who were pulling in the centre of the landing, a slithering heap of bodies and blanket. It was the Junior Sister, who had just come upstairs to see if we were asleep. She was so shocked, she couldn't say anything for a second; while she was sorting herself out and trying to get her breath back, we dashed off, blanket as well; the Sister scrambled to her feet, chased us back into the small dormitory; we were in bed, clothes over our heads! She said, 'Right! You will be reported for this little escapade, we will see what Sister Florence has to say about it!' Having recovered from the shock of colliding with four youngsters and a blanket, 'Now get to sleep, and don't let me hear of another sound!' Fearing tomorrow and the punishment we would get, we were sound asleep before the big boys came up.

The next morning at breakfast, Sister Florence made the announcement, 'The four little boys who had been caught sliding up and down the dormitories on blankets,' and so on, and so on. 'They will be punished!! They will pay for behaving so abominably, they cannot be trusted," and so on, and so on! While this tirade was going on, I looked over to the big table at my brother. Spencer was smiling, Lewis was frowning hard at me, Phillip had his hand over his mouth, stopping himself giggling. Lewis looked annoyed – to think his young brother was mixed up in this business was too bad! I looked back at Sister Florence, who was repeating, 'They will receive punishment, all of them, they will report to the Staff Room at tea-time.' So we had to wait until the evening.

Teatime arrived and the four of us stood outside the Staff Room door. As we stood there the boys went in for tea, the doorsteps went past on a long tray, the tea-urn passed through the serving hatch, followed by the Sisters and their tea trolley with the silverware, sandwiches, cakes. The grace was said and the tea came and went. I didn't hear Sister Florence give out the lesson for the week, but no doubt she did. We wouldn't have to worry about the lessons for a while as we couldn't read yet – it was for the older boys. The lesson wouldn't affect us until we were out of Kindergarten and Class 3.

After tea, Sister Florence appeared and said, 'You won't be having any tea today, you'll stand there until it is time for your bed!' No tea!

Nothing until breakfast, next morning! We stood there grim faced, until the Sister had disappeared in the Staff Room, then one of the older boys came up and winked at us; as he passed he said, 'I'll see you at six-thirty!' At 6.30 p.m., Sister Florence opened the door of the Staff Room, and said, 'You may get ready for bed now, boys! Don't let it happen again!' With that, we dashed for the washplace, through the swing doors and bumped into the boy who had said he would see us at 6.30 p.m. He said, 'Right! come with me.' Through the swing doors and just past the staircase was a small door under the stairs. 'In here,' he said, and under the stairs were sacks full of potatoes, carrots, turnips and onions. 'Here, help yourselves!' We stuffed our jerseys and our socks with carrots and turnips, he opened the door just wide enough to see the coast was clear, then said, 'Right, out you go!' We said, 'Thanks' and nipped upstairs. This would fill us up a bit, we all said, and stuffed the contents under the pillows, hopped into bed and waited! The duty Sister would be up in a minute – no riding on the blankets tonight, just good little boys, who had learnt their lesson!

The Sister came up and said, 'You have got into bed early haven't you, it's surprising what a bit of punishment will do, isn't it?' and disappeared as quickly as she came up. No 'Goodnight!' to us either! Anyway, we were fixed up with nice fat juicy carrots; did we have a feed that night!

The bell clanged at 6.15 a.m. Today would be the same as any other day, or so I thought. We got dressed, made our beds, *no wet bed* last night! Thank heavens! We disappeared downstairs through the swing doors to the washplace. Lewis, my brother, was busy brushing down the stairs, but keeping his eye on the potty boy above him on the landing. I said, 'Hello, Lew!' thinking he would be pleased to see me, but no! He looked up from his job of cleaning down the stairs, gave a grunt and carried on. I thought, 'Oh dear, he's in a bad mood this morning!'

At breakfast, Sister Florence said, 'The two new boys, namely Phillip and Mervyn will report to the Boiler House for a haircut after school!' At 4.15 p.m. we stood at the rear entrance of the Boiler House, where a man answered the door and said, 'You've got to wait inside over there!' There was a big boy already sitting on the stool, with a man standing over him with a pair of clippers, clipping away. We waited until he'd finished, then he said, 'You're next!' pointing to Phillip. I stood back against the wall and waited.

Down at the end of the Boiler House stood a great monstrosity. The outside was white, several feet across and stood as high as the ceiling; it had a large steel door, about four or five feet from the bottom, and next to the door, standing several feet away, were two men leaning on their shovels. Every two or three minutes one would open the door with his shovel, apparently it was too hot to handle, and the other man shovelled several shovelfuls of coal onto the red-hot fire beyond the door. You could almost feel the heat from where I stood; it was what they call a furnace! The other man would shut the door quickly with his shovel, as it was nearly red hot.

One of the men beckoned me over to look at the furnace; at first I refused. But curiosity never killed the cat! So over I went, but I was afraid of the heat; it was a fiery furnace, like a great monster! He grabbed me, lifting me off my feet; the other man opened the door with his spade, he then approached the furnace holding me head first, closer and closer; the heat was scorching my face. Surely he's not going to throw me in? Then, with a push I was at the front of the furnace, with the enormous fire within inches. I'm going in! I thought. I was within an inch of the door opening, getting closer; I couldn't open my eyes because the heat was so intense. I screamed! And put both of my tiny hands out to save myself, full on each side of the door; there was a searing pain on my hands and up my arms, the front of my head felt burnt, my hair felt as though it was alight, there was a strong smell of burning skin. I screamed and kept on screaming! I pulled myself free and ran, I ran out of the Boiler House like someone possessed, and ran through the back door of John Fowler House, through the washplace, across the hall and barged into the Staff Room!

Sister Florence and the Junior Sisters were taken aback by the sudden outburst, but just one look at me was enough, with my eyes looking as though I had been to 'hell and back', full of fright! Sister Florence reached for her youngest boy. My face was scorched, the front of my hair just fell away like sawdust, my hands were so painful and stiff, I stood there and just shook with fright, unable to speak! Sister Florence picked up the phone. 'The Governor's House, something terrible has happened,' and she went on about 'an inquiry, dismissal of the people responsible', and so on. I left with a Junior Sister for Newton Hall Sick Bay, where the Nurse examined my hands and face, saying, 'What were they doing, trying to kill him? There will be hell to pay for this!' I had some stuff put on my hands, and had them all bandaged up. I sat down, they gave me a cup of tea and I began to think clearly for the first time, it was a terrifying experience for one so young, I wasn't six years of age! This was to be the first of many hair-raising experiences I was to go through during my years at the N.C.H. & O., Frodsham; some were accidental, others were not, but by and large, I had a rough passage!

Upon returning to John Fowler House, I spent the next half an hour or so giving Sister Florence a full account of what happened in the Boiler House. I only went there for a haircut, I wasn't interfering with anyone. I never heard what happened at the inquiry, it all passed over without me knowing. I was too young to understand such things, but one thing I do know, nobody was sent to the Boiler House for a haircut, it was done in the respective houses. The Boiler House was demolished after a few years.

What effect that had on me, I don't know, what I do know is, that after that episode, I started wetting the bed regularly, and continued to wet the bed until I was eight or nine years old, when I was taken to Newton Hall to be circumcised. That cured me once and for all, no wet beds from then on!

In 1924, I moved to Class 4. I remember it was winter time, the hut was timber built with concrete flooring. In the centre of the classroom was a coal stove, which the teacher, a lady, had to fill up every half hour. Anyone sitting over four feet away never felt it at all. I remember my feet used to get really cold, and my legs used to get stiff with cold; it was terribly draughty too. The teacher was a woman with black hair and black eyes to match; she was a bit of a martinet; we used to call her 'The Witch' but how wrong little girls and boys could be; it was her appearance that gave her that nickname! One Friday afternoon she opened her desk and took out a large tin and several packets of tiny little bags. They were triangular and held about an ounce of Dolly Mixtures in the old days. She called us out to her desk, first the girls, then the boys, gave each of us a bag, then filled our bags with the tiny little sweets. We all said 'Thank you!' then each one of us thanked her in turn. It came as a bombshell to us children, who only had a sweet *once a year*, if we were lucky; this happened every Friday afternoon, until we moved to a higher class. We were a well-behaved class from then on. We found out that she owned a little sweet shop down in

Howey Lane, just a few jars of sweets in the front window. This we found on our Saturday afternoon walks in Overton.

At about this time, when I was about six, Phillip and I had to go to Newton Hall for vaccination against TB etc.; they pricked our arms four times on the left upper arm, so we had four very large scabs which took a long time to clear. Today, seventy years later, I still have four scars, the size of half pence, just like the dice of four!

In the last year or so, of having been there, life at John Fowler House hadn't changed much; the only thing that had changed was the boys! Older boys had mysteriously disappeared, emigrated to the Colonies, while other boys had come to take their places, some as young as I was, other boys were older, and so the daily pattern continued. We still had our meals on wooden tables, with just a strip of American cloth that went down the centre; it was still tin plates and mugs, no sugar in the tea, no marg on the bread! Breakfast seemed to be the same summer and winter, porridge with lumps in, like golfballs, two doorsteps with jam or treacle on them. Dinners were mostly stew of sorts, with the occasional dumpling, if you could find it. Afters would be prunes, rice or sago. I cannot remember anything different, except later on, when a new sister joined John Fowler; she cooked a bread and cheese pudding! Great lumps of cheese between slices of bread – it was delicious! In the season we always had an apple or a pear for pudding, or a lettuce leaf, or two, for tea, but not very often.

Mondays were always new prayers for the week, every week, year in, year out. On Fridays we were called on to say them; the Sister would pick on any boy, so they had to learn the passage, being reminded on Mondays and Fridays with a Bible and a hymn book alongside each plate, otherwise they were kept in two stacks at the end of each table. On Sundays, it was always outside church party in the mornings, Five Crosses Church, or Holy Trinity, for every house, girls and boys. There was no cooking on Sundays, just the tea and porridge in the morning, otherwise it was cold meat, mostly fat, and cold potatoes, with lashings of salt in a big jar; in the winter it was beyond a joke, with a pear or an apple, or a piece of treacle tart, no other vegetables or bread – *that* would be a luxury.

I never saw any money in the first six or seven years. I only got a halfpenny now and again because I used to go out to the farm next door to the orphanage and volunteer to do any little job that the farmer wanted doing. He would take pity on us, but it only happened twice while I was there. I was about twelve at the time, just old enough to start using my brains, otherwise we never saw any money and to go out of the orphanage to scrounge, or earn a copper, was strictly forbidden. Severe punishment was meted out if they had ever found out. We had no pockets to put any money in anyway; if I earned a penny or a halfpenny, I had to spend it right away; it was no use harbouring it. We tried all ways to get the stitches of our pockets undone, but it was no use, they were machine stitched. It was hell in the winter as we never had any gloves or scarves or coats!

I used to walk up to the kitchens at the rear of the Main Hall, where there was a large grid in the ground that used to have hot steam pouring out of it nearly all day long, when I was frozen with the cold on a winter's day. I used to nip up to this grid for half an hour, till I felt the heat coming through the soles in my boots and up my trouser legs. I never caught a cold, but I did have terrible chilblains on my hands and my legs, and I used to feel chapped.

Every so often, we used to be lined up in the hall before breakfast, with our mugs in our hands. Sister would appear with a large and long enamel jug which would contain senna pods, and would give each boy half a mugful of 'senna'. We had to drink it on the spot, failing that, we would have a dessertspoonful of 'cascara'!

The Sisters lived much the same, with their beautiful gatelegged table, lace tablecloth, silver teapot, milk jug and bone china. It looked wonderful to us boys, with napkins beside their plates; at tea-time there was a cake stand next to the table, with an array of cakes on it.

Three times a year there would be a Sister's birthday! On that particular day, the Sister in question would be absent. It was always done at breakfast, the duty Sister would have a large book, open at the ready on the breakfast table, with a pen in her hand. Honestly, as if any boys, who were nearly all orphans, would have any money! She addressed the boys, 'How much are we going to give towards Sister So and So's birthday?' Spencer, my eldest brother said, 'What are we buying her?' We never saw a shop; Frodsham was a mile and a half away! We only went to the shops three times in the eight years I was at the orphanage. 'A new tea service!' There were all sorts of replies, some unprintable, said out of earshot from the duty Sister. Well, the majority of the boys had no money, let alone any savings, but she called out half a dozen names, including the 'DOE' brothers. I never thought we had any money, the thought of it never entered our heads. I expect my mother sent us a shilling or two, so it came as a big surprise – we had, one shilling and threepence each. We were rich, but not for long, as it would soon be whittled away, three times a year, on Sisters' birthdays! Spencer replied, 'About threepence each!' 'Threepence from each of you, Spencer, Lewis, Phillip and Mervyn?' she asked, 'Yes!' Spencer replied. 'Good!' said the Sister. Well, there wasn't very much from any other boys. Somebody was going to dig deep into their pockets, perhaps the Governor and the Staff would make a substantial effort. I think it was scandalous, asking us, the boys of the orphanage, to subscribe to their birthdays!

In 1924 Spencer was sent to Newton Hall, and I was put into the large dormitory. Perhaps they had decided to split us up a bit. I later learned that Spencer had a weak heart; I would never have thought it, however, no more riding on blankets, that was the reason, split us young ones up a bit. The large dormitory opened up other possibilities – there were raids on the gardens, at night, scrumping! I wouldn't be old enough yet awhile, as it was for the big boys! The raids took place regularly in the late summer, down the fire escape, the boys had got it down to a fine art; shoes were smuggled upstairs on the said night! half their clothes were on under the night-shirts, and so on. Boys had been doing it for years, handed down from older boys to the young who were coming up. The fire door was always left locked until the Sisters had gone to bed, when everyone had settled down for the night; ;then it was opened, who by, I never knew, but one boy had a key!

Down the staircase, three boys would go; once in the yard, up the bank at the rear of the houses, through the play area, with swings and the trees, up the path to the gardens just behind Newton Hall. The exact location of the fruit had to be discovered during the daytime, when a boy would ask Farmer John if he could retrieve his ball that he had accidentally thrown over. Once in, it gave him some idea where to go and how to get in and where the best fruit was. The gardens were impregnable, with a high wire fence and a hedge all the way round, locked by a metal gate, but it was not impossible to get into. The spoils were divided when they returned, the pillowcases having been tipped on to the floor. Many a boy gave hair-raising accounts of being followed by a fox, or being called by an owl and there was plenty of both at

Newton Hall, as it was surrounded by trees on all sides; there were plenty of spooky areas. One boy swore he'd been followed by a man in black – it was that sort of place, very black in places, and we were close to the Delamere Forest!

After a while the novelty wore off, there was a limit to how much you could take. I remember there were only one or two 'Cherry Apple' trees, which were very rare, but there were plenty of ordinary apple trees and pears. Other than that, there were turnips and swedes in the winter, which we were glad of, until it was too cold to venture out at night, the winters were too severe in the 1920s, and three foot of snow was quite common.

In 1924, Christmas came, we didn't look forward to it very much; the children used to visit houses with lanterns, singing carols, in the evenings, and first thing Christmas morning we used to sing carols outside Sister Florence's bedroom. The house was decorated with coloured streamers, holly and evergreens; the Main Hall was a picture; you couldn't see the ceiling for streamers; every nook and cranny had holly, or evergreen in it. We never received many toys as most of them were sent from the people of Frodsham and the area was very poor just after the First World War. We had a toy each, but more often than not, they were either broken, or had a piece missing, or minus a wheel, but we were pleased with them. I had a toy horse; the Sister made such a fuss about this horse. 'It's covered with real horse hair,' she said, and that put me right off the horse. Sometime in the spring, it appeared from the Staff Room with Sister Florence holding it. She said, 'There you are, Mervyn, your horse,' and took a picture of me holding it, I never saw it after that!

We had a large tin of boiled sweets brought round, one each, then it disappeared for good. Chocolates we never saw at all, just a boiled sweet each, then it went into the Staff Room cupboard, and disappeared!

Christmas dinner comprised of a slice of roast beef, roast potatoes and greens, no peas, never a turkey or chicken; we did have Christmas Pudding and custard, no mince pies though. Sister had made a large fruit cake for tea as a special treat, but when it came to cut it, the knife went right through, it was hollow! Some boys had got into the larder, turned the cake upside-down and eaten all the underneath until it was a hollow shell, turned it the right way up and it looked a very nice cake, nobody ever suspected that it was hollow – there was hell to pay, for weeks afterwards, boys kept asking, 'Who had the Christmas Cake?' 'Do you know who it was?' *I did know*, but I never told anyone, he was one of my best mates!

In the New Year we all had mumps, and had our throats painted with iodine but my glands remained swollen. I was later admitted to Chester Infirmary to have my tonsils out, or so I thought, the same day; I returned to the orphanage with a very sore throat. After two or three days, my throat got better, but my glands remained swollen until I was *twenty years of age* and in the Royal Navy, but more about that later. I returned to John Fowler House.

Spencer was at Newton Hall while I was there and I spent an evening with him, as the eldest Doe he was like a father to me. I admired him so much, he was very good looking and clever with his hands; he was a brilliant artist, his work always used to hang up in the Main Hall for all to see. He was busy making a crystal set, the forerunner of the radio we see today. How had he got all the wire that he had got round a magnet, how did he get all the parts? At school mostly, I think! Mr Hunt, the Headmaster, would always help boys who had promise: he must have known the basic theory of the radio!

He helped me in later years with my bows and arrows, and helped me to try to make a crossbow; he was a very interesting man and a first-class teacher.

In 1925 we had our own Scouts, Guides, Brownies and Cubs, known as the 1st Newton and Frodsham Scouts. Spencer was in the Troop and I joined the Cubs as soon as I was old enough. I was the youngest member; Lewis and Phillip were occupied with the choir activities. In the summer of 1925 the World Scout Jamboree was held in Chester, on what is now known as the 'Roodee', the racecourse. Lord Baden-Powell was the founder of the Boy Scouts, Lady Baden-Powell was the founder of the Girl Guides, and they were both coming to the Jamboree.

We were taken to Chester on lorries as there were no buses in those days, just the odd charabanc, which were a sort of coach, open deck, but were few and far between and not available for the orphanage. Sandwiches were packed in large hampers and a large tea-urn was provided for the trip. I remember arriving in Chester; we had a long walk to the Racecourse, not through the City but through the Sealand area. We started walking with a handful of Scouts; soon it was several hundred, then a thousand; it became imperative that we remained together as a unit. I was only a little boy, so I found the Scouts from everywhere in England a bit overwhelming and hung on to Spencer, who was with the others, for grim death. We had Chinese one side of us, with Scottish Scouts in their kilts on the other, and so there were thousands of Scouts to the left and to the right, with every colour, race and uniform. We kept very good order as we approached the racecourse; there were no white wooden railings, in fact, I didn't know if it was a racecourse. It was a large open space with the railway going behind us on a viaduct; we assembled en masse over by the arches of the viaduct, and waited. Lord and Lady Baden-Powell and the Mayor stood and watched us. There were scouts from every corner of the globe, from China, Malaya, India, from far away islands in the Pacific, America, Canada, Europe, Middle East, South Africa, Australia, New Zealand; the best and the most colourful were the Scottish clans in their beautiful array of kilts.

The saluting dais was over against the City walls where the new pavilion stands today. Lord Baden-Powell beckoned us, with a wave of his hand, to come over to him. The multitude of scouts slowly moved forward; there must have been several hundred thousand of us, a sight I have never never seen since, just one vast mass of colour. Spencer kept a firm grip on me as we went forward with the others, until he raised his right arm, then his left; we had reached the rope barrier which separated us from the dais and we stopped to a man. He called the Cubs and Brownies to the front, but I preferred to remain with Spencer.

He came down from the dais, taking his time, looking all around, left and right; we kept perfectly still – he was like a God to us and was all over the world, he must have felt proud. The first scout troop he had founded had turned into a brotherhood of man, worldwide; he had become a legendary figure, truly a great man. He talked to us all through a megaphone for quite a while; we gave him three cheers and sang Auld Lang Syne; he thanked us all for coming, especially those who had come from the other side of the world. We cheered him, again and again, until he was eventually lost in a mass of Scouts who had thronged around him. What happened after that I can't remember, I do know that we made our way back to the lorries, where the Staff were waiting to give us sandwiches and tea. We all sat down, amongst all the scouts coming and going, trying to take in all what had happened; it was a great occasion, and we might never see the likes again. We left eventually for Frodsham.

The year 1925 was an eventful one – King George V made a visit to Frodsham and Spencer went down to Main Street for the parade of Scouts.

During the summer we used to take our tea out in a great big basket hamper and a tea urn carried by the big boys. Saturday afternoons were so peaceful, long before the days when the motor car would monopolise the place – there was only the horse and cart. If you saw one car a day, it would seem like an event. We used to go to the Dell, which was only a ten-minute walk out of the rear entrance, passing the Frog Pond on your left, up a cinder lane, round to the left and there was the Dell, so quiet and peaceful there, away from the orphanage. It was a sort of hollow, made up of grass and bushes, the ideal place out of the sun, or to get out of the wind. We used to spend many an hour there, exploring wildlife, birds and insects.

One Saturday afternoon we went to Overton Hill, now called Mersey View, with the village of Overton halfway up its frontal side. The orphanage was situated at the base of the hill, to the rear, looking towards Northwich. We would go out of the rear entrance, past the pond, past the Dell on our left, going uphill, through Sandy Lane, with huge towering rocks on each side of the lane, which used to crumble with time and turn into tons of sand at the foot. You could not go through the lane without getting your shoes full of sand, which used to be nearly a foot deep. With Cromers Lake on our left and we would eventually turn right down a country lane, passing two caves on our right; it seemed odd two caves, a hundred yards apart in the middle of a field, quite dark and menacing, they always looked. Then we would cross a junction with another lane, still climbing all the way; after about ten minutes, the lane would fizzle out, and the ground would appear rocky. The first thing which caught one's eye was the Helter-Skelter; from a distance it looked like a lighthouse. Once round a bend, you got the most magnificent view, and had to sit down to take in the whole panorama; it took quite a while to acclimatise your eyes to the height and the terrific view. You were several hundred feet high, with the small town of Frodsham was lost from view, tucked underneath the foot of the hill; the only thing that could be seen was the railway from Chester, passing through Helsby, then it disappeared underneath the foot of the

Tea in the Dell, 1925.
Author, on the extreme left, with a 'doorstep' in his hands!

Overton Hills. To the left, about three or four miles distant could be seen Helsby Crag, a range of hills about the same height as ourselves, the top of which was sheer rock; so was Overton originally, all rock in the 1920s.

You could spend all day, just admiring the view, it was extreme, with Chester to the left, the Welsh Mountains as a backdrop in front of you, you had Port Sunlight, The Wirral and Birkenhead. The Mersey went from our right, behind I.C.I. Runcorn, Speke and Liverpool, and out to sea. To our sharp right, there was Warrington, Manchester and the Pennine range! Ahead of us lay the Frodsham Marshes, the River Mersey at its widest part, while beyond that lay Widnes; you could see deep into the heart of Lancashire.

If you had good eyesight and patience, you could see a lot of things going on, for instance, there were the huge three-masted sailing ships, full of grain, making their way up the Manchester Ship Canal, to Manchester from Australia and New Zealand. The canal was approximately eighteen or nineteen miles long, a terrific feat of engineering, built recently at great cost in lives of the men who worked on it.

There was the River Weaver, and next to it, the Weaver Canal, which joined up with the Mersey and went to the right under the fifteen arches viaduct of the railway from Frodsham to Warrington, to Northwich, which lay to the right of the orphanage. You could see several coloured barges, making either their way up to, or down the Weaver to Ellesmere Port; to the left of Helsby, every now and then, there would be a train passing underneath, like a little toy train.

After we had taken in the view, one or two boys started exploring the area, and the first thing that caught the eye was the Helter-Skelter. I was too young to climb that and slide down on the mats provided; in any case, it cost one penny (old money), and I hadn't got a penny! Alongside the Helter-Skelter was a stall which supplied lemonade and an assortment of small toys. I worried the Sister about a halfpenny whistle, which was an inch long, made of metal, and would last me for ages, or so I thought. The Sister bought me one. I think I was the only boy who had anything bought for him. I thanked her very much for it, so much so, that for the next hour or so I blew continually on it. I didn't realise I was blowing on one note, and nearly sent them crazy, until a Sister said, 'For heaven's sake!' Someone else said, 'Give him a ride on the donkey!' There were three of them, standing idle at the rear of the stalls, but it would cost a penny a ride, however the man said it would not cost us anything, as he could see we were from the orphanage. He picked me up, sat me on the saddle and gave me a free ride. Sister Florence took possession of the whistle, which I didn't see any more, then took a photograph of me on the donkey; you could see the girls' boots I was wearing, laced up down the front. I said, 'Thank you!' to the man. I could just clearly hear someone say, 'That will keep him quiet for a while!'

The hills in those days were covered with yellow gorse, which used to look a picture, provided you kept well clear of it, otherwise it would tangle up with your clothes. On the slopes of Overton Hill there were masses of land berries, like blackcurrants, about a foot high. Crab apples could be found here and there, but they were bitter to eat, so we left them well alone. Lastly, there was the heather, pink and purple, that used to grow everywhere on the hills; it grew in abundance in those days. Now I have a job to find a sprig of heather, and can't find any land berries! In 1925 the top of Overton Hills was nearly all rock, a red sandstone; we used to sit on the rock jutting out and let our legs dangle over the edge into nothingness. You couldn't see hardly anything of

The Author on Overton Hill.

Frodsham as it was tucked underneath the foot of the hills. You could see the railway coming from Chester, through Helsby to Frodsham Station, then it would go to the right over the fifteen arches viaduct, the River Weaver and next to it the Weaver Canal, before the line would disappear into a long tunnel before coming out at Runcorn East and then Warrington, eventually to Manchester.

In 1925, I had reached the age of seven. I was considered a baby no more, the same applied to my other three mates. Other youngsters had arrived and were the babies of the House, while older boys had mysteriously disappeared from the orphanage. My mates and I were brought in to help with the chores on the following Monday morning. I was given the job of washing down the outside front seven steps, about ten yards from the front door; they took you down on to the drive which went round the Circle, and they had to be washed and scrubbed before 7.00 a.m., before breakfast, every morning, winter and summer! Summer was alright, just a bucket of water was slung down them; occasionally, they would get a scrub. But a winter's morning, that was a different kettle of fish; salt was the order of the day and plenty of it. I used to stop at kitchen door and ask for 'Salt', sometimes they would say, 'No salt'. I used to say 'I will report "no salt" to Sister Florence.' That would do the trick, as it was imperative that the steps should be clear of ice and snow. I had the job of washing down the front steps the whole time I was in the orphanage, eventually getting it down to a fine art after five years, when I was twelve, and left Frodsham for good.

Sister Florence had slipped down the steps one day and hurt herself; she was no lightweight, a very stout lady, but that was before my time. She never spared anything as far as the front steps were concerned.

Monday evening we had a Bible and hymn book alongside my plate, as did the others of my age group. So it was true, us four young ones had got to learn the prayers for the week, and from then on!

Sister Florence mentioned it when we sat down for tea. She seemed to derive a great deal of pleasure from it, and went on, 'How the young members of John Fowler House will be kept fully occupied from now on!'

However, she gave us the passage from the Bible, the 23rd Psalm, and four verses from a well-known hymn! Most of the big boys said, 'It's easy!' But it was done for our benefit, and so we learnt the lesson for the first week. The following week it was a different story – it was a difficult passage, and as Friday approached I couldn't remember it, so was relieved when another boy was called on to get up and say the prayers for that week. What a relief that was! As the weeks passed into months, we got used to reading the first two lines, then saying them from memory, over and over, until it came gradually, then it came as a matter of course.

On the following Tuesday, I was just returning to school, at ten to two when I heard someone shout at me, saying 'Spen's leaving!' My eldest brother was leaving! I turned towards the Main Gate and ran. I ran as if I were possessed, as if I were late for school; it was too bad, I was going to see 'Spen' before he left. I arrived at the gate just as he was leaving. I just had time to say, 'So you're going home then?' and he was gone, in the Governor's car, with a Sister. The car just sped off! I knew instinctively that I would never see him again. I was so taken aback by his sudden departure that I cried all the way back to school. I would miss him dearly; there would be a void in my life; he was a father to me as well as a brother. Lewis and Phillip were close together and didn't bother about me; they had friends in their age group, and what with the choir, they were quite apart from me. I had my mates in my own age group, and we grew up together, which helped a great deal; we would be involved in many a scrape together!

On Saturday we played in the large field, opposite the Main Gate on the other side of the Kingsley Road, outside the boundary of the orphanage as we knew it. We were allowed to go out of the Main Gate, to the football ground once a week on a Saturday and watch the football match between local teams. That afternoon we got a little bored with the match and went to have a go on a thing, which I could only describe as a sort of a maypole. It had an iron pole in the centre, on the top of which was a large round thing which used to revolve; attached to this round thing was a dozen chains with large round rings attached to the end of each chain. The general idea was for a dozen boys to take a chain each and swing, round and round the pole in the centre; the faster you went, the higher you would go, until your feet were clear of the ground. I hung on for dear life until I could grip it no longer and off I came, just as though I had been sprung from a catapult. I was flung outwards, hit the ground head first and knocked myself out; when I did come round, I walked round in circles, until I had to sit down. It was 'Goodbye' to the maypole!

Another Saturday afternoon we got tired of watching the older boys playing football in the large field, and three of us started exploring the hedge which ran along the bottom of the field near the maypole. We could see through the hedge in places – what was that we could see? A wire fence on the other side of a lane, and beyond was an orchard, surrounded by a high hedge, as well as a wire fence! We looked for a gap in the hedge and through it we went, crossed the lane and went through the wire fence and high hedge on the other side. It was no trouble to us, being small; we could get through where big tall boys couldn't.

We found ourselves in a very large orchard, with apple trees to the left and to the right; it was all too easy. About 200 yards away was the house of the owner; there were two dogs sniffing around it, but they kept their distance. We could easily nip an apple or two, and get back the way we came. We picked up a small ladder that was lying on the ground, put it up against the tree and I started to climb. No sooner was I up the tree, picking the apples and letting them fall for the other two to pick up, when there was a shout, 'He's coming this way!' I looked up to see the man slowly walking towards us; the dogs were coming as well. I let the ladder drop with a thud, came down as fast as I could and dropped to the ground. Then he saw me, and shouted, 'Hey, you there!' The dogs gave chase, but I was off, making for the hole in the high hedge; the other two had a head start from me and were through the hedge. I said, 'Come on! Come on!' to the second boy who was taking his time, but it was too late – as I bent down to get through the hole, I felt a strong pair of jaws get hold of my shorts; he was growling and trying to pull me backwards; he wasn't going to let go; with that, I wetted my pants on the spot! I heard the man say, 'It's alright, I've got him now my beauty,' to the dog. With that, I was wrenched backwards, out of the hedge, by two strong hands. He said, 'You come with me!' and gripped my arm. The two dogs were jumping up at me all the way back to the house. 'I'll teach you children to steal my apples!' My trousers were feeling wet and uncomfortable, as they were made of a very coarse serge. We entered the house, where I was given a wooden chair which soon began to feel wet; the dogs were shut in the kitchen. I felt grateful that they would be kept free from me; the man sat down at his desk and was writing. Upon the completion of the letter addressed to the Governor, he gave the envelope to me saying, 'Now, see that this is handed to him, alright? And don't ever let it happen again, or, it will be the worse for you!' I got up from the wet chair and saw that I had left quite a puddle in the centre of it. I think the man saw it as well, because he let me go without a cuff round the ear, and kindly showed me the proper way out and into the lane. There was no sign of the other two boys as I made my way through the hedge – they had got as far away as possible from the orchard. I walked back to the Main Gate, turned right into the Governor's gardens and posted the letter through his letter box. On Sunday, nothing was said about the attempting scrumping, or on the Monday at prayers. It fizzled out. Little did I realise that within a week or two, I would be asking that man for help!

The adventures in the large playing field were not quite over, because on another Saturday afternoon, there wasn't anything to do. We were left to our own devices, so the boys said, 'What about climbing some trees?' I said, 'I have climbed all the trees!' That was not boasting, it was an everyday occurrence: the big boys climbed trees, so the youngsters followed suit; you learnt at an early age. I was never afraid of heights, it came as second nature, and was always a challenge! I said, 'I have climbed all the trees that are climbable!' One boy said, 'Not that one!' pointing to a poplar tree! That is a very difficult tree, all the branches are thin and there is hardly any room to put one's feet. 'I dare you!' said one boy; that was all I needed when a young boy, someone to say, 'I dare you!' Two boys bent down against the poplar tree. I climbed on their backs and was up, climbing for all I was worth. As I went higher it became more difficult, the tree got narrower and there was hardly enough room to put my feet between the branches. In fact, every now and then I got a foot stuck, only to wrench it free again. The branches of a poplar tree slope upwards, so it was slow work, but I was making progress. I was being very careful where I put my foot; as I went upwards the branches became much thinner, and I was thinking how thin they were and weak, when suddenly one broke. I suddenly had nothing to hang on to – I was off and falling! All in a second. One moment I was climbing, the next – I was off! A branch which was sticking up, went straight up my trouser leg! Then there was a ripping sound and it came out where my bottom was! And there I hung, completely upside down, a long way from terra firma! My leg felt as though all the skin had been ripped off.

There was pandemonium below from what I could see of it; the boys had nipped through the hedge and called the man from the orchard who came with a ladder and a long rope. The ladder was fully extended, the man had got himself halfway up the tree and was coming up with the rope, but, just then my trousers started to give way. I managed to reach a branch to steady myself and to ease the strain on my trousers. I felt a rope go round my shoulders and the stump of the branch that had broken, and felt myself being pulled upright again. I managed to get what remained of my trouser leg off the branch, and was able to get myself upright; then I made my descent to the ground, assisted by the very man who caught me in his orchard a week ago. He said, 'Aren't you the boy I caught in my orchard last Saturday?' I said, 'Yes sir!' 'Do you get into all these scrapes all the time?' he replied. 'It's just a case of having nothing to do!' said one of the boys. With that I hobbled up to Newton Hall for treatment to my leg. I can't remember the excuse I made, but the condition of my trousers were enough to go by. I know I was walking about with a stiff leg for weeks afterwards. It put paid to any climbing for a while.

About this time I complained about the girl's boots I was wearing; they had got too small for me, the toes were pinched up and the only relief I was able to get was to tap the heel against a large stone to take the pressure off my toes. I had corns on the small toes before I was any age. All the shoes were ill-fitting, passed down from older boys to the young ones, as they grew up. Boots were covered by metal heels, with studs from the toes to the insteps; they never wore out, and the uppers were given a good 'Dubbing' every night. When asked why the dubbing on our boots every night, I was told, 'A preparation of grease for preserving and softening the leather!' There is no answer to that!

My mate, who was smaller than I, had my boots, as can be seen in a photograph of the two of us. I was given a larger pair, more like army boots.

On Founders Day (they used to commemorate this day every year) the flag used to be flying at the masthead. It was a big day, and the staff went to a lot of work to make sure it was a success and that everyone enjoyed themselves. We young ones were dressed all in white, white jerseys, shorts, socks and shoes. Sometimes two of us were dressed in sailors' clothes, in white, with a blue jean collar ('blue jean' – navy for the collar) as sailors wear them, once a year, then at the end of the day they would disappear, till next year! The whole idea was to give the hundreds of people who used to attend Founders Day, which was open to the public, the best impression possible.

There were large tents and marquees erected by firms outside which would be placed all around the Circle on the grass, providing tea and lemonade, pastries and cakes, sales of work, all sorts of things which were made in the orphanage. There were sports and games for everyone to get involved in. Last, but not least, there was the procession led by the Frodsham Brass Band, followed by the Scouts, Guides, Brownies and Cubs, followed by the people from Frodsham. The festivities went on all day. I remember the weather used to be hot, never, ever a wet day, which seemed to be endless, with glorious sunshine.

I will always remember Christmas 1925. I had gone to bed at the

The Author with Eddie, 1926.

usual time of 6.30 p.m. in the large dormitory, with another boy about the same age as myself. It was dark at that time of the year, except for a solitary gas light, that used to flicker from a small jet, attached to a bracket on the wall. We might as well have had no light for what good it was, in the days before electricity was even heard of. We had just got into bed, lying there on our backs, waiting for the Sister to come round, when something made me look at the door, and there stood my eldest brother Spencer. He was as clear as he could be, and was trying to tell me something, but I couldn't hear a word! I turned to the other boy, and said 'Did you see him?' He said, 'Yes, who was it?' I said, 'It was my brother Spencer. But he's not at the orphanage now, he's nearly two hundred miles away!' I looked back at the doorway, but he was gone! I lay for a while just looking at the doorway, hoping he would come back, but no! So I said to the other boy, 'You saw him, didn't you?' he replied, 'Yes, I did!' Soon afterwards I fell asleep.

Next morning at breakfast, Sister Florence, having said grace, handed Lewis a black-edged letter. 'It must be bad news for the Doe brothers,' she said. It was a letter from my mother, saying that Spencer had died the day before in the London Hospital, Whitechapel, London. I wasn't given the letter to read; Lewis read it, then handed it to Phillip! I said, 'He appeared in the doorway of the large dormitory at about 7.00 p.m. last night!' Lewis and Phillip didn't listen, as they thought I was making it up; they didn't believe me. I am convinced, beyond a shadow of a doubt, that my eldest brother came to see me when he died. I was shattered by the news! I looked to him, with my Dad gone; he was my only hope. I cried and cried! Everywhere at school, back in the house. Spencer was fourteen years of age, I was then $7^1/2$.

I don't remember Christmas 1925 that followed. Spencer had died on 12 December, but life had to go on; my other two brothers would never be the same to me.

I worshipped Spencer, and as the days passed into months, time was the healer. In January 1926, we had a month of continual snow, which came right up to the window sills; everywhere was frozen up. I used to spend many a half hour standing on the grill outside the cookhouse, letting the steam warm through my boots, up my shorts; it was ecstasy. I used to walk away thoroughly warmed through. I had no coat, hat or gloves, no pockets in my trousers. I used to put each hand up alternative sleeves, like a Chinaman; my hands used to be terribly swollen with chilblains, and the inside of my legs used to be raw with the chafing of the coarse serge.

We all used to go out in the yards shuffling our boots along the ground, making a slide, the longer the better. After it had a couple of dozen boys sliding down a given strip, it was like glass; you only had to make a slight run and you went fifteen to twenty yards. In fact, sometimes if you got up quite a run, you seemed to go up to thirty yards; you were literally waiting in the queue; we kept it up for hours, and nice and warm we got too. The next morning, whoever got out into the yard first would be working up the surface, getting it like glass; this went on for weeks until the cold spell ended in late February.

The Frog Pond used to be frozen solid, so come Saturday afternoon we got permission to go up Sandy Lane to Cromers Lake. It was a huge lake and there on the lake was a big sledge, which some boys from Frodsham had built. I asked for a ride on it and was found room just on the back. The next thing, we were hurtling down the lake. I was hanging on to the boy in front of me. I thought it was good fun, and before I knew where I was, we were going down the lake at breakneck speed the way we had come, stopping at the road edge where we had started. The big boys who had been pulling changed places with the chap who had had a ride, and before we knew where we were, we were off to the far end of the lake, going like a bomb! When the end of the lake approached, instead of stopping, we slewed round so hard and at speed that I lost my grip on the boy in front of me, the sledge careered to the left so violently, that I shot off the back and hit the ice head first. I did not remember anything until I came to, holding my head with both hands on the bank. I had an enormous headache, but otherwise I was alright; it was goodbye to sledging in the future!

In May 1926, we had the General Strike. It affected everybody in the land, including we who were in the orphanage, and especially the north of the country because that was where most of the industry was. Everybody stopped work, the dockers, shipbuilders, steelworkers, coalminers, factories of every kind, the railways, the buses, in every trade or production, it stopped to a man! The troops and the Navy were brought in to help with the buses and the postal services.

The first we knew of it was on Sundays when we were going to church. The men were standing in groups on the pavement, dressed in their working dark grey, with the inevitable cloth cap; only the bosses wore a bowler hat. The flat cloth cap, that was the uniform of the day in the 1920s!

We used to pass them, every Sunday, on our way to Five Crosses Church or Holy Trinity Church, which was further down on the Warrington Road. They never spoke, or smiled, just a look of foreboding on their faces. It was a national tragedy, nobody knew where their next meal was coming from; in those days there was *no* unemployment benefit and redundancy pay was never thought of; it was a case of no work, no money – nothing! There were no savings. The pay was *not* sufficient to feed them. Savings – only the rich had money, or capital; the poor working people only had coppers in their pockets, never any silver; a pound note was hardly ever seen. You saw a ten shilling note, but only one, if you were lucky and in work. You were well off if you had half a crown in your pocket (two shillings and sixpence). You were paid in shillings and pence, four farthings to one penny, and I was lucky to earn one half penny, twice, when I was older, and that was all I ever saw. That was worth, today, half of a penny.

There was *no* Sickness Benefit, *no* family allowances, or Income Support, *no* holiday pay! There were *no* allowances of any kind! If you didn't work, there was *no* pay, nothing! You starved from day one!

Within a week, the country had come to a standstill and people were starving, especially in the north; food was held up in the docks with nobody to move it. That's when the government of the day called out the Army and the Navy; it took time before any food was getting to the shops, and then it was painfully slow.

The people were getting desperate now and the hunger marchers in their thousands were marching on London; they came from everywhere in the industrial north, Glasgow, Newcastle, Liverpool, Birkenhead, Manchester, Coventry and Birmingham. From every port and coalmine they came; many died on the way, *they were desperate men*! They were starving, their wives and children were starving too!

The hunger marchers marched every few weeks on London and continued right through to the 1930s, long after I had left the orphanage. The cause of the General Strike was *pay*! Pay was too low and men had to work long hours, for a six-day week, sixty or seventy hours a week for a mere pittance, while the bosses and owners of industry were raking in the profits. It was a case of the rich getting richer, the poor getting poorer!

The General Strike was beginning to have its effect on the orphanage, where a great deal of the food was donated from outside. One of the great benefactors was the family of Fowler from Liverpool, after whom several houses and beds in the dormitories were named. Many of these sources dried up with the strike; many food items didn't see their way to us or reach us, the orphans, and it got worse, but, more of that later. We suffered most with the strike in 1928 when there was nothing!!

A great amount of food was grown in the gardens, such as fruit and vegetables of every kind, but meat was scarce. An egg we saw once at Easter, that was all. They had chickens in the gardens, because I used to see batteries of baby chicks under netting out on the lawns in front of Newton Hall in the spring of each year, but we never had chicken!

In the latter part of the summer we used to have an apple or a pear on our plate for afters, but it was usually sago or some milk pudding. At teatime in the season, we occasionally got a couple of lettuce leaves, but they used to be short-lived.

We were tucking into this new-found luxury one day and I happened to glance at the boy opposite. He was helping himself to salt, which he was putting on the lettuce before going into his mouth, when I noticed a large black slug on the underside of the leaf, but, before I could say anything, he stuffed the lettuce leaf whole into his mouth, slug as well. I stopped eating, stared at him, and pulled a terrible face, imagining what it would taste like, but nothing registered on his face. He caught me staring at him with a sour look on my face, and he just winked! I thought that mouthful must have tasted juicy. His name was Tom Jenkins.

By the time I was eight, I was hardened to the long walks we used to make in the summer months, long Saturday afternoons, just walking mile after mile. Gone too were the white clothes we used to be dressed in on Sundays and special days, like Founder's Day or Christmas Day; that was for the five- or six-year-olds in future.

On another Saturday afternoon we walked to Helsby Crag, another hill, just like Overton Hill, about three miles away from Overton, in the direction of Chester, the last stop on the railway from Manchester. It was as high as Overton, but there the similarity ends; the whole of the top was sheer rock that sloped away in the rear to nothingness.

We left out of the rear gate, uphill, passing the Dell to our left, up Sandy Lane, passing Cromers Lake; instead of turning right to the top of Overton Hill, we kept straight on, coming to Fox Hill. Before the house was turned into a conference centre it was just a grand old house, surrounded by trees and gorse; in June every year it was a picture of rhododendron bushes. I don't remember the walk from Fox Hill to Helsby Crag, but I do remember it being all rock. We used to sit and let our legs dangle over the edge into thin air; what a view we got from there! Ellesmere Port and Port 'Sunlight' (the soap manufacturers) were just ahead, with Helsby tucked underneath the cliff; the Wirral was directly ahead with Birkenhead way over in the distance. We could see Chester clearly with the Welsh mountains as a backdrop.

On our way back to Overton Hill we came to 'Jacob's Ladder' at a place called Dunsdale. 'Jacob's Ladder' was approximately fifty or sixty feet of sheer rock from top to bottom and that was the only way down as far as I could see. Down the years people had left their footprints in the rock; you could lose your boots in the indentations, they were so deep. It was difficult to get down; once started, you had to go on, ending up going down on hands and knees; it was extremely dangerous, to me, a youngster it was hair-raising; you slithered on your bottom most of the time. I was greatly relieved when I got to the bottom; the Sisters took a wide detour to miss 'Jacob's Ladder!' We eventually came out by Overton Village passing Overton Church, Howey Lane, turning right into the Kingsley Road, passed Five Crosses Church to the Orphanage, what a walk it was, hour after hour, after hour.

Saturday evening was shower night. The shower consisted of a square cubicle about seven feet square, all red tiled, including the floor, which tapered down to a drain in the centre. The shower came out of a small rose in the ceiling, just above you and the drain. Two boys were let in at a time. The Sister operated the hot and cold taps just outside the cubicle, cold water was allowed through, thence a good rub down with soap, then a minute to rinse off with hot water, if you were lucky. More often than not it was lukewarm, then out, the next two were waiting on the duckboards. The shower was situated next to the back door and that was a draughty place to be, especially in the winter time. Summertime was bad enough; we soon came out in goosepimples; it was never a good hot shower. I was always greatly relieved to put on clean clothes and get out of the washplace.

I never seemed to see my other brothers, Lewis and Phillip, you would never believe they were in the same house. They spent most of their time together; there was only two years between them. They were always engrossed in the Day Room with their painting or drawing. Lewis was the clever one, always doing something good, not so good as Spencer, but he was quite the master of drawing or painting, or woodwork. Phillip was always the 'watcher', I never saw him doing anything. In fact, he was never happier than making himself a b***** nuisance to everyone. They joined the choir together, which meant a great deal of time spent in the choir hut, practising singing or rehearsing a school play. At school they were in the top class, run by a Mr Hunt, who was the Headmaster. He was a man who was liked by everyone, young and old, in and out of school, a first-class teacher. Once or twice a week, he came to tell us a story; every time he came into our classroom, there was dead silence, you could hear a pin drop. He would tell us exciting stories; my favourite was King Arthur and Knights of the Round Table.

Well, it was one of his afternoons he came into our classroom to read one of his brilliant stories. His class was on their own for about half an hour, on their best behaviour, engaged in woodwork at their own benches. Lewis was at the bench with a large mallet and wood chisel in his hands, chipping away, at something or other. Phillip was his usual self, skylarking about! Lewis had asked him not to mess about, but no, Phillip kept pushing Lewis's arm, but he pushed it once too often! Lewis's hand slipped; Phillip was right up against the vice and the chisel entered his pants where his left buttock was and buried itself in his buttock, right up to the handle of the chisel!

The first I knew of it Phillip was in bed, with a screen around his bed, a doctor and two Sisters bent over him. I was told he was delirious, in a terrible state and had lost a lot of blood. He nearly died, and was in a state of crisis for several days; he recovered, *but only just*. It was a near thing! I always felt that the accident affected him, for he was never the same afterwards!

In 1927 my mother came to Frodsham. Five years had passed since I last saw her on Leamington Station. She stayed at a cottage just a little way over from the rear entrance of the orphanage. She stayed for three days, but never came inside the orphanage or took a look at John Fowler House and the conditions under which we lived, never met Sister Florence or any member of the staff, as far as I know. I was allowed out, with Lewis and Phillip once, and once only. We walked up Sandy Lane, past Cromers Lake to the Overton Hills; it was a lovely day, weatherwise; we sat on an area that was covered with heather; my mother picked a sprig or two, and she talked. What about, I can't remember exactly, but it was something about why she had to put us boys into an orphanage; it explained why she was holding a baby, when she came to say goodbye to Phil and I at the station. She seemed to get worried when she said that she couldn't come to the orphanage carrying someone else's baby, that would have taken some explaining! I lost track of the conversation. Lewis seemed a bit put out, when he said, 'How many years have we to put with this place?' and so on. Why did she come all this way to see us? Apparently, it was partly due to losing Spencer, and the accident to Phillip, and she was now living near

Marylebone, London; her furniture from 30 Grove Street, Leamington Spa, was in storage. She had to break all ties with the people in Leamington, especially the Wesleyan Church in Dale Street, where we all went to church and Sunday school. After what seemed to be a short visit, and an unusual one, she was gone, like a ship in the night! Back to London. She obviously liaised with Sister Florence, because years after I left, letters were going back and forth from Sister Florence to my mother. As far as I know we hardly ever heard from my mother.

It was about this time in 1927, after my mother left, that I was admitted to Newton Hall to be circumcised, as I was still wetting the bed regularly; it hadn't ceased since I first came to the orphanage. One day previously, Sister had taken me down to the doctor on the Kingsley Road, near Five Crosses Church. He examined me and we returned to the orphanage. I didn't think any more about it until I was admitted a few days later. The operation was soon over; it was painful while it lasted, but within a few days the soreness wore off and I returned to John Fowler House, never to wet the bed again!

We never got a Christmas card, or a birthday card, or a letter from my mother. We couldn't send her a card either (a) because we never had any money, not even a farthing, a quarter of a penny, (b) we had no pockets, all machine-stitched up, (c) we never went down to Frodsham to the shops, never! Well, I went twice in eight years for about half an hour, but nothing in the way of sweets was ever bought for us. This over the years, died hard on me, so much so, that I grew up *not* remembering whose birthday it was, or when. The die was cast by my mother, so it was with me, until I had children of my own. Now, I must admit, I have a tendency to spoil them.

While I was in Newton Hall for my minor operation, I had an occasion to wander into the front of the house, which was up on a hill, with a commanding view over towards Warrington. There were about 300 yards of lawns and beds of rhododendrons, with a large entrance down the bottom of the drive, where there were, covered over with sheets of netting, hundreds of baby chicks sunning themselves in the afternoon sun, all chirping away. I had never seen a baby chick before, the sweetest things I ever did see!

Some Saturdays, we always picked a good day to go for a walk. In the summertime, we would take our tea to the Dell, which wasn't far to walk, or to Overton Hills, or we would go up the Kingsley Road and down to Pear Lane, but one day we went up the back way to Overton Hills, passed the Dell, Cromers Lake, through the lanes which housed the caves, and on to Overton Hill.

The top of the hill was mainly sandstone in the front, but this particular day we would change the landscape, a little off the top of Overton Hills. A lot of the sandstone was firm, and we could not move it, but here and there, it used to crumble and would turn into a rough sand; that's how it was in the 1920s. This particular afternoon, one or two of us had wandered off away from the rest of the boys and Sisters, who were stretched out in the sun; we couldn't be seen by them, pulling at the loose rock. As soon as it became free, it rolled down the hill, which was several hundred feet. We watched it bounce and bounce, it would disappear for a while, then you would see it hit the wall skirting the Chester Road, or go charging over the road to disappear in the Frodsham marches. There wasn't a soul to be seen on the paths, we had it all to ourselves; it used to be very quiet in those days. Although it was a major road, there *was* a bus from Chester to Frodsham, but I never saw it, and the cars were extinct; a bike you would see from time to time; that was the only means of conveyance, except a horse pulling a cart, from time to time.

And so it was on this sunny afternoon. We continued pulling at the loose stone, pushing it down to heaven knows where, until we got a large boulder free; all hands to this one. We got it to the edge, had one good look to see it was clear below, then let it go! It hardly touched the hill spinning in the air, then it hit a mound; up it went again until it disappeared to the naked eye; then we could see it again, going into the side of the hill, bouncing into the air again, fifty feet or more, then missing the wall at the bottom by about fifteen feet, clearing the road altogether!

We looked for a larger rock; they were getting bigger all the time; some were stuck fast and you couldn't move them; others just broke off. Finally, we all pulled an enormous one out; it took all three of us to get it to the edge. It was better than the others, being rounder. It would go like a bomb! Where the others were flatter and awkward shapes, this was ideal. The three of us concentrated on it; it would knock the wall down. We managed to get it to the edge and stopped for a minute to make sure that it was clear below. We waited for a minute or two, looked left and right, sure there wasn't anybody coming along the paths.

There were three paths which all connected with the centre path halfway up, and the centre path that connected to the top path which ran along the top, or went over the hill. Satisfied that it was absolutely clear, that nobody was coming along the road at the bottom, we let the monster go with a push. It must have weighed several hundredweight; we watched it spellbound! If it hit anybody, we'd be for it! We couldn't see a living soul; down to the bottom it went, gathering speed all the way down, hitting a mound here and there, which sent it spinning up in the air, careering over the centre path, going at an incredible speed. Then we saw it together! It made our hearts jump! A farmer was coming round the bend of the road from Helsby on his bike, ambling along as if he'd got all day, oblivious to all and sundry. I think he heard something like a great swishing sound, looked left, right and all around for a second, then looked up! He wasn't sure, unable to believe what he was seeing. It was no use shouting 'Look out' from that height – he wouldn't have heard us. His face froze on the spot, I should think! As if he was going to be devoured by a huge monster! We watched helplessly. The boulder, about three hundredweight, had bounced just before the wall at the bottom, which skirted the road, and went crashing over the road at about thirty feet. It would have demolished the wall if it hit it, but as luck would have it, it missed. Nothing would stop it, it went through the hedge opposite, as if it wasn't there and careered across the marshes and out of sight.

The farmer must have panicked, because, he and the bike went into the ditch opposite, after he had zig-zagged all over the road. It was a ditch full of water, next to the marshes, because when he came out, he looked soaked. He got to his feet, pulled the bike out, spent a few minutes straightening the handlebars and got on his bike again. He looked up the hill, then he looked left and right, going on his merry way, thinking he might have to complain to the Council of his experience. He must have thought, 'I had better see the Council about all the loose rock on the top of the hill, it's dangerous all that loose rock!' In the meantime, we had dropped to the ground when the boulder had bounced over the wall and cleared the road. We kept down, watching the farmer to see if he was alright. Satisfied that he was we went along and joined the rest of John Fowler House, keeping very quiet about the boulders! We returned to the orphanage.

Nothing was said by us or the authorities, but much later, we noticed a great deal of the loose rock had been removed from the top of Overton!

Another Saturday afternoon I was walking down to the sports ground to watch the football, going through the main gate and crossing the road, when I saw a lorry. No, it was a steam wagon, stopped where they had started to build a house, which I was later to learn was to be for the new Governor; it had delivered a load of bricks.

I went over to look at the steam wagon and found it empty, the driver and fireman having a cup of tea elsewhere, no doubt. What a massive thing it was, built for strength. It had a huge boiler in the front of it, where the engine would be, with a large funnel which came out at the roof of the driver's cab; there were two seats, one for the driver and one for the fireman; his job would be to stoke the boiler in the front of the cab and keep the steam pressure up, being a steam engine. The cab was very large, it had to be to keep a large amount of coal in it; it had two large windows in front, which were 'louvre' and diagonal to each other, with the funnel passing between the two; no doubt, it got very hot in the cab because the louvre windows were open; there was a huge hissing of steam; the fire was red-hot. The whole appearance of the steam wagon was of strength; the chassis and wheels were enormous, with solid tyres several inches thick. The advantage over the petrol lorry was that it could carry great loads, over greater distances and they were very economical to run; breakdowns were minimal. Their speed was about thirty miles per hour, but this used to decrease as it went uphill; you could get out and walk faster.

I was fascinated by it, it seemed alive somehow, and yet it was empty, the driver and the fireman not being around; neither was anybody else. Saturday afternoons were very quiet at the orphanage, there wasn't anything on the roads and there wasn't a soul about, the ideal time to do a bunk, get away for good! I looked around to see if there was anyone watching me; it was all trees, both sides of the road; there was just Mr Schofield's, the Governor's house, just twenty yards away, but there the house looked quiet and still. One last look over my shoulder to see if the men were coming back, one foot on the rear wheel and then a foot over the side panels, and I was in! I lay down flat on the boards, at the top end, so they wouldn't see me, and kept still, listening for the two men to return to the steam wagon!

After what seemed like an eternity, the driver and fireman came back. No doubt they had been longer than they thought, for they seemed to be in a hurry to be off, and didn't bother to look over the side panels; they had unloaded bricks, so it should have been empty!

There was a lot of shovelling of coal, followed by the hissing of steam, then a jerk, more hissing of steam, then a big jerk, a 'chug, chug', and slowly we moved off. 'Chug, chug, chug', she went, smoke coming out of the chimney above my head, and she settled down to a 'chug, chug, chug'. After a while I got used to the noise and we settled down to a steady speed. The roads were empty; we had the road to ourselves, downhill to Five Crosses Church, then the junction with Howey Lane and two turnings on the right. Church Lane started from here, which became a very steep hill all the way down to the station and Main Street with all the shops on the right side of the hill. It was all rock, thirty feet high, with houses perched on top of them. I kept down on the boards, seeing just an occasional building here and there, then we came to Frodsham station, went under the bridge and stopped temporarily at the junction with Main Street. Which way shall we go, to the right to Warrington, or to the left, to Chester? I had no sooner wondered which way we were going, when we quite suddenly swung to the left. 'Ah, Chester!' I said to myself. In no time at all, we were chugging down Main Street with all its little shops. There were more people down here, so I kept my nose just below the side panel. We came to the end of Main Street, where the road to Helsby took the left fork and became narrow; we passed the spot where the farmer came off his bike and I found myself looking upwards to Overton Hills; then later we came to Fox Hill, nearly at Helsby! Oh, God! I thought, what am I going to do for money? I hadn't a farthing! I would need lots of money to go to London! I had to think quickly – the steam wagon was putting miles between me and the orphanage! We came to a hill just before Helsby and gradually slowed up a little as all steam wagons do; they go so much slower up a hill. I'll wait until she reaches the top, I decided, then slide off the end of the tail board. The fireman was off his seat and stoking the boiler; this was my chance; I waited until it had slowed right down, slid off the tail board, dropped to the ground and took one dart to the hedge on the side of the road. 'Phew, that was a near thing!' I murmured, gathering myself after the ride on the steam wagon. I looked to see her going over the hill and disappearing down to Helsby.

I could see Overton Hill in the distance, so I walked along the way we had come until I could climb over the wall and pick up the lower path which would eventually take me to the top of Overton. Once I was past the Helter-Skelter I would soon be home and dry. So, I walked, and walked. I was used to it by now and I knew the terrain from many a Saturday, and the route back to the orphanage. I could either keep walking as I was, and would come to the village of Overton, which would take me down Howey Lane, the long way back, or climb Overton Hill. It would be uphill, but it was the quickest way back to the home! Did I feel alone, or lonely? No! I was used to being on my own, and felt as though I had been on my own for ever! No father! No mother, hardly! No brothers – hardly ever saw them! Spencer – I missed him!

In no time I was up on the middle path, making my way slowly upwards, keeping the Helter-Skelter in view. I climbed ever upwards for several hundred feet. I never knew how high it was; it could be seen in Chester, and that was a long way away. Eventually I reached the top and sat down for a while, it was quite early, about mid-afternoon, so there was plenty of time to get back. I passed the Helter-Skelter and made my way past the field which had the caves. We were never allowed in that field as it was private property and I never saw anyone near them at any time; they became foreboding. It was downhill all the way now, past Cromers Lane, down Sandy Lane, past the Dell to my right. I entered the rear gate, past the Frog Pond, the Boiler House, round the back of the Main Hall, and there I joined one or two of my mates in the yard of John Fowler House. Nobody ever knew that I had done a bunk from the orphanage without being seen. I had abandoned it, only to realise I couldn't get any farther than Chester without money. I would have got home if I had had the fare. I played with my mates until teatime and went indoors; nobody was any the wiser. I never thought of doing a bunk again; the thought never entered my head, because of the money! There were several attempts by boys to do a bunk or run away, but they all failed, mainly because they took the wrong route. One boy was caught trying to cross the River Weaver to the south and was caught after he had fallen in. The River Weaver was a natural barrier because it ran from the Mersey right round the back of the orphanage. The only way out was by road, to Warrington or Chester; there were no rivers that way.

In 1928, I was ten years old; at school, I had gone up to Class 6; next class in the hall was Class 7. Lewis and Phillip were in that class. The mornings were either arithmetic or composition, but in the afternoons, the subjects changed considerably. I used to look across at Class 7, to see what Lewis was up to; he and Mr Hunt were always leaning over a bench. There was always a strong smell of paint or dope; they were making a shield made of wood; others were making swords and daggers painted silver, so that they looked authentic. About a week after, they started making bows and arrows. The bows were about five feet in height, the arrows were about two feet, just over, with steel tips in the sharp end and feathers in the other end, all correct, just like the real things. The tips and the feathers were spliced into the shaft at each end – they looked lethal weapons!

Sister Ida, who was in charge of the choir, announced that she was going to launch her first play at the orphanage; it was to be 'Robin Hood and his Merry Men'. It would be put on at the Main Hall, which was ideal for it; Lewis would play Robin Hood, and Phillip would play Will Scarlet. I saw them in their full costumes, green for Robin and red for Will Scarlet; they looked the real thing, complete in every detail, including the five-foot bows and the sheaths with the arrows slung over their heads, so that they wore them properly, right arm free to get the arrows on the right side. They had their photos taken in costume.

I fancied a bow myself. Some boys had made bows about two feet long, with long bits of wood for arrows. My bow would be four feet long, as tall as myself. I spent days looking for a tree that would make a good bow; it would have to be springy and bend so it wouldn't snap. I found one, up in the gardens, a sort of Weeping Willow, just the right thickness and springy. I got some cord from the Headmaster which was just right for my bow. I put a whipping of about five inches exactly halfway on the bow where the arrows would fire from. For my arrows, I split long, straight lengths from a box I had managed to scrounge. I shaved them down till they were as thick as a pencil and as smooth. They were spliced at either end, for the tip made of metal, and for the flight of the arrow, four large feathers, inserted in the rear end of the shaft, spliced with wire. I made eight arrows like this for my bow.

The day came to try my bow to see if I'd got my arrows perfectly balanced. The most important thing was the flight of the four feathers, which had to be exactly spaced, ninety degrees between each feather, and very tightly spliced with thin wire. I went up into the top field which overlooked John Fowler House. It was clear of trees; it had had wheat in the previous year, but this year it would be pasture, as the grass was already about four inches high, ideal to try out my new bow. I took an arrow from the sheath I had made, and put, or placed it, on the five inches of whipping at the halfway mark, raised my bow skywards and pulled slowly back on the chord. It would not break, neither would the bow; I was confident in how I had made it. I let it go, my first arrow – it went up, clean as a whistle! I followed its flight until it reached the top of its arc, and it came down way out in the centre of the field, the tip stuck out of the ground as clean as could be. So I tried another arrow, with a bit more tension on the bow; I really pulled back, wanting it to go high up. My second arrow went faster and farther than the first; it seemed out of sight, was this how it was in the old days with the longbow? I thought. Then I saw it come down in the other half of the field.

I was proud of my bow and arrows, and always stood it on end when showing it to my mates. It was nearly as tall as me, and the craze soon caught on; for several weeks the boys were coming to take a look at my bow, until eventually there were at least six bows up in the top field; in no time, there were bows and arrows everywhere. We would have to have order, as there were boys shooting off arrows in all directions. We agreed that the next Saturday afternoon, we'd all come up together and stand on one side of the field.

The next Saturday afternoon the boys from John Fowler and Albert Fowler Houses walked up to the top field together. For some reason or other, I was late getting to the field; when I did arrive, it was absolutely chaos – some of the boys had wooden swords and shields, those that hadn't a shield were using dustbin lids. 'We are not having a battle?' I said. Some who had bows were firing their arrows all over the place; somebody was going to get hurt! Some were firing correctly, and the arrows were landing way out in the field. Others had no idea, shooting their arrows parallel to the ground, which could be fatal. I tried to get all the boys who had bows to one side of the field; some came, some didn't, it was those who didn't which caused the trouble. Some arrows were coming down vertically, some were coming down parallel. Then it happened – wham! An arrow went straight into the side of my right knee! I went to step forward with my left foot and literally tripped over the arrow. I grabbed at it, but it was in deep. I managed to pull it out and then I don't remember anything else – I must have fainted! I came to in Newton Hall, in bed, and the pain was terrible, my knee was giving me hell!

The nurse had applied a tourniquet somewhere up near the top of my leg and was busy looking at her watch. Then I heard her say, 'I think it should come off now!' After some fiddling with it, she said, 'It's stopped now.' With that over, they dressed the knee, then sent for the doctor, who said, 'Not you again, you really get into the wars, don't you?' I replied, 'Yes, it was Agincourt this time!' which brought a smile to his lips! I stayed in Newton Hall for three weeks.

I returned to John Fowler House, with a bandage on my knee. Sister Florence approached me, and asked if I was feeling better. I said, 'Much better, thank you!' She said, 'This bow and arrow business you started has got to stop forthwith!' She saw a bit of the rebel in me, not like her darling Lewis, and so it was – I was a bit of a rebel!

My leg healed with time; it left quite a scar. Even now at seventy-nine years of age, I can put a finger in the indentation, a slight hole in the left side of the right knee the size of 1p!

The sisters had been round all the boys' lockers in my absence, confiscating all the bows and arrows that could be found, mine included. That was the only time we went up to the top field that I can remember. Some of the boys had gone up to fight a battle between John Fowler and Albert Fowler Houses. Well, they were wrong! Nothing was farther from my mind; so it ended – but going round the lockers left me bitter!

The play, 'Robin Hood and His Merry Men', was cancelled, but we never heard what the outcome was!

A few weeks passed and I was taking the same route after dinner that I had done, when I saw the steam lorry! I had gone down to the Main Gate, when I saw a car stopped round on the girls' side of the Circle, which was out of bounds to the boys; it was also the rear entrance to the Governor's house, Mr Schofield; it was the first and only car to be seen in the orphanage. I wanted to go and have a look at it, so round I walked, not very far, not even in front of the girls' houses; it wouldn't do anybody any harm, just going to look at a car! It had a completely round radiator, all polished like brass; at the top was a blue badge, which said in three words, 'Morris Cowley, Oxford', which later I was to learn was the 'Bull-nosed Cowley', complete with a temperature gauge on top, so you would know if the engine was overheating. It had a canvas hood, complete with a running board on each side; on one side there was a spare can for petrol, on the other side, a spare wheel; the starting handle was stuck into the front, at the bottom of the radiator. There was no chromium in those days, all brass and enamel paint; it was painted an olive green, and looked quite smart with the polished radiator and door handles.

I was walking round and round the car, looking for further improvements, when somebody shouted, 'Hey, you there! Don't you know that you're out of bounds, what do you think you are doing?' I turned round, it was old fiddling moustache himself, the Governor! He had come down the pathway from his house, having had his dinner, hidden by a high hedge, and appeared at the last minute, when he came out to the car. 'What's your name?' he said. 'Mervyn Doe,' I replied. 'Oh yes, you are the boy who started this bow and arrow business, aren't you? I've heard a great deal about you!' I thought, I could tell you a trick or two, that you don't know! When I did a bunk on the back of the steam lorry to Helsby! and many more stunts just as good! 'Me, sir?' I said. 'You, my boy!' he replied. His moustache nearly took off, and he settled it with a quick twist of his left fingers, giving it a couple of twists. 'Well you got hurt, didn't you?' he said, with a smile of satisfaction. 'Fortunes of war!' I replied. 'Now, don't be insolent!' he replied with a frown. 'You are the youngest of the four Does. I had a lot of dealings with your eldest brother Spencer!' That did it!! Pig, I thought. 'My brother passed away just before Christmas 1925!' I said. That shook him! He knew that he had left a couple of years before, but he didn't know that he had died. 'I'm very sorry to hear that!' he said, and with that, he appeared to let me off, 'Anyway, this side is out of bounds to boys, don't let me catch you again, is that clear?' he said. 'Yes, sir!' With that I dashed off to the Main Gate, thanking my lucky stars that I had got away with it, not many boys got away without being punished, not from Mr Schofield, the Governor, they didn't!

I went down to the playing fields and watched a football match being played by two teams from Frodsham. When it was over, I was returning to the Main Gate and John Fowler House for tea; just as I was about to cross the road, who was coming out of the Main Gates, but the Governor in his car. He looked a bit put out, having been all afternoon trying to start his car. He turned right in the direction of Kingsley and I watched to see him go until he was out of sight. I said to myself, 'A damned good riddance!' I believe that he ruled the orphanage with a rod of iron to cover up his misdoings; it was not just a case of discipline, as we were all afraid of him; we just couldn't breathe with him about, everyone felt uneasy when he was around. He retired to Kingsley, which was only a few minutes up the road on the way to Northwich, not before an enquiry was held as to how the orphanage was being run. I didn't know it at the time, it was in the National newspapers, and went on for weeks. There were rumours of pilfering on a grand scale: food that was intended for the children never arrived, the staff received it, sweets, cakes, eggs and meat, then it disappeared, month after month; the children went without, somebody was disposing of food and making a fat profit out of it and the finger pointed at Mr Schofield. It was never proven, but he was dismissed as the Governor, though it was all hushed up!

The General Strike was to blame mainly, for there was a shortage of food, and it encouraged any pilfering that wouldn't happen normally. There was one thing that used to stand out to us boys, which happened regularly: some very kind benefactor used to send us a huge round tin of boiled sweets once a month, several pounds in weight; it used to stand at least twelve inches high, enough to last us a year if not longer. Sister Florence would produce this large tin after we had had our tea, saying someone had been so kind to send us this huge tin of sweets, but we could take one only. Removing the lid, she walked round the tables until we all had our *boiled sweet*, and I think, we all said, 'Thank you'. She said, 'I will write and thank them very much, on behalf of you boys!' then she would disappear into the staff room; we would never see the sweets again, never. We could never say we hadn't had them, but we were told to take one only. It was always the same each year, and was a fiddle!

So it was with eggs: we only had one a year, but there were dozens and dozens of chickens. Remember how I'd seen the chicks? There must have been at least a hundred chicks under netting, sunning themselves at Newton Hall, when I went for my operation, but we never, ever had chicken at the orphanage!

On Sundays we had a little meat, served up cold, winter or summer, as there was no cooking on Sundays! Cold white fat, I remember! There was never any lean on my plate. Cold white fat! That used to make me retch then, on my way back from Five Crosses Church and still does on a cold day, week after week, month after month. A little salt was placed in a white earthenware jar on the table; all the boys helped themselves to lots of salt, as there wasn't anything else to eat, you had to eat or starve. Red meat I never saw, or lean; I never saw a sausage, or any other meat during the whole time I was at the orphanage; we must have been vegetarians! We had dumplings about as big as golfballs in our stew, quite a regular dinner with plenty of vegetables in it. We had fish regularly, once a week, a large piece of cod, steamed, no sauce, plain, just a large whack of steamed cod and boiled potatoes. I didn't like the cod by itself, as it had a funny taste to it. The boy opposite me was very partial to fish, and would eat the skin as well. I used to push my plate across to him and say, 'Fancy my fish, Tom?' 'Coo, yes not half!' he said; great lengths of skin he would devour. He was the same chap who swallowed half a lettuce leaf with a huge black slug or a snail underneath it! Tom Jenkins was his name.

In the summer of 1928, a bus service was started to Frodsham which caused quite a stir. It was the first ever bus which used to stop outside the Main Gates of the orphanage; till then, a motor car was a very rare occurrence. Mr Schofield's car was the only car to be seen. This was the forerunner of the buses which run locally and in Chester today; this service ran from Northwich to Frodsham every hour, then to Chester; it was called a 'Crossville' and was a single-decker bus, painted red and white.

One Monday morning in August 1928, before breakfast, Phillip and I were asked to go to the Staff Room as Sister Florence wished to see us. We were told that we were going on holiday that morning, to London for fourteen days! Our mother would be at Euston to meet us. Our minds were in a state of turmoil at the news. We had our breakfast, then a hot shower, changed into special clothes that befitted us for a holiday, said goodbye to Sister Florence, and to the other two Sisters, and we were off down the drive to the Main Gate; there we were joined by another Sister, who said she was coming as far as Chester to see us on the London train. I don't remember the ride on the bus, or the train journey to Chester, but I do remember Chester! I suppose I was excited to be going home at last.

We pulled in to Chester, a huge station, my first impression was of noise! There were several red engines, puffing great clouds of smoke, some going this way, some the other way, people rushing about, hadn't got a minute to live, you could hardly hear yourself speak! I heard the Sister say that we'd got to go over the footbridge to catch the London train.

Within a few minutes the train came, a long train, pulled by two red engines, though not as big as they are today. One thing that caught my eye was the huge pistons driving two wheels, two small wheels in the front, two large wheels, connected by a piston rod. I didn't know it at the time, but I later learnt that an engine which has four small wheels in front, followed by four large driving wheels was called an 'Atlantic' type. Later we had four, six wheels, called a 'Pacific' type. So we were going to be pulled by two 'Atlantic' type engines but, hang on! we had a third on the back. This engine, I learned, was used to help push the long train out, and would break off once the train got going!

There was a long shrill on a whistle, and slowly but surely, we were off! I sat down in a corner, Phillip was half out of the window shouting goodbye to the Sister who brought us to Chester. We were free after six years of being in an orphanage. I had been too young to understand why we had been so abruptly sent to the orphanage; my mother knew it would be a few years before I would fully understand, there was a baby, who my mother was holding, on Leamington Spa Station in 1922; but my father had died shortly before I was born. *I* would be the last Doe! Who was he? The train trundled on, I looked at the railway line opposite, watched the sleepers going faster, faster; it was a different life outside, no longer having to be woken up by the clanging of a bell, or dashing downstairs for a bucket to wash the front steps on a cold and frosty morning, no more doorsteps for breakfast, with no butter on the bread, no more boiled potatoes with their skins on, no more Sunday dinners of white fat instead of meat, with lots of salt to help it down with, no more prayers to learn from the Bible, every Monday evening before tea, and, no more ill-fitting boots that gave me bad feet, or ill-fitting clothes, with no pockets to put your hands in when it was wintertime, no coat, or gloves either – there was no limit to the hardship and deprivation of the 'National Children's Home and Orphanage', Frodsham, Cheshire, in the 1920s, and the Staff who were responsible for it. I was only four years of age in 1922!

'By the way, where's Lew [Lewis]?' I said to Phil (Phillip).

Sister Florence said, 'Lewis will be going down to London later.' What we didn't know was he'd be going home for good! Lewis was now fifteen, old enough to out to work. Would we stay here until we were old enough to work?

The train slowed down and came to a stop at Crewe; it had the same huge glass partitions that Chester had between each platform, which went as high as the roof and were the entire length of the platforms. They were for the smoke from the engines!

We were off, once again, on a long journey, with nothing to eat; they didn't think about sandwiches in those days, which were unheard of; the buffets on stations were very small; you had a job to find it, if you had a penny or two, to spend on a cup of tea, and we didn't have any money, not so much as a farthing (a quarter of one penny) so refreshment was out.

Phillip went to sleep; he hardly ever spoke to me; I was the youngest Doe, the baby as far as he was concerned. I wished I had one or two mates with me, and eventually dropped off to sleep, to be rudely awakened by someone shouting, 'This is Rugby!' Another station as big as Crewe, with glass partitions between each platform for the smoke from the engines! People got off the train, people got on! The train moved off slowly, in no time it gathered speed. I tried to look at the scenery, but it was going too fast. I wasn't interested in houses, which looked very much the same; it seemed as though we had been on the train for hours and eventually I dropped off to sleep again.

I heard someone shout, 'We'll be in Euston in a few minutes!' I woke, startled, the train was slowing down. I looked at Phil, who seemed to have had a good sleep, and walked out into the corridor to get some fresh air. I turned round and said, 'Have you got the tickets alright, Phil?' He said, 'Yes!' He took the tickets out of the top of one of his socks, and produced them for me to see. The train was slowly entering Euston station, the corridors seeming to fill up with people and their baggage. 'We'll never see Mum amongst this lot of people on the platform!' I said. The train stopped, we got off and were pushed and jostled to the ticket barrier. Phil gave up half of our tickets and kept the return half for our return in a fortnight's time, when we would have to return to Frodsham. Mum had seen us pushing through the crowd; she had been waiting near the barrier, and there she was! She said, 'Hello, did you have a good journey?' 'Yes, not a bad journey!' we replied. 'A bit hungry!' said Phil. 'We'll soon be home!' she said, with that, we walked out of Euston Station into the streets of London, bustling with people and traffic. Mum hailed a bus, funny looking buses they were too, painted red with the word 'General' printed on the sides. They were double-deckers; you got to the top by climbing the spiral staircase outside, at the back of the bus; they appeared top heavy, as they seemed wider at the top and narrower at the bottom. The wheels were of solid tyres several inches thick and racks fitted between the front and rear wheels, to stop people from falling between the wheels. They were known as the General Omnibus Company for years; antiquated they were too!

We went inside the bus, the ticket collector came for our fare, and Mum said, 'One and two halves to Baker Street please!' He gave three rings on his cancelling machine, which was slung around his shoulder, clipped three tickets and gave Mum one penny and two half-penny tickets, then she gave each of us a ticket; we felt tickled pink with our tickets and decided to keep all the tickets from the buses on our holiday.

The ticket collector shouted 'Baker Street Station next stop!' Mum said, 'We get off here!' Baker Street tube station was on the other side of the road; we got off, and walked in the direction of Regent's Park over to the right. We took the next turning on our left, crossed over the road, then finally we took the next turning left, a cul-de-sac called Lynhope Street; on the right-hand side was no. 49 Lynhope Street; it was all fenced off, and the railings were painted black. Every house, both sides of the road, were the same to the other end of the cul-de-sac, but this was home, old and dilapidated and run down, one of thousands of slum dwellings in London. All the children played in the road, so that there was the noise of children in the road all day, every day. We climbed three steps and went inside the front door; it was pitch dark inside. Mum opened the door to our left and found ourselves in the front room, the light from outside barely coming through the window. I sat down on the first chair that I came to; after a few minutes I saw there were other chairs round a plain wooden table, a paraffin lamp on the table. Mum had just removed the long glass to light the burner with a match. After it was lit, we could see a bit better, but it wasn't exactly bathed in light, when suddenly I could see an elderly man with a beard, sitting in a corner; he had an old cloth cap on his head. Mum said, 'Say hello to Grandad!' I said a mumbled, 'Hello, Grandad!' with that he shuffled his feet and produced an enormous red handkerchief which he spread out on his lap. I soon found out that it was a habit of his to always have his dirty old handkerchief on his lap; he never, ever put his hanky away.

Eventually my eyes got used to the dark half light; the paraffin lamp gave some light, but mainly just around the table. I could just see a big black cooking range in a recess under the mantelpiece. Mum lifted up the front of it and revealed a warm glowing fire; she proceeded to rake it with a poker, putting a huge black kettle on it.

Tired of sitting, I got up and said to Mum, 'Can I help you with anything?' She replied, 'Yes, there's a tablecloth in that drawer of the table!' I got the cloth out and spread it out over the table; knives and forks were in the same drawer. Mum was bending over the cooking range, opened the door of the oven and produced a whole lot of fish and chips, with slices of bread and butter, salt and vinegar, and a pot of tea; we had our first real meal of the day. Afterwards, we cleared the table; hot water from the kettle soon had everything washed up and dried on a towel that I found hanging up.

After tea, I went exploring round the house. There was no electricity, it had not been invented when they built this property; no gas, one water tap, outside the back door on a wall! No bathroom, it had not been invented, and no kitchen, also not invented, just four rooms, two downstairs, and two upstairs. The lavatory was a 'Black Hole of Calcutta!' at the end of the yard, which didn't flush with water – you had to fill the bucket, outside the door, with water, to flush the lavatory. I never knew what colour the walls were, if there was any paint on it at all, it was so dark inside. There was a yard between the back door and the lavatory, a coal place was just outside the back door and next to it was a huge zinc bath hanging on the wall. Did Mum do the washing in that, or did we have a bath in it? Any water for tea, cooking or washing in the morning, or at night, had to be collected in the big kettle outside the door.

The second room downstairs was for Grandad, and the two bedrooms upstairs, both reasonably large, were for Mum and the other boy, with the other for Phillip and me. Lewis was still at Frodsham.

My mother had a small round crystal set (very early radio) which used to go only when it wanted to; there were a pair of wires attached to a pair of earphones, and you could, if you were quiet, hear music on them; from time to time, a man's voice could be heard saying, 'This is 2LO calling!' the broadcasting station at the time; the early radios were very primitive, with only one person able to hear through the earphones at a time. The whole building was in complete darkness all the time, so we lived with a candle in our hands.

We didn't spend much time at home during the day, when we had washed from the only tap outside, had breakfast, done all the chores; we were off, down to Regents Park, which lies to the left of Baker Street, glad to get out from the house and its dark interior. We stayed near the lake with Grandad on a seat; Mum went off to work at a house near Baker Street for three hours and left us to our own devices. At twelve o'clock Mum returned with some cheese rolls which we ate for lunch.

After we'd eaten our cheese rolls, we made our way by bus to Edgware Road, and went into a shop to buy a pair of plimsolls for Phillip and myself. Plimsolls, were a white, lightweight shoe, like tennis shoes. The man behind the counter was a cobbler, who said, 'What size do they take?' pointing towards me; with that, I took off one of my boots, and said, 'About this size!' He said, 'Good Heavens, where on earth did you get these from?' turning them over and over, first to see the soles, then the uppers, continuing 'I have seen army boots, but nothing like this!' 'We wear them in the orphanage, steel bars on the soles and heels and studs,' I said. 'They certainly don't want you to wear them out, do they?' I left it to the end, I said, 'These are my best ones, you want to see the pair I wear every day, I have corns on my little and big toes!' He replied, 'No!' I took off my socks and showed him my feet. 'I do see, my boy!' he said, looking up at my mother. 'He certainly can speak up for himself, can't he?' he said, and went on, 'This is a disgrace, I'd like to keep these boots and display them in my window!' Mum said, 'I'm afraid he's got to go back in them!'

Mother then purchased two pairs of plimsolls, one pair for me and one pair for Phil, which we wore right away and right through the holiday.

We went into a new store called Woolworth's next, a store that was springing up in every city in the country, so my mother said. As you went inside it took you aback, the smell of perfumes and new things on display; there were rows of counters to the left and down the centre and down to the right; it sold nearly everything, but to me, I had only eyes for the toys, especially train sets and cranes.

Every article was either threepence or sixpence, nothing more or less, and so it remained, the threepenny and sixpenny store, right through the 1920s and 1930s. It originated in the USA and caught on like wildfire over here, in England.

Mother bought us each a 'snake' belt, as they were called at the time, owing to the fact that it had a fastener on the front just like a 'snake', in metal, and clipped together. You could purchase them in various colours, red and yellow, red and grey, or green and yellow, for sixpence each. I wore a red and grey one – nearly everyone was wearing a snake belt in the summertime; it became a craze that went on into the 1930s.

Finally, Mum bought us a small fishing net on the end of a four-foot cane, especially for catching 'tiddlers' in the Regents Park lake; they cost threepence each; with a couple of jam jars, with a loop tied around the neck of the jar, we'd be fully occupied in the mornings, catching tiddlers.

A day or two later, Mum didn't have to go to work that day, so we caught a bus in Baker Street, a General omnibus to Trafalgar Square. We soon discovered the big shops down Oxford Street, Selfridges, I remember. Eventually we came to Trafalgar Square, where Mum pointed out places of interest like the Tate Gallery, St Martins-in-the-Fields, the Admiralty Arch, South Africa House, Whitehall and Nelson's Column and the fountains; before we could say 'Jack Robinson' we were off down Whitehall, passing the Admiralty on our right, then we alighted near the Cenotaph, crossed the road and there was a Life Guard, all in shining armour, sitting on a black horse; he looked magnificent. We walked through an archway which brought us out on the Horse Guards Parade; at the far end was St James's Park, to the right of the park stood the Guards Memorial, so we were told, surmounted by five guardsmen – Grenadier, Coldstream, Scots, Irish and Welsh guardsmen. Keeping to the left we entered St James's Park, walked to the far end of the park and came out opposite Buckingham Palace where the changing of the guard was about to take place. The band and the guard could be heard coming from Buckingham Palace Road; within a few minutes they could be seen approaching; the streets were lined with crowds of people, so much so that we could only see the bearskins on the top of their heads and the band and the guard disappeared through the gates into the forecourt or parade ground in the front of the palace. A few minutes later a drum and fife band, complete with a guard, came out and marched up the Mall to St James's Palace, which is situated on the left of the Mall, there to change the old guard, so I was told! The changing of the guard seemed to take a long time, I thought. All I could see was the backs of crowds of people. I looked up and I could see a gold coloured flag fluttering from a mast. I said to Mum, 'What flag is that?' She said, 'That is the King's Standard; when it is flying from the masthead, he is in residence!' I said, 'What king is that?' Mum replied, 'King George V.'

We walked back the way we had come and sat down in the park, Mum produced some sandwiches from a bag she was carrying and we tucked into these; we sat for about an hour, before tracing our steps to the Life Guards Parade, turned to the right and saw a building with words 'The Treasury'. We continued towards Big Ben and the Houses of Parliament. Turning left we approached Westminster Bridge, turned left again and walked along the Embankment alongside the Thames, where we sat down and watched the traffic on the river. What was all that noise? I quickly turned my head to see – trams, loads of them, they don't half make a noise with all the rattling they made on the rails, all turning left over Westminster Bridge in the direction of Kennington, so it said, on the front of the tram.

Later we caught a bus in Whitehall, which took us back through Trafalgar Square, passing through Leicester Square, Oxford Street, finally turning right into Baker Street and home to Lynhope Street.

One day of our holiday, Phil and I were taken to the public baths in Edgware Road, where for sixpence we could have a luxury bath, with as much hot water as we wanted. I had never seen a public bath before, they were huge and the taps were enormous. The attendant came in and gave me a huge hot towel and soap; he ran the water; it gushed out, all steaming hot; when he was satisfied that the water was alright, he left saying, 'Ring the bell, if you want anything!' I said, 'No, it will be fine!' We left Mum in the waiting room, she, no doubt settled the bill. I never had a bath like it since, everywhere was so warm; I came out not only clean, but I felt several pounds lighter.

We returned to Lynhope Street just in time to catch the 'Walls Ice Cream' man, who came on his tricycle into our street twice a day; he used to ring his bell and shout, 'Walls Ice Cream! They're lovely!' He used to ride a three-wheeled tricycle; supported on the front two wheels, was a huge refrigeration box, painted blue with white letters, which used to read, 'Walls Ices, Stop Me and Buy One!' He wore a uniform with a peaked cap. He kept all sorts of ices down to the halfpenny 'Snowfruit' which Mum bought us. These Walls Ice Cream tricycles were known and seen all over the south of the country in the summertime.

One day we went to the Zoo in Regent's Park, I remember. I didn't care to see all the animals in cages and tanks, it didn't seem natural to me. I soon got bored and went back into the park.

Phillip, Mum and myself went to Windsor Castle on a lovely summer's day; how we got there from Lynhope Street, I can't remember. I know we had a photo taken on a large round tower, but other than that, I don't remember much of the castle.

No holiday would be complete without a visit to the old 'Met', the Metropolitan Music Hall in Edgware Road; we must have gone to an afternoon's performance with variety on the stage. I was thrilled with all the coloured lights which shone on all the singers, the indicators on each side of the stage, from one to ten, as each act finished, so the number changed from one to two and so on; the orchestra put in a good performance too. The Met was demolished after the War.

I had my photo taken in Regents Park, beside the lake, where we had spent so many hours catching tiddlers with our nets; one thing which stays in my mind, the beautiful flower beds; there were enormous blooms, which must have been dahlias or peonies, they were so large. I'd never seen such gardens, and so our holiday came to an end. Monday morning we would discard our nice clothes, white shirt, with a snake belt, nice socks and our white plimsolls; the boots would hurt my feet as before, the old clothes would have to be worn again!

Monday morning, I said goodbye to my Grandad; he was my Mother's father. The other boy, who was he? Why did Phillip and I have to go back to the orphanage, and he was staying behind? It didn't seem fair to me! Who was he? He was not a member of my family. I was the youngest Doe, that was for sure! He was probably adopted – yes, that was the answer. We never knew until much later!

We caught a General omnibus outside Baker Street Station for Euston Station, where I said goodbye to my mother, thanked her very much for our lovely holiday; I didn't say any more, but got on the train in numb silence. I didn't know what to say, it all seemed so wrong and bewildering, going back, having been home. I don't remember either of us kissing my mother, or asking when we were coming home again, or how long we had to stay at Frodsham. I don't remember Phil saying anything either, he was struck dumb too, I think!

The train moved off very silently, one minute Mum was there, the next minute she was gone. Phil was waving frantically out of the window, then we sat down in a compartment, and just looked at each other in absolute silence, then turning, looked at the scenery going by, there were no tears from either of us; we had got used to being 'shut off' in the orphanage, the only tears I had were for Spencer. Nothing else. I was hard!

Phil prematurely opened the case and took out some sandwiches that Mum had packed for us; we helped ourselves to them. I let my mind wander over the last fortnight. It had gone all too quickly. There was my Grandad! Where had he come from? He wasn't at 30 Grove Street, Leamington. Neither was this Mr Miles who kept putting in an appearance every time we went anywhere. My mind wandered from one thing to another; the time passed quickly, until I heard a man shout, 'This is Rugby Station, Rugby!' I came to with a bump. I looked across at Phil, who was fast asleep. I looked down at my boots, which were beginning to pinch my toes. I must see Sister about my boots, must get a larger size. Gone were the plimsolls; they were so comfortable. Yes, I would ask Sister Edith; she was the nicest Sister; she would help me, so different from Sister Florence, the Senior Sister. I was her baby! I don't think so, the old die-hard, made to measure for the National Children's Home and Orphanage. Time she retired – punishment was the operative word in her vocabulary. Her full name was Florence De Walklett, and she came from a well-to-do family in Oxford. She was about fifty years of age, rather overweight, suffered from gout from time to time and had to be wheeled about in an invalid chair. As a Senior Sister, she was always dressed in a dark navy blue gown that came down to a few inches above her black shoes. She had a large white starched collar at the neck and six-inch starched cuffs at her wrists. A very large gold badge, complete with gold chain, in the form of a lifebelt she wore in the centre of her white starched collar, which read on the outside rim of the lifebelt, 'To Seek and To Save'; underneath the lifebelt it read, 'The National Children's Home and Orphanage'. She wore rimless spectacles, which to me used to make her broad head appear more masculine than it was; she was to all us boys, a typical matron type. I was 'Her baby!' so she said when I arrived at the orphanage – heaven forbid! The only thing I haven't mentioned is the headgear. All the Sisters wore the same, a small pillbox hat, held on to the top of the head with hat pins, made of a dark blue, pleated material fixed to the rear of the pillbox hat which used to hang folded down the back for approximately three feet, which made them look similar to nuns, or sisters of Holy Orders. The Junior Sisters wore exactly the same uniform in grey material, with a badge at the centre of the white starched collar in silver, with the same inscription.

Sister Edith was a Junior Sister, having only been at Frodsham a short while. She was Irish, and a natural Irish beauty. I used to admire her in my own boyish way; she was very strict, but was very kind; she and another Junior Sister did all the work, bathed us, cooked for us, did all the mundane jobs connected with the boys; she was a lovely person, but her life ended tragically in 1930, as we shall see!

My mind was so wrapped up in the orphanage that I hadn't realised we were stopping at Crewe; it had some high glass panels between the platforms, as high as the roof; the only reason for this was to stop all the smoke spreading all over the station; it went upwards instead. I went outside, stood in the corridor and watched red engines coming and going. Phil was fast asleep, I felt so alone; I felt like crying, but the tears wouldn't come. I hadn't cried before, not even at five years of age, so I wouldn't cry now. I suppose I had become hardened with the discipline of the orphanage; later on I would be grateful for the discipline and the stiff upper lip that was being meted out to me every day of my life. I looked at the track opposite, it was whizzing past me, taking my brother and I farther and farther away from home. How long would I have to endure the orphanage? How old would I be? Fourteen? Fifteen? Had I done something wrong to be shut away like this? Would we all go to Australia or New Zealand, Canada or South Africa? When we are fifteen like so many of my past mates have done, never to be seen by us ever again! The holiday seemed all a dream now. I came to with a jolt, we were coming in to Chester. 'This *is* Chester!' said a guard who was coming through the train shouting. I looked at Phil, who was just stirring himself. I said, 'I wonder if there is anyone here to meet us.' The train pulled to a stop; I helped to get the case down from the rack and made for the nearest door. I got out and looked around, nobody for us! Then suddenly, there she was – Sister Edith! I rushed to meet her; there was that smile again, my troubles left me. 'Hello, Mervan!' she said with her Irish accent. 'Hello, Phillip!' she said. 'Hello, Sister!' we both said. I looked up into her face, when she said, 'Did you have a nice holiday?' 'Yes, thanks!' I said. She took our case with one hand and reached for my hand with the other. She had never held my hand before; it was a touch of motherly instinct, anyway, I felt as though I was wanted! We went over the bridge to get the train to Frodsham; the train was already in, just as if it was waiting for us; we climbed aboard and sat down in a compartment which said 'Third'. I was just about to ask her about the 'Third', when she said, 'You're looking well, both of you!' Phil said, 'Yes, we're fine.' Her face seemed to light up, when I looked at her and said, 'Yes, I'm feeling much better now, thank you.'

The little old engine, with its three small carriages slowly moved out of Chester Station and chugged away to Helsby, very soon we saw Helsby Crag loom up and in the distance was Overton Hill. My heart sank and my stomach turned over, the atmosphere changed dramatically. I thought at once of lumpy porridge, two doorsteps of bread and grease on tin plates and enamel mugs on bare wooden tables and forms, cold fat for lunch on Sundays; but worst of all, the learning of prayers every week, for every month of the year; there'd be no lying in in the mornings – the seven steps would have to be washed down before breakfast! I could see Sister Florence picking up her Bible, saying, 'The reading for this week will be from the book of Matthew, Chapter so and so!' oh dear! for every Monday, for every week of the year!

Phillip searched for the tickets and handed them to Sister Edith, as the train was now pulling into Frodsham Station; we got out and walked over the footbridge, through the side gate, handed the tickets to the man who stood there at the gate, down some steps which brought us out by some shops in Church Street.

I laughed as we stood waiting for a small 'Crossville' bus. Sister Edith said, 'What are you laughing at, Mervan?' in her Irish accent. 'I remember the last time I stood here in 1922.' I said. 'The Governor couldn't start his Morris Cowley; he was a full fifteen minutes trying to get it started. Well, I saw him the Saturday before our holiday, the day he was leaving the orphanage, and his car wouldn't start then!' 'Oh dear, poor Mr Schofield!' said Sister Edith. That's not what I thought about him. With that the bus arrived and within a few minutes we were stopping at the Main Gate; we made our way up the left-hand drive, round the Circle to John Fowler House, where we were greeted at the front door by Sister Florence. 'Have a good holiday, Phillip and Mervyn?' We said, 'Yes, thank you!' She said, 'You will see a few changes since you have been away.' (Not before time, I thought!)

I thanked Sister Edith for coming to meet us; she gave me a warm smile and said, 'It was a pleasure!'

We went into the Dining Room and had tea, two doorsteps again, smothered in some sort of grease. 'Now boys, your attention please!' Sister Florence began. 'The reading for this week will be from the book of St Matthew, Chapter so and so, verses one to . . . and you will learn hymn number so and so, the first four verses' – we were back!

I retired to the Day Room with my Bible and hymn book and studied the reading for the week and the first four verses of the hymn till bedtime, which was later now I was ten years of age. I was none the wiser, although I had gone over it time after time; bedtime came and I was glad to feel the pillow and the comfort that it brought and so I slept.

The clanging of the handbell woke me up with a start. The Junior Sister was giving it all it was worth. For God's sake stop that infernal din! I thought. So there's been one or two changes, has there? *Not* as many as there's going to be! The clanging of the bell will go – for a start! I watched where the Junior Sister put the bell – I see, upon a ledge above the door. Right! I made a mental note of it for that evening, before anyone went to bed.

When I had dressed, made my bed, rushed downstairs, had my wash, been to the cupboard under the stairs, pinched a couple of carrots out of a sack, retrieved the bucket, scrubbing brush and a cloth, dashed into the washplace, drawn some water, proceeded to open the front door, turned right for some ten yards and stopped at the head of seven large steps, it was quite daylight, not too bad at this time of the year. Come winter, when we had three feet of snow, and it was dark and slippery, you couldn't see your bucket! But you could now. Swoosh! Down the steps it went. I made sure that each step was clean and had received some water – that was my job until the following morning. Then went into breakfast, sat down and waited for the other boys to come in after completing their allotted tasks.

Sister Florence walked in, followed by Sister Edith and the Junior Sister carrying their breakfast and coffee on nice bone china with silver coffee pot and silver milk jug. 'Good morning, boys' she said. 'Good morning, Sisters,' we replied in unison. Down came the lumpy porridge on tin plates, followed by two great slices, doorsteps, two each, with some sort of grease, not dripping, just axle grease. When everyone was served with 'an insult to a breakfast' there was a total hush. Sister Florence said the grace: 'For what we are about to receive, May the Lord make us truly Thankful!' We all said, 'Amen.' the boys tucked into the porridge as though it was delicious, helping themselves to salt, which was always the only thing that was on the table; things hadn't changed very much, I thought!

After we had cleared away the breakfast things and washed up, I went off to school. We had a male teacher for the first time; it didn't take long to find out why the class was so quiet and well behaved. He caught my attention from the outset; he was very tall and slim, with broad shoulders and a back as straight as a ramrod; he had a lean cut face, quite good looking, marked only by the loss of one eye. Here was a military man, his whole manner was one of a man used to giving orders; he'd lost his eye in battle no doubt; his name was Mr Peagum. I shall always remember, he was most efficient. I admired him, here was a real man, someone you could look up to; I remember that he always had a well-behaved class.

During the morning break, I noticed that the school was inundated with workmen everywhere you went. I said, 'What on earth is going on?' One boy said, 'They're putting in electricity.' ELECTRICITY! For months the men worked on every house and public building, putting wires through ceilings and walls, fitting various types of globes and switches.

Gone were those horrible fishtail brackets, with a single little 'Bunsen' burner that had to be lit with a match by the duty Sister, before anyone could see to get into bed, and when she had lit the bracket, which was always near the door, you could just find your bed. Now the place seemed to be flooded with light just with a flick of a switch!

The new Governor was taking over; he was everywhere, seeing to this, seeing to that; everywhere he went, he was followed by a multitude of children; he always had a smile on his face and had time to talk to the children. He became very popular and turned out to be the finest governor we had at Frodsham; his name was Mr S. Snell.

The first thing he did was to provide every girl and boy with a new pair of sandals; he thought the existing boots (not shoes) were diabolical; that was over 300 pairs of sandals! That was only for the summertime, of course, in the winter we went back to our boots. The corns on each of my little and large toes persisted well after I had left the orphanage. Not until I joined the Navy, nine years later, did I get them removed and have never suffered from them since.

Evening came, we had tea; everyone was excited by the new electric light, it was daylight everywhere, especially out in the washplaces and the toilets. The Sisters were so engrossed – I saw my chance! I shot upstairs to the landing, found the bell, removed the clapper by means of turning a screw, which came away quite easily, replaced the bell as I had found it, wrapped the clanger in a rag and stuffed it into my shirt, not having a pocket, and raced downstairs, through the swing doors to the washplaces, through the back door, into the yard, whereupon I threw it as hard and as far as I could into the bushes, up on the bank, which ran along that part of the yard.

Nobody would ever look for it up there. That was that then!

The following morning, I awoke to a terrible commotion going on. The Junior Sister was put out! Someone had removed the clapper from the bell; there was no way of waking the boys up properly. Oh dear, what a shame! The Sister had to go round waking every boy separately; how peaceful it was, no clanging of the bell, backwards and forwards, up the dormitories. Naturally, nobody had touched the bell! Somebody had taken it! Who took it! Questions were asked among the boys. I left to go down to the washplace – I wasn't going to own up to it! I left the Sisters on the landing still examining the bell.

There was an uncanny silence at breakfast that morning. Sister Florence said, 'Quiet please!' The grace was said and other than that, there was absolute silence!

The conclusion after weeks of silence was that the clapper must have got loose, eventually falling off and rolling away somewhere. There was no other conclusion. Anyway, they never had it repaired or replaced, so *that* was the end of the bell. A great improvement all round!

A week or two later we were going up to Overton Hill. I remember it was a very hot day and my garters were irritating my legs as they were too tight, so I hung about near the back door hoping to see Sister Edith to get them changed. I walked up a steep bank at the rear of the yard; on the right-hand side was a high wire mesh fence; several boys were on the other side heaving great granite stones over the fence. The first one missed me, it was as big as a pudding basin, followed by the second; it caught me fair and square on the top of my head and knocked me out. I remember coming to being carried by a fireman's lift by my brother, Lewis, who was running down the bank with me, to John Fowler House. I opened my eyes for a second, but closed them immediately; blood was pouring down my face; it seemed as though I was losing pints of it! In actual fact, it was running down into my eyes. I said to myself, 'Keep your eyes shut tight!'

As we approached the back door of John Fowler, Sister Edith rushed up to help, saying, 'What on earth has happened to Mervan [Irish accent]?' She took me to the washplace and ran the water; my head was immersed in cold water; when I opened my eyes again, all I could see was a basin of blood; my head was being held firmly in an effort to stop the flow!

After a while, the doctor came. I don't remember being asked to sit down, as I felt very dazed, all I got from him was, 'What you again?' and he bent over to look at my head. 'What wars have you been in this time?' he asked. I said, 'I haven't been in any wars – I was just minding my own business!' He said, 'That's a change! Now keep still a minute, I'm going to examine your head!' He poured something on it, 'Ow! it hurts!' I said. I think it was Iodine on an open wound. 'He's lucky there's no fracture!' he said to Sister Edith; he had stopped the flow of blood and was putting a dressing on it, followed by a bandage, which went round vertically, under my chin, and horizontally above my ears. In the end, I looked like an out-of-work rugby player. 'Keep that on, and I'll come and see him, in a day or two,' he said to Sister Edith.

I still didn't sit down and rest, as it was dinnertime so I went into dinner with the rest of the boys, which was a sort of mutton stew, with no dumplings, followed by prunes, with no custard – we never, ever had custard.

After dinner, I felt a bit better, my headache was clearing. Sister Edith said, 'Do you feel like a walk this afternoon, Mervan?' I said, 'Yes, I'll be alright, thank you Sister. Oh, by the way, could I have a pair of garters, these are too tight, they're hurting my legs.' She said, 'Yes, certainly, come with me to the Clothing Store!' We went to the store and soon got me fixed up with a more comfortable pair of garters. 'Thank you very much!' I said, I caught her smile!

At two o'clock we left for Overton Hill, Sister Florence, Sister Edith and about twenty-five boys. It was a hot day in late summer as we walked out of the back gate, passed the Frog Pond, up the cinder road, passed the Dell, walking all the way upwards for nearly half an hour before coming to Sandy Lane, which slowed us up considerably, because it was all sand, nearly a foot deep for nearly 300 or 400 yards; caused by the high rocks of sandstone on either side of the cutting. We pressed on and came to Cromers Lake, which was big enough to sail a small dinghy on. Turning right we eventually came to the large caves on our right; nobody was ever seen near them; they were some distance apart from each other. The first thing which we saw as we reached the summit was the Helter-Skelter which stood out like a lighthouse at the top of the hill.

We all sat down for a while to get our breath back and to take in the panoramic view, which had to be seen to be believed. It was a fantastic sight there; suddenly there was a little train, a miniature train making its way along to Helsby, several hundred feet below; you couldn't hear it, but you could just make out the smoke going, 'Chuff, chuff, chuff!' on its merry way – suddenly, I felt dizzy. I mentioned this to the Sister who said I shouldn't have come out that afternoon. 'Sit next to me, it will pass if you sit quietly!' I said, 'Thank you, Sister!' She smiled, and I thought, how nice it would be if she was my mother.

We would go home eventually – when, we didn't know. Spencer had left and died, all in less than a year. Lewis was the next eldest, he was due to go home shortly, so I was told; he was fifteen years old. Phillip was just over a year younger than Lewis, at fourteen years of age. Douglas, who was being brought up by my Uncle Harry in Haverhill, in Suffolk, was twelve years of age. I was the youngest brother, then ten years of age. It seemed as though we had been here a lifetime; it was to my brothers and myself a form of punishment, which would stay with us all our lives; it was especially so to Lewis, as long after, years later, he was bitter to my mother, and when she died in 1968, he let rip, and told her just what he thought of her. In fact, he said things that he shouldn't have done, to a woman, my mother, who was dying; even if I say so myself, it was unforgivable. When I came down from Norwich to

Shoreham, I saw my mother, who was heartbroken, and then she died, in pain! That was 1968. That's how bitter we had become.

Life was much harder at Frodsham than I have written about – one has to experience it; people who were born in the nineteenth century were brought up very strictly with a code of living that is hardly ever seen today. They were people of character and a sense of pride of oneself and of one's country, England, and its Empire, were paramount; they were a hard people, who lived a life of hard work and discipline and duty; mix in the word 'punishment' and you get some idea of how the orphanages were being run while we were there!

Mr Schofield, the retired, or sacked, Governor, was a tyrant or worse, a sadist who kept his sticks or canes in a jar of vinegar to keep them pliable; he punished boys with them for nothing at all. Spencer, my eldest brother, was punished regularly with a big stick, because he collected birds' eggs. He told us that he only took an egg if there were several in the nest; if there were only two or one, he would leave the nest alone. I for one believed him; he had a valuable collection, which he took home with him.

When you sit at the top of Overton Hill, you have the time to take stock of life around you, and today was just one of those days. We made our way back to the orphanage, downhill all the way; my head had cleared, but still felt sore. Sandy Lane was an obstacle – it filled your boots up with sand, taking it back to John Fowler and emptying our boots at the back door.

The doctor called to see my head, and said it was alright, but to keep the dressing on. He said, 'You will have a large scar there when it clears up!' I was doing well for scars, one on my right knee, now, one on my head; I was living a charmed life!

Sunday was outside church, marching to Five Crosses Church; there were no buses to worry about; we would continue marching in the road as we always did. The new buses that had started running from Northwich to Frodsham, didn't run on Sundays. Sunday was still a day of rest – there were no shops open, people were not encouraged to spend money on a Sunday, and the churches were full. We were never allowed to walk on the pavement, the pavement was for the Sisters only.

Sunday dinner was the same as usual, cold, mostly white fat and cold potatoes; it never changed, winter or summer; there was no cooking on a Sunday; there was always this large jar plonked in the centre of the table, salt! I used to use a lot of salt as it helped down the fat; there was no bread, but there was an apple or a pear for afters, in season; afterwards we helped clear away and wash up.

Every Sunday afternoon was spent in the Day Room either painting, drawing, or just reading. Sometimes Sister Edith would play on the piano; she could play well and soon would have a lot of the boys round her. I would stand on her right side and turn the pages; they were the songs of the day. She wasn't playing for long before she broke into quiet singing and we used to join in. I remember one that comes to mind:

> I vow to thee, my Country, all earthly things above,
> Entire and Whole and Perfect, the Service of my Love,
> The Love that asks no question, the Love that stands the test,
> That lays upon the altar, the dearest and the best,
> The Love that never falters, the Love that pays the price,
> The Love that makes undaunted, the final Sacrifice.

We all joined in singing 'I vow to thee my Country' and many more, like 'Jerusalem the Golden.' As I stood there next to Sister Edith, my eyes always went to the picture above the piano, the 'Boyhood of Raleigh'. I looked to where the old sailor was pointing out to sea. I thought, would I go to sea one day? The afternoon passed very quickly because the next I knew, the Junior Sister was calling out 'Teatime'. We all went into the Dining Room; when everyone was settled and in their places, Sister Florence said the grace. We all tucked into the doorsteps that each boy had on his enamel plate, and all looked forward to our weekly ration of one slice of seed cake on Sundays.

This was followed by the opening of the bookcase, which allowed us a book of our choice once a week. I always chose books of the sea, about the big liners of the day and the Royal Navy. The time went very quickly, soon they called all the boys to get ready for evening prayers in the Main Hall.

The Governor, Mr Snell, took the service; halfway through he produced several slips of paper. We knew the meaning of the slips of paper; silence fell on the whole assembly; they were reports of the latest batch of boys who had been shipped to Australia, New Zealand and Canada, several months ago. I listened – some had settled down on the sheep farms, some did very well, others, not so well; they were all orphans. Not in every case, not in the Doe family.

The days passed with monotonous regularity, except that morning we had to fall in, in the hall, in a line, with our mugs in our hands. Sister Florence came from the kitchen carrying a large enamel jug. 'Get your mugs ready, boys!' Just half a mug full of senna pods was poured into each cup and we all had to drink it down, on the spot. We were lucky, last time it was 'Cascara'! And we all knew how terrible that was; we used to have a dose of one or the other every three or four weeks.

One day I was up in the Upper Playing Area, where the swings were amongst the trees, when I heard a most unusual sound coming from above the trees; suddenly I saw it, it was an aeroplane; it shone all silver. Round and round it was going. It looked as though it was coming down, getting noisier every minute, then it landed in the field where we had had our battle with bows and arrows and disappeared after taxying quite a way over the hill, down towards Frodsham. I learnt later that it belonged to the millionaire who lived in a large house, surrounded by trees and bushes, known as the 'Castle' at the foot of Overton Hill. I had seen my first aeroplane!

In the autumn of 1929, Lewis, now the eldest Doe, left the orphanage and Frodsham. I wasn't told he was going, the orphanage was like that – people were there one day and gone the next. I would have liked to have seen him before he left. I learnt several years later that while Lewis was on the Chester-Euston train, he had a conversation with a man, who asked Lewis if he would go to the Buffet Car and get some cigarettes for him, which he did. The man asked Lewis his name and address, and he said that he'd just left the orphanage at Frodsham. He said he was a Mr Dutton of Dutton's Engineering Co. He gave Lewis his card, and told him to make an appointment when he got home, which he did. He got the job as a heating engineer, and worked at Dutton's for close on thirty years.

Winter came with a vengeance that year, bringing heavy falls of snow before Christmas. Cromers Lake was frozen over, so was the Frog Pond near the rear entrance. The slides in the back yard were in abundance, terrific long slides, whole stretches of ice, which kept us warm running backwards and forwards; the only parts that suffered were our hands and knees; my hands used to swell up with no gloves in those days. My legs used to feel red raw with the chafing of the serge trousers.

Early in the morning, the clearing of the seven front steps became a terrible job as it was dark and freezing cold. I brushed them down as best I could without slipping down; the amount of salt I used didn't last the week; more had to be ordered; Sister Florence saw to that. The front steps had to be kept clear at all times as she had fallen down the steps one day long before my time. She was no lightweight and hurt herself badly, so when I said, 'There's no salt,' the Sisters were up to the Cookhouse for more.

Two of my mates and I went up to the Frog Pond in the dinner hour one day during the big freeze; each of us dared each other to walk over the pond to the other side. The pond was quite large, large enough to have a huge slide about thirty or forty yards; it was frozen solid except where the bushes overhung the pond. The ice near the overhanging bushes looked black to me and it looked very deep that end. I walked quite gingerly out from the edge; turning round, I said to my mates, 'It's as solid as a rock.' I kept walking until I reached the centre, turned round and said, 'There you are, easy.' I noticed that the ice seemed to turn from white to a dark grey. I stopped in my tracks and gently turned round to go back the way I had come. The next second it gave way, and crash! I went through the ice. I grabbed at a whole sheet of ice but that just sank; I was up to my armpits, only my head and arms were above the water. I tried to climb on to ice, but it gave way every time. I kept treading water, making for the bank, until I managed to get on to thicker ice. Eventually I got out, soaked to the skin. Where could I get dry? I went shivering in to the Main Hall, knowing there was a huge central pipe inside the door which was very hot. I wrapped myself around it until the bell sounded for school; it stopped my shivering. I don't remember whether I got dry, although I suppose I must have to a certain extent because I went back to my class until 3.45 p.m. and returned to John Fowler House none the worse, except for my boots, which kept squelching away; and next day, no cold at all!

Christmas came and went with plenty of decorations in the house and the Main Hall; an enormous amount of greenery was used, and there were toys sent to the orphanage. As usual they were broken or had a wheel missing. Large tins of boiled sweets were sent, as on previous Christmases. Each tin held several pounds, but the Sister walked round the two tables, offering a sweet per boy, then we wouldn't see the tin again. We got used to this ritual, us older boys, as it was repeated every year. We also knew that a great deal of food of different kinds was sent for us, the orphans and children, but it got as far as the Staff Dining Hall and the Kitchens, which was the same place as the Bakery that was adjoining. What went on there, we never knew. The children never went into any of these premises, or were not allowed near them. What we did know was that the staff benefited greatly by the generosity of people outside, time and time again, not only at Christmas. Regular donations of food were sent but we didn't receive them because the daily diet didn't change one iota. In actual fact, we were short of food the whole time I was there. I cannot ask anyone else because they were all shipped out to the colonies up to the War, or are dead, but I have an excellent memory and it died hard with me.

The Principal of the National Children's Home and Orphanage, Dr Stephenson, was due to be coming up from the headquarters at Highbury, North London, in the New Year of 1930. His visit was overdue. When Mr Schofield was dismissed as Governor in 1928, there was a public outcry as to the way the orphanages were being run; pilfering was suspected, but it was hushed up and nothing came of it.

I was eleven years of age by now having taken my place on the long table a year or so before. I had taken my share in the household chores, like clearing away the tables after meals, not forgetting the washing down of the seven front steps at 6.30 every morning.

The books I was allowed to read now from the bookcase on a Sunday evening were not children's books, but were huge books in picture form of the Great War. France and Belgium were the battlefields of slaughter and everywhere poppies grew in abundance; it made a great impression on me.

I remember reading books on great liners, ships of the White Star Line, of Cunard; there was the *Oceanic*, *Olympic*, *Majestic*, *Titanic*, also the *Lusitania*, *Berengaria*, *Aquitania*, the *Mauritania*, long before the *Queen Mary* and the *Queen Elizabeth* were built. I enjoyed reading books of the sea.

The spring of 1930 came early that year. I was breaking all the rules of the orphanage, playing on the wrong side of the Circle, on the girls' side, on the lower part where Mr Schofield had caught me looking at his car. I was playing football with two or three other boys; one boy had received a football for Christmas and we were racing along with the ball towards the Main Gate, dribbling with the ball. I was acting as goalkeeper; one boy rushed at me with the ball and I rushed at him but he was not getting past me! We collided with an almighty 'bang', so that we piled up on the ground – he got up, I didn't. I went to get up, but my right leg collapsed and gave me a nasty jab of pain. I had broken it in two places above the knee and at the ankle. The other rule had been broken too, playing football on a Sunday!

Within a few minutes I had a crowd of boys around me, someone had gone up to Newton Hall to summon help; after what seemed an eternity, a stretcher and two boys arrived, I was put on it and carted up to the Hall. Once there, the doctor set the splints; they would examine me further when I arrived at the Chester Infirmary; the splints were a temporary treatment.

I arrived in the dark and was wheeled into a long ward where I fell asleep, was woken by the pain. The doctor and staff were around my bed, which was covered by a red rubber sheet; they were in the process of setting the leg, putting it in plaster, which seemed to go on until the early hours of the next morning.

I seemed to sleep for a short while and was awoken by a duty nurse with a bowl of hot water and a short hand towel. 'You have a wash,' she said. 'Sorry, I can't get up, besides I have no soap or anything,' I replied. She disappeared for a minute and returned with soap and flannel, and washed my face and hands; a quick lick and I was finished with. I lay on my back and took a look at my surroundings. There was a goalpost affair, with one post at the foot of the bed, and another one at the head, with pulleys attached in two or three places; on my injured leg was all plaster, with an iron calliper, which started at my groin and went down each side of the leg, finished up beyond my heel with a screw attachment. This was in case the leg shrank – they could give the 'Calliper' a few turns which would stretch my leg. Each side of my leg were sandbags, used to keep my leg still. The leg did shrink while it was in plaster – to this day it is half an inch shorter than my left, and would give me more trouble late in life.

Eventually, the nurse was coming round asking the patients what they wanted for breakfast. As my bed was out in the centre of the ward, she didn't get round to me until the end. 'And what does our young man want for his breakfast, an egg?' she asked. 'No, I haven't got any eggs,' I said, 'Oh dear,' she said. A man nearest to me said, 'You can have one of mine, if you like!' I said, 'Thanks very much, that will be a treat, I've never had an egg for breakfast.' The Sister came into the ward, called the nurse over and had a long chat with her. From then on, butter wouldn't melt in my mouth – apparently what was said was that I was from the orphanage at Frodsham. They provided me with eggs for my breakfast, apples, oranges and grapes. I felt completely overwhelmed by the generosity of the staff. I thanked them all most sincerely, saying, 'Really, I am not used to it. I never have them, so I don't miss them, but thank you very much indeed!'

One day, one of the nurses bought me a small compact from Chester, with a comb one side and a mirror on the other. She said, 'You hadn't got anything, so I bought you this!' I felt so embarrassed by all the gifts and everyone doing so much for me, that I kissed her on both cheeks and thanked them again, saying, 'I never have anything, so I don't miss them, it's as simple as that.' She blushed, much to the delight of the men patients, and we struck up a friendship that was to last all the time I was in Chester Infirmary.

I was happy in the ward and got to know the other patients. The days passed into weeks; the doctor called to see me from time to time, examined my leg and asked if it was comfortable. I thanked him very much – there was only one thing I had to complain about, my bottom was getting quite sore being on my back the whole time, so he left instructions with the Sister, that I was to have my back rubbed every morning with ointment.

I had no visitors from the orphanage, but Mr Snell had not forgotten me. He sent me the *Boy's Own Paper*, once a week and later a box of Cliptico, similar to Meccano, it just clipped together. In the *Boy's Own Paper*, there was a picture of Sir Henry Segrave, the first of the speed kings of the day, and a picture of his Golden Arrow at Daytona, USA; his speed record in 1929 was 231 m.p.h. There was another picture of a speed king, Kaye Don, in his Silver Bullet. He was going to attempt to raise the land speed record further. A great, long, silver car with a double tail, to act as stabilisers, there were several of these men whose life was racing at Brooklands; it was all the rage; it fired me, they were the most important men to me. At eleven year of age, they were like tin gods! All I could think about was Brooklands, the speed records and that one day I would be a speed king.

There were men like Captain (later Sir) Malcolm Campbell, Sir

Henry Segrave, Kaye Don, George Eyeston, John Cobb, Captain Goldie Gardner, Sir Henry Birkin, Earl Howe, Clive Dunfee and his brother, and several more.

The Cliptico was much quicker on assembling models: they just clipped together. The first thing that I made was a four-foot model of Segrave's Golden Arrow, identical to the actual car; every part was gold like the car; it had a tail, disc wheels complete with rubber tyres and identical cockpit with steering wheel inside. It looked the real thing and was my pride and joy.

At about this time, my bed was moved over to the side, last but one nearest to the door. There was a young man next to me in the corner, a very nice fellow he was, several years older than I. We got on like a house on fire; he would have made a good brother. Wednesdays and Sundays his mother came to visit him and she often looked in my direction and smiled. Her son must have told her that I was from the orphanage at Frodsham; she became very interested in me, visiting me at the same time as her son. I soon became quite attached to them. I liked her and her son very much; she said she lived at Main Street, Frodsham. I said I knew where Main Street was and that it backed on to the railway station (it is now built on, by a new store and a car park). She wondered if I would like to come to tea one day, when I was better? I said, 'Yes, I would love to come,' but she would have to ask Mr Snell, the Governor, first.

The day came and the young man left; they both came to say goodbye to me; she said she was sorry to leave me, but that she would get in touch with the Governor of the orphanage. I said, 'Thank you. I will look forward to it very much.'

I received the first parcel I had ever received from my mother, a chocolate Easter egg. I had never received one before, but Sister Florence must have written to her telling her of my accident and that I was in Chester Infirmary. She wrote to my mother from time to time and continued after we all left. I was 'over the moon' to get an Easter egg; with it was a letter in which she wrote that she and Mr Miles had bought a house together at 7 Brookside, East Barnet in Hertfordshire. Who was Mr Miles? Who was he? I didn't like the news she gave me at all. I couldn't write a letter on my back, so it would have to wait for the time being as I had no pen or writing material, let alone stamps. There was no way of contacting my brother, Phil, either.

About three weeks later I got rid of my goalposts over my bed, but the calliper stayed on.

Eventually, with the warmer weather, I was moved out of the ward, through double doors, out on to a small balcony with one other bed, which was pushed back every night, 1st floor up.

The first thing I noticed was how close we were to the City walls, which came from the right, close to the Infirmary, then went down and joined a tower at the bottom of the hill before turning to the left, disappearing in the distance to the 'Roodee' racecourse.

Next to the wall was a railway tunnel quite close also to the Infirmary. This was the main line from Chester to Llandudno, and Holyhead; it was at that time the LMS (London, Midland and Scottish Railway) from Euston. It ran from the tunnel on a long viaduct over the River Dee, and disappeared in the direction of Rhyl, North Wales. Next to the railway and the tunnel, ran the Shropshire Canal, complete with a vast array of locks. Eventually when the Canal had reached a low level, it turned right and went in the direction of the Wirral.

There was plenty to occupy my day – the railway came so close out of the tunnel, you could see the passengers on the trains; from time to time I got a wave from a passenger who was passing on his way. The Irish Mail express ran regularly. Every carriage had on its side roof a board, in black and white, saying 'The Irish Mail'.

On the Monday, I had a letter from Sister Edith, saying that she was going on holiday to Ireland, leaving Chester at 10.30 a.m. on the Tuesday, on the Irish Mail express for Holyhead. I got the nurse to prop me up and I waited. I had a good view from where I was, and would be able to see her. At 10.30 a.m. I heard the express surge forward from the tunnel with an almighty roar, a big red engine followed by red carriages. I looked as they passed and there she was standing at the window waving a white handkerchief. I raised my arm as if to wave – and she was gone! I wondered whether I would see her again.

About a fortnight later I received a letter from Sister Florence in which she wrote that Sister Edith had been run over by a bus whilst on holiday in Dublin, and had been *killed*! I read the letter again, and couldn't believe it. It wasn't true! She was the most beautiful lady, an 'Irish Beauty', so gentle and understanding. She had become part and parcel of my life. Without her at John Fowler House, life would not be the same; I suddenly dreaded going back.

My bed was moved inside the ward again. I wondered why. The doctor arrived in the afternoon and said they were going to remove the plaster. The calliper was removed and they started cutting down the edge of the plaster, then the other side, carefully removing the plaster in two sections. Suddenly the leg felt quite naked, and my leg started to quiver and jump. I had a job trying to keep it steady, slowly it settled down, but it felt as though it would collapse again without support.

Satisfied, the doctor replaced the calliper and told me to rest it for a day or two. They never at any time measured each leg; if they had done, they would have found that my right leg had shrunk by half an inch!

This oversight on the part of the doctors, was unforgivable – I would pay for it later in life, and pay for it, I did!

Each day I tried to lift myself out of bed, I carefully tried to put the leg down on to the floor with the calliper on; it seemed like jelly, so I left it till the following day, when I tried again and it was a little better; so I just sat on the side of the bed. There was no physiotherapy in those days, you took advice from the Doctor or Sister; one got things done by one's own efforts, so I sat on the bed and just generally moved the leg about, from one side to the other.

The next day, I would try and stand on it; and so I stood upright for a minute. Next day, I tried to walk to the end of the bed, then sat on it. Within a week, I was greatly improved and could just make it to the toilets, unaided and back. And so with each day I got stronger; I was feeling my old self again.

The day came when I left the Chester Infirmary. I was helped into my trousers; my right boot had a hole in the heel to take the end of the calliper, and eventually I stood fully clothed once again, ready to say goodbye to all my friends. I went round to them all saying farewell and thank you for all they had done for me, especially to the Sister and the nurses. A special goodbye to the nurse who bought me a compact mirror and comb; everyone had been just wonderful to me. I will always remember Chester Infirmary and the happy days I spent there.

I arrived back at Newton Hall by ambulance, with spring well underway. It was early in May 1930, the weather stayed sunny during the weeks of convalescence. I was given a single bedroom upstairs in the back of the house, looking out onto gardens. As far as I knew, I was completely on my own. I walked gingerly downstairs and out through the large lounge, through these enormous French windows, with shutters which seemed to begin at the ceiling and ended up at the floor, with ottomans at the side. The gardens were beautiful at this time of the year. I walked out on a lawn looking at the flower beds. Newton Hall had at one time been a country mansion under private ownership before the orphanage was built. It still had some of the trappings left of its heyday, with the decorating kept at a high standard; the gardens had regular men to look after them.

I was never bored at Newton Hall. We used to have coffee at 10.30 a.m. every morning. I couldn't stand coffee in my young days as it was made with milk and I couldn't stand the skin appearing on the surface. I would appreciate it more later in life. I had a regular supply of oranges every day, which were very acceptable. There was a small library downstairs, which I found most useful to spend the time reading.

One afternoon as I lay on my bed reading, when suddenly I heard a drumming noise! Whatever's that? It got louder and louder. The noise filled the room. I raced to the window and saw the biggest thing I'd ever seen. I stood with my mouth open. It was coming directly towards me, only a few hundred feet. It was, I thought, several hundred yards long, and had several engines and propellers. It filled the whole window – and then it disappeared. The roof shook with the noise as it passed overhead. I saw the letters 'R.100' on the side. I learnt later it was the Airship R.100 which was returning from a test flight over the sea and was making her way back to Cardington, in Bedfordshire, where she was built. I was to see three giant airships in the next two or three years.

The following morning, I was told that I would stay at the Hall for about three weeks convalescence, then, I would go back to John Fowler House. I can't remember what I did during those three weeks; having an iron calliper on my leg restricted me somewhat. The days passed slowly, but pass they did, and I was preparing myself to meet Sister Florence. Would I receive some form of punishment for breaking the rules, i.e. playing football on a Sunday afternoon, and for being out of bounds, on the wrong side of the Circle? All these things passed through my mind. The orphanage always had strict rules and woe betide anyone who broke them! But Mr Snell was the new Governor now, not Mr Schofield.

I rejoined my mates in the Day Room of John Fowler House. I expected to see Sister Edith in the room, but no matter how I would look for her at certain times of the day, she would not return ever. I looked at the piano she used to play on a Sunday afternoon; the picture, 'The Boyhood of Raleigh' still hung on the wall above it.

Sister Florence soon broke the spell I was in. 'Hello, Mervyn, are you feeling better now?' she said. 'Yes, thank you, Sister,' I replied. (He's my baby! – Heaven forbid!) She said, 'You won't be going back to school for a while, tomorrow is to be a special occasion.' I replied, 'May I ask what is going to happen?' She said, 'Yes, you may, the Principal of all the orphanages, Dr Stephenson, is arriving at the orphanage tomorrow, and he wants to meet you, especially, at John Fowler House.' 'It's going to be a special occasion' and so on and so on. She was full of it, did *I* remember him? I replied, 'Yes, about a year or two ago, on a Founders Day, wasn't it?' (I remembered meeting the old duffer!)

There was no mention of being punished for breaking the rules – the less said the better! She was so full of her own importance at the moment, having to receive the 'Head of all the Orphanages'. Well, the mind boggles, don't you think?

I said, 'Why me, what have I done to be involved with the Principal?' She replied, 'Nothing! It's just that he has broken his leg too and he has his in a calliper too. It's a great honour to be singled out like this!' I said, 'Oh yes!' sarcastically, 'I don't suppose he was playing football on a Sunday afternoon too?' She replied, 'No! hardly a thing for a gentleman of the cloth to do! Don't be so cheeky!'

On the morrow, a huge black Daimler saloon pulled up outside John Fowler House. The chauffeur assisted the Principal who was having a job getting out of the car. He was all in black, dressed like a bishop, with a large-brimmed black hat, long black coat, with some sort of decoration of 'his office' around his neck, long black stockings and shoes. The only thing which spoilt his appearance of grandeur was his calliper on his left leg. As he turned to come in, I noticed he had a monocle! He made heavy work of walking with a calliper on, and had to be assisted up the seven steps to the front door. He was a huge, fat man, or, gentleman, of middle age, and looked red faced – too much 'Port and Over Ripe Pheasant', I expect. The Junior Sister and I waited in the centre of the hall; Sister Florence showed him inside the front door, assisted by the chauffeur; the Junior Sister was introduced, then he turned to me, 'Oh yes, we have met before, haven't we, Mervyn?' he said. 'Yes, sir!' I replied. 'A year or so ago, on Founders Day.' He said,

'How are you, my dear boy?' Then he said, 'I remember! You're the boy who was reluctant to smile, when we were having our photographs taken. Anyway, how's your leg? Give you much pain?' I replied, 'No, it's quite comfortable now, thank you, sir!' He said, 'I wish I could say the same, you don't get over it so quickly at my age!' With that Sister Florence beckoned us to retire to the Staff Room. It was laid out with the best silverware and crockery on one table, with an assortment of sandwiches and cakes on another.

A cup of tea was handed to his Lordship, followed by sandwiches and cakes; everyone was involved in talking to someone! I had to stand to one side; everybody had a chair except me. Hmm, like that is it? We shall see! There wasn't any room for another chair, the Staff Room wasn't that big, so I remained where I was; eventually I was passed a cup of tea. The talking went on and on: how I broke my leg, being sent to Chester Infirmary, playing football on a Sunday, being quite a good goalkeeper, that raised a few eyebrows round the room. Sister Florence was in her element, going on about me to the Principal, saying that I was her baby, coming to the orphanage at four years old. I tried not to listen, but I kept getting smiles from one and the other. After what seemed like an eternity, they decided to go out of the house, to the bit of lawn in front and have a photograph taken. The Principal was helped by the chauffeur and Sister Florence, a chair was put out for him and there he sat; the Sisters realised it would look funny, him sitting, and we all standing, so more chairs were brought – now we looked a group. Sister Florence produced her Kodak folding camera; the chauffeur was going to take the first shot – the Principal sat in the centre, with me on his left, Sister Florence on his right. This was the day to remember – me being taken with the Principal of the National Children's Home and Orphanage (I don't think)! We all looked at our front, just as he said, 'Ready!' At the last second, I looked up at the sky. 'Click', it went. The chauffeur, he wasn't satisfied: somebody had moved. Who moved? He came over to whisper to Sister Florence to have a word and they both looked in my direction. The chauffeur went back and tried again. Sister Florence bent forward and said to me, 'Come now, Mervyn, you can do better than that' I thought, I know what I will do, I'll smile, then, when the camera goes 'click', I will quickly turn my head. It gave a click, I moved my head! Sister Florence gave me the blackest of looks, went forward and took charge of the camera, saying, 'I think I will take one of the Principal and Mervyn alone.' I smiled beautifully, then just as the camera went click, I went deadpan much to her disgust.

I don't remember the farewell scene, but I do remember him being helped into the car and driving off, without even a smile for me!

I remember it going round the House that I had had my photograph taken with the Principal; it went round like wildfire, but was short-lived. I never saw the photo, neither did my mother, apparently it went into the monthly magazine, instead.

That night I went to bed with mixed thoughts, as I suddenly realised there weren't many boys in the dormitory. I had missed some of them at teatime – what had happened to them? I was older now and able to think for myself. They had quietly emigrated them, fourteen- and fifteen-year-olds to Australia, New Zealand, South Africa and Canada; it had been going on under our very noses for years and years. No wonder we always had those reports at prayers early in the morning, every so often, every month, or so, year in, year out!

Normally, there were thirty boys or girls to a house, in John Fowler House the number fluctuated from thirty to twenty boys. While I had been in the Chester Infirmary, the number had decreased, and a lot of my mates had suddenly disappeared. They were truly orphans with no parents to go home to. We, the Does, were lucky, we had a mother to go home to, or were we lucky? I can name seven or eight boys who suddenly went, disappeared off the earth, even now, over sixty years later. I can still remember them by name. Liverpool was not far away, just the other side of the Mersey; the train would have got you there in under half an hour; very convenient. There were over 200 homes under the National Children's Homes. There were a lot of children to find jobs for and it must have been a headache for the Head Office at Highbury, North London.

I didn't go back to school, but I was informed by one of my mates that at the Woodwork Class one of the older boys had succeeded in making a crossbow. What an achievement! I just had to see it. I went to see the Headmaster, Mr Hunt, he said, 'Of course you may see it, as you were one of the boys who started the bows and arrows.' It was kept in a cupboard and worked perfectly. I said, 'I would have loved to have fired the crossbow,' but, as Mr Hunt said, it was more than we dared do, in view of the restrictions on bows and arrows in the orphanage. I thanked him for letting me see it – little did I realise at the time that I wouldn't be seeing him again.

Sister Florence was very friendly with the Sisters at Annie Fowler House, the first girls' house, the other side of the Main Hall. They asked me if I would like a drive in the Riley saloon which was parked outside Annie Fowler House; a friend had called to see them and they were taking a drive round Helsby. I said, 'Yes, please.' The car came round in the afternoon, so I hobbled out with my calliper on, looking forward to this treat. The time was late May, the weather was perfect, just nice and warm, the gardens were at their best, the air seemed full of scent and blooms were everywhere. Helsby was beautiful at this time of year; it was a marvellous trip. I thanked them for letting me see the gardens – I shall always remember my trip to Helsby one day in May! Soon after this trip, I discarded the calliper on my leg; it felt strange at first, the leg seemed lost without it and seemed to collapse at the knee joint; other than that it was less restricted. I was issued with a new pair of sandals for the summer. I was now nearly twelve years of age and this was the first pair I had ever had. Since 1922 I had had a pair of ill-fitting boots, girls' boots too, with iron bars on the soles and heels; my feet gave me a lot of pain over the years, so to be suddenly issued with a pair of sandals, was heaven. I was walking on air, grateful to the new Governor, Mr S. Snell, for his efforts in getting the orphanage fitted out completely with new sandals; it was unheard of in those days.

Sister Edith was sorely missed; every day I looked for her, but it was not to be, a new Sister came to take her place. I think the Sister's name was Sister Ida, she put herself out to be nice to us all, and would insist on being at the washplaces every morning, washing all the boys' faces and necks; like a breath of fresh air she was, always smiling, always trying to help, but it was to be short-lived – she was getting married soon, in the summer, and was going to Chipping Norton in the Cotswolds to live.

Monday morning arrived, the boys were called by the Sister with no bell clanging away. We made our beds and rushed downstairs through the swing doors to the washplaces. After my wash, I got the bucket from under the stairs, filled it with cold water, went out of the front door, turned right and went along for a few yards to the seven steps; the sun was about to come up over the horizon. I took a look at them, they looked clean, so I slung the water down the steps and returned the bucket to the cupboard, just in time to fall in line with my mug for 'medicine' again. Sister Florence appeared with an enamel jug which held about a gallon of senna pods; we put our mugs out, which in turn were half filled, and drank it down on the spot.

Prior to breakfast, there was the same old ritual: the Junior Sisters came in with their cooked breakfast on a trolley, a silver teapot and jug, the best china, with napkins with silver rings around; we stood there until the Sisters took their places, then we sat, silent, until Sister Florence said the grace.

On Monday morning, we sat there, and had a big surprise for breakfast – we had new china plates and mugs; the old tin plates had disappeared.

I didn't see anything of Phil, my brother, who seemed to hide himself away. I didn't see him at prayers in the Main Hall; Mr Snell took the service, and when he walked down the Hall to the pulpit, I noticed that in his hand was a bundle of reports, from Australia and New Zealand, Canada and South Africa, which he always read out at the end of the service. 'So and so, was not getting on very well,' so it rambled on. I didn't listen as after a while, it seemed to me, that the majority of them were sent under duress; one thing, they were not going to get me on their boats to Australia!

I learnt later that day that I wouldn't be going back to school yet, but I was going home on holiday, not Phillip, just me. I put my Bible and hymn book back in the cupboard; I could repeat the reading 'parrot fashion'; it came easy after years of the Bible; we would have made good theologians for the Church; we had good training.

In the morning, I had a shower, put on some fairly good clothes, including my recently acquired sandals, had breakfast with my mates, gave my porridge with lumps in to my mate next door to me, and was glad to finish off the two doorsteps with 'cartgrease' on, with a sprinkling of salt.

I said goodbye to Sister Florence. She said, 'Goodbye, Mervyn. Have a good holiday, see you when you get back.' 'Not if I have anything to do with it, you won't!' I said under my breath. With that I walked out of the house. The Junior Sister handed me a small case, saying it was for the holiday, and we walked round the drive of the Circle. I didn't realise then, but it was to be for the last time!

We caught a little Crossville bus to the station and the Sister got the tickets for us both – one return to Chester, one single to East Barnet, via Euston. I said goodbye to the Sister at Chester, and clambered aboard the express to Euston with a wave; we were off! I wouldn't be going back to the National Children's Home and Orphanage if I could help it! No, sir! They wouldn't send me on a boat for Australia at fourteen.

But what of the house I was going to, 7 Brookside, East Barnet, Hertfordshire? Would I be happy there? There was Mr Miles who half owned the house, and Mum wasn't married to him! There was Grandad, my mother's father, and there was also the other boy, born after my father's death. Who was he? I would have to wait and see! My Grandad didn't have a pension as they didn't give you one in those days. Mr Miles was constantly out of work. My mother had her widow's pension which in those days before the War was very small, and didn't go far. She used to supplement it by doing cleaning at various houses twice a week.

So it was hardly the type of home that I could feel happy about. But Lewis was at home. I was now twelve years old, hard and disciplined, with harsh years behind me, and *no* love from my mother during those young formative years. It was a case of survival of the fittest, *no* tears were ever shed for my mother and I got no help from my two brothers after I lost Spencer. I was on my own as always.

And so the time passed, the journey passed very quickly too; it was 1930 and I had passed a milestone. Would I always be alone? I always seemed alone, nobody ever to guide me. Would my Mother guide me? She hadn't so far, neither had my brothers. Only 'Spen' (Spencer), but he left in 1925 and died before the year was out, poor old 'Spen'. I missed him and still miss him today! I felt terribly alone, so I would be a loner.

The train jerked suddenly; we were slowing down. I looked out of the window as we pulled into Euston Station.

Chapter II

In July 1930, I arrived at Euston Station, after a long and uneventful journey from Chester, feeling somewhat relieved that I had got away from the orphanage after what seemed like an eternity.

I walked towards the ticket barrier, through the crowds, and there was my mother, but I made no attempt to kiss her. She made no attempt to kiss me and so it was all the time I knew her. I knew then that I wasn't wanted, I was the unwanted baby. I felt there was no motherly love in her. She said, 'Hello, Mervyn, how's your leg?' looking in the direction of my right leg. I said, 'It's better thanks.' With that we walked out of the station and caught a bus to King's Cross station, which was only a few minutes journey down the road. Upon arriving at King's Cross, Mum went to the ticket office and got an extra ticket for me to Oakleigh Park for East Barnet; within a few minutes we caught a train which stopped at every station: Finsbury Park, Haringey, Hornsey, Wood Green, Southgate, and finally Oakleigh Park, for East Barnet, where we alighted and turned left for East Barnet.

As we turned left out of the station, Mum said, 'It's a new house, just completed; there is so much to do, trying to make it liveable; everything is left as the builders left it.' We walked down the hill from the station, along Capel Road, turning left at the bottom into Churchill Road, where, in the distance, we could see the shops in the form of a triangle, which make up the centre of East Barnet, with a clock tower above the centre of the shops, little more than a village really. We turned right past East Barnet Methodist Church, which was to become involved in my life later; just past the church was an unmade road; this then was Brookside and in front of it ran a brook known as Pym's Brook, which came from Hadleigh Woods the entire length of Brookside and beyond.

Mum pointed to the house, the fourth from the end; the first half a dozen were completed, the remainder of the road being in various stages of construction; so were other roads on the estate which when completed would amount to 500 houses comprising the Little Grove Estate as it was to become known as time went by.

The estate was on the side of a hill known as Cat Hill, with our house on a higher level than the roadway, which remained unmade till after the War. We went through the front gate, up some steps and reached the front door. The house had a large gable on the roof, with a large casement and a small casement window below it, plus a large casement window on the ground floor – different from 49 Lynhope Street, Marylebone! This was a three-bedroom, semi-detached house, one of several hundred being built in the area prior to the War for £650 to £750 freehold, a lot of money then!

We went into the roomy house, still smelling of plaster and paint wherever we went; there was plenty of light due to the large windows, and the French windows at the back, in the dining room, which led out to the large concrete yard and the rear garden, which sloped upwards to the back gate.

I was introduced to my Grandad, who I had seen at Lynhope Street. At that moment a big military man stepped into the room who introduced himself as Mr Miles. He was a heavily built man, with a wax moustache that pointed out from both sides of his face, which was heavy jowled, with a very flat nose. We learnt that he got it from boxing; he was every inch an ex-soldier; I was right on both counts. He informed me that he was an ex-regular Sergeant Major, third Battalion Grenadier Guards and had served at Mons, Battle of the Marne, Ypres and the Somme; he was wounded three times, in the legs, through the buttocks, and had his left lung shot away. For that he won the Military Medal twice, and had seven other medals, including the Mons Star. He was the boss of the house, as I was to find out, who threw his orders right and left and we had to obey them, which didn't go down very well with me. I had had my doubts about him when Mum wrote and told me in Chester Infirmary.

Lewis was working at Dutton's Engineering in London, and didn't seem surprised at seeing me when he came home; he seemed to have other problems on his mind, so much so, he took jobs away from home for twelve months or more, as he was not happy at home.

I spent the fortnight's holiday helping to get things straight. Mr Miles was shouting about, giving orders, a foretaste of what life was going to be like, ordering us boys about as if we were soldiers – we had to jump to it!

Every Friday, Mum and Mr Miles used to go to Caledonian Market, in London; the fare was cheap in the 1930s. They used to go from Oakleigh Park station until 1935, when the Underground, as we used to call it, was extended from Bounds Green to Cockfosters, when it became known as the Northern Line, then they got direct from Enfield West, now Oakwood Station, to Caledonian Road. It was a cheap ride on the tube, only costing a few pence; there was food of every description, dirt cheap. Mum always came home loaded, and most important there was furniture for a few pounds, which they got from time to time; the whole house was fitted out from the Caledonian Market.

The time came when I had to go back to the orphanage. I saw that Mum had a home, why should I go back, so I said, 'I'm not going back to that orphanage!' Mum said, 'But you have to go back, Mervyn!' I stood my ground and said, 'I am not going back, nobody can make me!' Mum looked at Mr Miles – What's it got to do with him? He's not my Dad, I thought. It was *then* that I realised, they were together, Mum and him, Living as man and wife. It put a new light on everything: I had jumped from the frying pan into the fire! I did not like it, not one bit, I'd find a way out of this mess, when I was older, but not now!

Eventually Mum said to Mr Miles, 'What can *we* do then?' I spoke up first. I said, 'I am twelve years old, another two years in that orphanage, and I'll be shipped out to Australia, or somewhere like that!' It hit Mum like a thunderbolt. 'Shipped to Australia?' said Mum. 'Of course you won't be, I'm your mother!' She looked at Mr Miles for an answer, but before he could answer I said, 'You don't know, nobody outside the orphanage knows. You are all kept in the dark about what goes on.' Mum said, 'They wouldn't take you and Phillip!' I said, 'Wouldn't they? I knew boys who had parents – they went!' My mother and Mr Miles looked at each other, spellbound, lost for words! They both looked very uncomfortable, but eventually my mother said, 'I will write to Mr Snell, the Governor of the orphanage, saying that I have decided, in view of my new home, I have decided to keep my son, Mervyn, at home, and that Phillip be transferred to N.C.H. & O. Harpenden, Hertfordshire, as soon as is possible and that he will come home later!' Harpenden was the nearest to home.

It was a bombshell to my mother and Mr Miles, as people were not so well informed as they are today; it had been going on for years and years, but the public didn't know, they were kept in the dark.

Mum had a reply from Mr Snell. I never knew the contents of the letter, or ever saw it. A Bible was sent for me, which had his signature in it, dated July 1930.

Within a week or two, Phillip was moved to Harpenden in Hertfordshire; eventually he came home, as he was at the age when he could get a job, which he did, at Maws Surgical Suppliers, off the Bulmer Road, New Barnet, which brought in much-needed money as Mr Miles, for all his shouting, giving us orders, was out of work, up to the time when I eventually left home later.

Grandad never received an old age pension having never paid into one. He used to get a small amount of thirty shillings every *three months* from the Sons of Temperance which he used to belong to. He died later aged ninety-three years of age, before they paid a small pension to people who did not get one.

It was a wet and windy night at the beginning of October 1930 as we were listening to the radio – it was the 4th to be exact – when at 8.00 p.m. we heard the 'Drum, drum, drum, drum' which got louder and louder. Mum said, 'Whatever is it?' I said, 'It's an airship.' It was dark, so we opened the French windows and there she was, flying with her nose down slightly and going at a bit of an angle, not surprising as the wind was strong and it was raining hard; we could even see the lights in her cabins. She came from Cardington, Bedfordshire, eventually Hatfield and Potters Bar and went in the direction of Southgate and the East End of London. Mr Miles said, 'It's the R.101, she is going to India!' A natural remark, at the time was 'She'll be lucky to reach the south coast, the way she is flying!' And he went indoors and thought no more about it.

Next morning, on the radio, it said the R.101 crashed at Beauvais in France at 2.00 a.m. Of the fifty-four people on board, crew and passengers, only six walked out alive – what a disaster it was!!

The R.100, the sistership, flew to Montreal, Canada and back, just after I had seen her at Newton Hall, Frodsham, at the end of July 1930, but owing to the R.101 disaster, the R.100 was later dismantled, and that was the end of the airships as far as Britain was concerned.

It was a Saturday morning, and everyone was numb with shock, I remember it as though it were yesterday! A lady who I knew lived at Capel Road, said to me, 'I have lost a nephew on the R.101.'

Lewis took long contract jobs in various parts of the country which lasted one year, and even two years in some cases; what arrangements he made with my mother, I don't know, but Mum used to tell me, 'Lew will argue over a halfpenny!'

Mum was still drawing her widow's pension and that wasn't very much before the War. There were six of us living in the new house in 1930, we all had to be fed and clothed, and a mortgage to be paid; there was Grandad, Mr Miles, my mother, Phillip, me and the other boy.

I immediately got myself a paper round from a bookstall at Oakleigh Park Station; later I worked on Saturdays at Anderson's, the bakers. I used to help deliver bread in the area, and kept this up until I left school at fifteen years of age, although I should have left at fourteen. Owing to the time lost with my broken leg, Mum decided that I should stay on until I was fifteen; I helped as much as I could, giving *all* the money I earned to my mother.

The only school there was in the area was the Margaret Road School; the other boy and I attended; it was situated in New Barnet, at least a mile away off East Barnet Road.

It was at Margaret Road School that I met and made good friends which lasted for years. I realised that I had missed out a great deal of my schooling, and was behind in many subjects, especially Arithmetic, known today as Maths.

I was put into Standard Five to start with. I had a terrible time with my Arithmetic as I did not know what they were talking about. I struggled on into Standard Six, when I was put next to George. He was mustard at Arithmetic and every other subject. I told him that I didn't know it and he helped me, and with any other lessons that I didn't know. I soon picked it up and there was no trouble after that; George and I became very close friends and we stayed together, sharing the same desk through Mr Carpenter's class (Standard Six), Mr Lockwood's class (Standard Seven) and Mr Haynes's (Headmaster) Standard Eight; we had a great deal in common, especially band music and the drum beat.

While I was at Margaret Road School, I had joined the Boy Scouts, the third East Barnet Troop, which was at the East Barnet Methodist Church, situated in the village opposite the Clockhouse Parade which was a parade of several shops superimposed by a large historical clock. It was the centre for most of the shops; the East Barnet Methodist Church and the chapel occupied all that side of the triangle opposite; the church was no more than fifty yards from our house; we all used to go to the church on Sundays; in time we spent most of our time there. I used to go to the church on Sunday at 11.00 a.m. for morning service; 3.00 p.m. Sunday School; and at 6.30 p.m. Evening Service, every Sunday, wet or fine; and later on, to several activities during the week.

Lewis was made Assistant Scoutmaster for the short time he was at home. I passed my Tenderfoot Badge, eventually being made the Bulldog Patrol Leader, my mate becoming the Lion Patrol Leader. One weekend in the summer we undertook the Second Class Test: we walked, complete with a full pack of food, tent, blankets, billy cans (2), canvas water bags (2), including our staffs with the Bulldog and the Lion on our flags, a clipboard apiece to mark out the route, and a compass to the Chase, Enfield, along the Ridgeway to Potters Bar, seven miles there, seven miles back, fourteen miles altogether, in a heatwave, with a thunderstorm during the night. We trudged back the next day to a rousing reception from the troop on our return, to be congratulated by the Commissioner of the Scout Movement in Barnet and presented with a luxury-style billy can. So we became second-class scouts, and wore the second-class badge.

My mate, George, who shared my desk throughout my school days at Margaret Road, used to tell me all about the Boys Brigade that he belonged to; in fact, boys from Standard Six, Seven and Eight, were all in the Brigade. He said, 'I play in the bugle band, and we are now turning over to a brass band. I have learnt to play the trombone in preparation for the changeover.' I said, 'I would like to learn to play the cornet.' George said, 'Why don't you come along on Monday night, it's band practise at 7.00 p.m. – I'll call for you.'

I joined the 1st New Barnet Company of the Boys' Brigade at the Congregational Church, Plantagenet Road, New Barnet, where I met many of my school pals from Margaret Road School.

Captain Alan J. Ridge, was the Captain of the company, the Lieutenant, Cyril Hayes, was the Bandmaster; they were all proud of the 1st New Barnet, and what a fine company it was, second to none in the whole area; the strength of the company was never less than ninety-five, run on military lines. Discipline and Drill were carried out by army officers once a week. During the Great War, the company carried rifles and was drilled in the use of small arms, just like being in the Army. The Boys Brigade was so disciplined that it was sent out to France and fought in the Battle of the Somme.

It was the senior company of the Battalion, which consisted of several companies in Barnet and the adjoining towns. The 1st had repeatedly won every conceivable cup and shield so many times that we were awarded these trophies to keep. The Daily Telegraph Shield – our name was on it so many years, we were told to keep it for good, so new cups, shields and colours had to be produced for competitions for further years. Morale was high, competition was great and rivalry existed between us, the 1st New Barnet and the 1st Barnet Companies.

In 1897, a William Smith formed the 1st Boys Brigade in Glasgow. Two years later, the 1st New Barnet Company of the Boys Brigade was formed; it had a reputation to live up to; when we marched through the town on Sunday parade, we were proud of our company.

I sat that first night with the brass band, who were learning to play together after the bugle band had been disbanded. I was given my cornet to take home, plus my music, and spent the rest of the week learning the rudiments of it. I said to George, 'I can't get a note out of it.' As luck would have it, George's family moved from Netherlands Road to 23 Brookside, just down the road from me, so we were able to converse about the cornet.

After continual practise and learning the music, I advanced from 4th Cornet to 2nd and eventually rose to 1st Cornet and played the melody! I was coming along in leaps and bounds: practise, practise, practise, was the order of the day. When George and I were together, we would automatically strike up with 'Sons of the Brave' or 'Our Director' or 'Standard of St George'. We were brass band mad!

In 1934 we had a new headquarters built at the other end of Plantagenet Road on the left, named Anchor Hall; it had a large Drill Hall/Gymnasium, Changing Rooms/Toilets, Band Room/Trophy Room, a Chapel and a Club Room, brick built, with all the modern conveniences, and a noticeboard at the entrance; there was something every night of the week.

Monday night was band practise, and what a noise we used to make, with much hard work by Cyril Hayes, the Bandmaster; as the months went by we all became quite proficient with our instruments, but there was the odd time when he would say, 'There's somebody out of tune somewhere,' and would run through all the instruments. 'Give me a "G" please.'

We won the Battalion Brass Band Contest at High Barnet that year; it was quite an achievement as we had only been a brass band for a few months; we celebrated with another cup which we all drank from. Later we had invitations to play at various functions.

In 1936 we took part in the London Brass Band Contest for the Boys Brigade; there were some super bands there. Several of us went to the Guildhall, in London, later, including the 1st New Barnet Brass Band to rehearse for the Annual Boys Brigade Display at the Albert Hall; there were the best ten bands there, making it over 200 bandsmen in all. We fell in outside the Albert Hall, in double file outside and came in down two staircases, even then we had a job to get into the arena; there must have been at least 250 of us.

George was a trombonist in the front row; I was so close to the people on the right-hand side, that I was sure they could see that my music was upside down. I was playing 'Our Director' from memory! I knew it backwards, I'd played it so often; we played the 'Finale' and 'God Save the King'.

I used to go to the B.B. as we knew it, every Monday: Band Practise; Wednesday: Gymnasium; Thursday: Drill Night; Saturday: Club night; Sunday: Parade in the morning – in the evening: Bible Class (Church).

It was run on military lines, with discipline strict at all times; smartness was the keyword, trousers were always in their creases and the white haversack was starched, not a crease in it. The belt used to be an art in polishing the buckle, smothered in bluebell metal polish, held over a gas flame for a few minutes, polished with a brush 'like hell' – you would see it glitter like gold. Shoes would need a good polish and with a soft cloth afterwards to enable you to see your face in them.

At Drill Night, every Thursday, we were always inspected prior to the evening's drill. The Corporal of each squad took the inspection; he was never satisfied with the shine on my buckle and it was always the same remark, 'You'll have to get a better shine on that buckle, Doe.'

The East Barnet Methodist Church was only a stone's throw from our house in Brookside, on the opposite corner; eventually it was called Brookside North, with a Brookside South on the other end of Oakhill Park, which used to commence at the end of our road.

It was the rule in our family to go to Church three times on a Sunday: Morning Service at 11.00 a.m., Sunday School at 3.00 p.m. and Evening Service at 6.30 p.m. There was no way of escaping it; even after I left the Scouts, I used to dash out of church at 7.00 p.m., and just catch a bus outside to Plantagenet Road, to the B.B. Bible Class (Church) at 8.00 p.m. sharp.

I realised for some time that Mum was trying to get me involved in the Church. One day I saw her talking to the Sunday School Superintendent, Mr Warren. The result was that I was asked to be a Sunday School Teacher. I said I would try it, and started at fifteen years of age, stayed in the Primary School till I was sixteen, then moved up into the Intermediate for older boys and girls who were bent on skylarking about the whole time. I found it difficult, reading the lesson from the Bible and keeping them in order at the same time. I knew my Bible, life in the Orphanage had taught me that, but somehow I felt out of my depth, although I stuck it out for a long time.

Life at home was becoming difficult. My mother, with the support of Mr Miles, used to control us boys with a rod of iron. Every Saturday morning, after I had done my paper round, we were expected to clean the house from top to bottom, cleaning the brass door knobs, front and back, brass treads under the doors, front and back, and sweeping the front steps leading down to the gate; for that, we used to receive *a penny*!

Eventually, I used to work at Anderson's, the bakers, doing a morning delivery of bread and helping in the bakery in the afternoons, which got me out of cleaning the house from top to bottom. I gave the money I earned doing my paper round, plus the money I earned at Anderson's the bakers, on Saturdays, to my mother.

When I left school at fifteen, I had various jobs, plus my paper round, plus working on Saturdays at Anderson's, until I got a job at the Barnet Gas and Water Company, in Albert Road, New Barnet, as a fitter's mate. Most of my mates who were, like me, at Margaret Road School and in the Boy's Brigade, were employed at the Gas Company, the biggest employer in the district, so we were happy, being at work together and being in the B.B. together, a very close community, we were at that time, pals for life. The person who was responsible for this was Captain Alan J. Ridge, Captain of the 1st New Barnet Company of the Boys' Brigade. His was the influence, and he used his good offices to get his boys in a good regular job, for which all of us could be eternally grateful to him.

I was happy to be in good surroundings, fitting gas appliances, from meters to cookers, from refrigerators to Ascot water heaters. There was always the odd shilling or sixpence at the end of the job. In those days, the customer was always right and we saw to it that they were always right, with a touch of the peaked cap; when we left, it paid dividends to do your job to suit the customer. My wages I gave intact, in the pay envelope, to my mother, every week without fail, and lived on the tips that I used to get from customers from time to time.

Evening classes were compulsory in the Gas Company, we used to attend on Tuesday Evening (Theory) and Friday Evening (Practical) – at Elizabeth Grammar School for the Theory and at the Gas Works for Practical on the bench. I passed the City and Guilds Certificate, Grade I, after my first year.

Now I was fully occupied, Mondays: Band Practise, B.B.; Tuesdays: Evening Classes (Theory); Wednesdays: Teachers' Preparation Class; Thursdays: Drill Night, B.B.; Fridays: Evening Classes (Practical); Saturdays: Club Night, B.B.; Sundays: Church, three times, plus B.B. Bible Class (Church). I was a busy young man!

My job, the Boys' Brigade and the evening classes, I could stand; in fact, I enjoyed my life to the full, but one thing I could never stand was the unnatural atmosphere created by Mr Miles and my mother. He was out of work so long and there was *no* unemployment benefit as there is today; we boys were working, bringing in the money every week, intact. They were living together as man and wife, going to church every Sunday, and they were the days when a man and woman living together were frowned upon. We boys were completely dominated by both of them – they had my pay as a gas fitter's mate, except eighteen pence, which I used to keep as my pocket money; they also had the money from my paper round and what I got from my Saturday job at Anderson's, the bakers. I consider that not only paid for my keep, but contributed considerably towards the mortgage repayment. Anderson's used to give me half a dozen free cakes every week.

I thought, 'Who the heck is he, bossing us boys about? He's not my Dad and never will be. And so the resentment grew. Lewis was taking more jobs away from home; when he did come home there were always rows about money, and I would have to work out what I was going to do. When that opportunity presented itself, I too would be off!

One of my mates, Arthur, who lived in Lancaster Road, New Barnet, who was in the B.B., said he was going to enlist in the RNVR at HMS *President*, on King's Reach, the embankment of the Thames, London, one night a week to start with. So I went with him.

Wednesday was the most convenient night – the Teachers Preparation would have to be given a miss from now on.

We enjoyed going down to HMS *President* once a week, going aboard an HM ship, learning all the nautical terms for everything, learning extra knots that I already knew from the Scouts, taking drill from a Petty Officer, and Stand Easy, when a ten-minute break meant a glass of beer from the canteen. We looked forward to the Pipe, Stand Easy!

My mother didn't say anything at the time, thinking it was just a boyish fad that would soon pass. How little had she thought of me; she had underestimated me; *I* was deadly serious about the Royal Navy, but I said nothing about the evenings aboard HMS *President*. I kept my feelings in check for later; it turned out the solution to my problem at home. The die was cast!

At about this time I went to a Church Annual Meeting one day with my mother – she was always trying to get me involved with the affairs of the Church. We met Rev. John Waterhouse who used to spend any free time at our house, trying to convince me that the Ministry was the A and Z of everything. I didn't know it at the time, that Mum's ambition was to get me into the Church – that is why I always sat in the front row in church, next to a Rev. Milton-Brown, a retired minister. I would have been a lay preacher no doubt. During the evening, several things were discussed, including a nomination for the new Foreign Missionary Secretary for the church – I knew that my mother had a hand in this because one of her friends, a Mrs Brown from the local dairy, got up and said, 'I nominate Mr Doe as the new secretary,' and they all said, 'Hear! Hear! Excellent choice,' and so on.

I got up and said, 'I am greatly honoured at being nominated, but I must refuse. Every evening of the week is fully occupied, so it is out of the question. People argued for and against me, so much so that I got up and walked out of the meeting and the church, never to return. My mother had shot her bolt!

In 1936, when we played at the Royal Albert Hall in a mass band, it was to me the proudest moment of my life – it should have been a guide to me as to what I wanted to do – I should have enlisted in the Royal Marines. I could play a kettledrum as well as I played the cornet. I could have been a drummer/bugler, if not in the Band, or I could have gone to the School of Music, Deal, Kent, in the Royal Marines.

However, at nineteen I was a bit headstrong, all I wanted was to get away from my mother and Mr Miles, away from the home called 7 Brookside, East Barnet, and all that it entailed; that was why, when she asked me from time to time down the years, 'Is there anything you want?' my answer was, as always, 'Nothing thanks.' Even just before she died, when she asked me, 'Is there anything you want?' I said, 'Nothing thanks.' My other brothers had more than their fair share; they were like vultures, not me, it could not make up for all the miseries of the past. I could forgive, but as long as I shall live, I can't forget words said about me while I was away fighting.

On 13 December 1937 my mate, Arthur, and I joined the Royal Navy; my mother told friends and neighbours that Mervyn, her son, had gone to the devil! What, the Royal Navy?

We enlisted at Whitehall, as it was then the recruitment centre for London, for twelve years active service and eight years on the reserve. They said there were only vacancies for stokers, cooks, etc. – no seamen required. I said 'no' to a stoker, and to a cook, 'no'! The Chief who signed us on initially said, 'If you sign on as a cook, you can always transfer to another branch inside, when the vacancy arises!' I fell for that one! We both signed and passed our medical.

We came home and I told my mother what we had done; she was speechless, thinking I would never leave home again, but she was wrong. In my early years, I had had plenty of practise with eight years away from home. I was the unwanted baby, put on a train with Phillip from Leamington Spa to Frodsham, Cheshire, and I wasn't four years old at the time!

Within the week, Arthur and I travelled up to Whitehall, London, where we joined thirty other new entrants and were given travel warrants and Meal Vouchers. We caught a train from Charing Cross Station to Chatham, Kent.

Upon our arrival at Chatham, we turned right out of the station, down the hill to the military road at the bottom, where we caught a bus for HMS Pembroke, the RN barracks. On arrival, we showed our credentials to a petty officer, who had been expecting us.

After ticking us off on a clipboard which had our names on; he said, 'Come with me.' We marched in double file up onto Terrace Road, which runs the entire length of the barracks and beyond the Gunnery School to East Camp. The first building on our right was the Wardroom Block, which housed the officers, where the colours hung from a mast out on the lawn. Reveille and Sunset would be sounded at these colours each day by a Royal Marine bugler.

Ahead on the right were the six blocks, four storeys high, which housed the main personnel of the barracks, approximately 5,000 men in peacetime. On the left of Terrace Road and twelve feet below it, was a huge parade ground, which ran the entire length of the barracks from the canteen, which was opposite the Wardroom Block to the Sick Bay, which was opposite the Gunnery School. On the other side of the parade ground was a drill shed, which was of great length and could house the entire personnel of the barracks. Beyond the drill shed and attached to it were various offices for the running of the barracks. The road turned left, went into the dockyard main gate opposite the clock tower, then ran on to the entrance of the RN barracks again, making it a circular road. Access to the parade ground from Terrace Road was by three flights of steps at three points; once on the parade ground, all personnel, I mean *all*, had to double across it – to walk or amble would be an offence!

The first two blocks, after the Wardroom, were left half and right half, Nelson; next was left half and right half, Anson; and left half and right half, Duncan, making seven blocks altogether. Next was the Gunnery School with a large anti-aircraft battery in between; beyond that was East Camp, an overflow camp, additional accommodation for 3–4,000 men, galley and dining rooms, washing facilities, finally the Gas School, where everyone went to do a gas test on one's own personal respirator, which *everyone carried at all times* at the outbreak of hostilities in September 1939.

When we first arrived at left half Duncan Block, we halted. The Petty Officer said, 'This is to be your home, until your basic training is completed, then you will move into the other blocks according to your branch.' With that we walked 'aft' under a covered way and passed a place called the 'Scran Bag', a place where every article, clothing or otherwise, left in the messes and unattended, was collected by the people who ran the Scran Bag. To collect or retrieve the said article of clothing or otherwise, one had to pay one and sixpence to retrieve it. It was against the rules to leave anything lying about during working hours. Also, on the ground floor were the washplaces, lecture rooms, and various Divisional offices.

We went to the rear entrance, up several flights of stairs which took us up to the second floor; the door on our right said '2MM', which was known as 'Two Double Monkey.' On our left it sad 'New Entries', our home for the next fortnight. We opened the door and there stood a Chief Petty Officer; he looked fearsome and had been waiting for us to arrive. He said to the Petty Officer, 'We'd better get them fed first.' 'You four, with me,' said the Petty Officer, and away we marched, down to the lower floor, to the galley, where we picked up two long trays. He said to the cook, 'New Entries, about forty hands.' The cook fixed us up with knives, forks and spoons, plates, sausages and mash, prunes and custard, and we marched up the way we had come, fully loaded, plonked the two trays on the table and let another four hands dish it up. After dinner we cleared away and washed up, returning the trays and mess tins back to the galley.

At 1.00 p.m. the tannoy sounded, 'Out pipes, hands carry on with your work.' Every day, we would hear the tannoy giving the orders. We would get used to it and there would be choice remarks made in reply!

'The Chief, as he became known, got us all together and gave us a lecture on the rudiments of the Royal Navy. Firstly, we would go *below*, and not downstairs, we would go *up top*, and not upstairs, we would look out of a *porthole*, and not the window, and so on, and so forth. We would all go below to the Bedding Store and draw a hammock and one blanket each – one blanket! We were not going to be very warm tonight! We went below and drew a hammock and one blanket, and what a blanket! It was four times thicker than a civilian blanket, what beauties they were.

He showed us how to sling our hammocks. 'There's a right way and a wrong way to sling hammocks! If you sling it wrong, as soon as you get in, it slips, and down on the deck you fall! If you sling it right, it will stay up for all eternity,' the Chief said. 'At seven feet high, just over, there are hooks on the girders every four feet and at six feet there is a polished bar. The hooks to lash your hammocks to each end, the polished bar is to grab, to help you get into your hammock; just jump up, grab the bar and lift yourself into your hammock. It's easy, right? Now we shall all sling hammocks; it should be up high enough to walk under all hammocks when at sea. Right, away you go,' said the Chief.

Well, if ever you saw Fred Karno's Outfit, a comedy act in the 1920s, it was nothing compared with what followed. Some chaps slung their hammocks alright, but in their enthusiasm to get into their hammocks first time, grabbed the bar with lots of gusto and went straight over the hammock, missing it completely and hitting the deck on the other side of the hammock with an absolutely almighty crash. Others just didn't quite make it, they had got their feet in, but in so doing, just pushed the hammock away, and the more they pushed with their feet the worse it got and they ended up swinging on the polished bar, with no hammock, as they dropped to the deck.

When the Chief Petty Officer had finished laughing, he said, 'Well, you had better get it right, because that's where you will sleep from now on!' Everybody decided to leave them up and practise getting in and out of them. Then he said, 'I'll show you how to lash them up, which you will have to do, lash them up every morning, every week, and every year of your life in the Navy.'

He showed us how to lash the hammock up, 'Which you do as soon as you get out, besides, it makes more room, every morning at 5.45 am. and woe betide anyone if it's done any old how,' he said. He showed us how to fold the mattress and the blanket, so it was just under the length of the hammock, then seven turns (for the seven seas) with the lashing or rope round the hammock, 'So tight that you are unable to get your fingers between hammock and lashing. If your hammock is lashed correctly, it should keep you afloat in the sea for twenty-four hours, so look after your hammock, it could save your life at sea!'

For tea, we had herring in tomato sauce and beetroot, taking it in turns to go to the galley, four of us for 24 hours; we fetched the bread on a large wooden tray, also, a large billy can for the tea; the two chaps queued up for the 'herrings in'. How many times would I have 'herrings in' when I was down in the South Atlantic? Six weeks of it, every day for dinner, we had nothing else; stores had run out, we only had one other thing – 'boiled rice and herrings in' until the supply ship met us; we were somewhere off Antarctica, protecting the whaling fleets, having completed 112 days at sea without a break! It was freezing cold, with very little food.

When we finally got into our hammocks at 9.00 p.m. that first night, you could hear someone crying in his hammock; in fact, I think it was more than one, but they would get used to it in time. I went off like a rock, used to being away from home, and slept contented.

Next morning, at the crack of dawn, we were awoken by a Royal Marine bugler, who it seemed was trying to blow his guts out by playing Reveille twice over; the second time was played in double time, twice as fast as the first. I came to the conclusion that he was dying to go to the heads (toilet). 'I heard you the first time!' someone near me shouted. Suddenly the door burst open with a rush, revealing the offending bugler, followed by the duty Chief Petty Officer, who before he'd got into the door was shouting his head off, 'Wakey! Wakey! Wakey! Rise and shine! The sun's scorching your eyes out! Heave ho, Heave ho! Lash up and stow!' 'Who's that shouting so loud, so early?' said one bloke rubbing his eyes. 'He's got a nerve,' another offended bloke said, 'who the hell is that? Coming charging in here like that?' as he tumbled from his hammock and hit the deck, six feet below. 'Who pushed my hammock from underneath?' he said, and was about to give him a piece of his mind, when he found himself staring right into the hardened face of a Chief Petty Officer, Gunner's Mate, the most feared men in the Navy. I laughed and said, 'Good morning, Chief!' to which he replied, 'Step lively there, get lashed up!' and passed straight out of the mess, without batting an eyelid, as if I hadn't spoken, and went charging into 2MM mess and frightened the living daylights out of the blokes in there with, 'Wakey, Wakey! Rise and shine!' and so on! The bugler was having a whale of a time, blasting mess after mess, with his rendering of Reveille. You would have thought we were a mile up the River Medway. What a rude awakening that was! He was a good bugler, though.

I quickly got dressed and started lashing up as the Chief had shown us yesterday, mattress and blanket folded up inside the hammock, get the lashing (rope), start with a half hitch, pull it tight to start, then it's like packing a parcel, seven turns for the seven seas round the hammock and pull it tight all the time, I mean tight; each turn, you pull it tight, for all you are worth, and another half hitch at the end, tuck those in between the turns. Providing the hammock is tight, so as you can't get a finger under a rope anywhere, you've lashed up correctly; stow in the rack provided, six feet high, well clear of the mess deck. I then turned to help any other chap who was having difficulty, and found that all the chaps had been watching me.

After we had all washed on the ground floor, we made sure that the decks were cleared of any hammocks, and that the tables were clear for breakfast. 'Cooks to the Galley' sounded on the tannoy, and we who were detailed the day before got off to a flying start as there were queues; we collected on our trays, bacon and tomatoes, bread and butter, and a large dixie of tea. After breakfast we washed up and squared the mess ready for the Chief's inspection.

'Today,' the Chief said, 'we will go down to the Kitting Up Store and draw our bedding. You will learn how to make your hammock out of a piece of canvas, approximately six feet square; you will learn how to make a 'whipping' and an 'eye splice' and everything appertaining to making your own hammock from scratch, because every man in this man's Navy *makes his own*!'

I thought, It's a good thing I was in the Scouts, it gives me a head start. I had learnt six different 'knots, whipping', 'eye splice', and normal splicing of rope. The Chief concluded, 'So, it's got to be right, as it will have to last you all the time you're in the Service.'

Everybody received a large piece of canvas, six feet by six, two large rings, a long piece of lashing several yards long, several yards of thinner rope for the thirty-two 'nettles', sixteen at each end to attach to the hammock, and ten feet of strong rope for the two 'clues' on each end of the hammock. The Chief saw to it that we had enough twine, needles and palms to put on our right hand for sewing, and two bars of 'pussers' soap, for rubbing into the ropework when finished, as it helps to preserve the rope! *I* was in my element, with a crowd of chaps, going through it together.

We returned to the mess with all this clobber, every man issued with a sort of 'Type', with his name on, to stamp his kit, starting with his hammock, everything he was issued with.

The Chief said, 'If you don't know anything about sewing, now's the time to learn, and learn good. I'll see to it!'

We spent one week making our personal hammocks under the expert guidance of the CPO when all the 'whippings' and 'eye splices' were finished, the nettles were attached to the large rings, sixteen nettles to each ring, and sixteen nettles to each end of the hammock, then there was one 'clue' to go on each ring on each end of the hammock. When that was done our bedding was stamped with our name, official number and CH, for Chatham; they were stamped in large type, so they could be seen at a glance, when 'stowed away'.

During the second week, we drew our uniforms; there was the No. 1 best uniform, Canadian doeskin; No. 3 navy-blue serge, working rig; No. 6 white uniform, working in the galley; tropical uniform would be issued later; gym gear, shorts, blue jersey, gym shoes. We were issued with a wooden 'diddy box' with our name on a brass plate. This was for shaving gear, soap, toothbrush, etc.; official shoe brushes, clothes brush and writing gear; an enormous kit bag, which stood on its end, nearly five feet high; the bottom was reinforced with rope and it was completely waterproof, with our name and number on the bottom. 1 great coat; 1 oilskin; 2 caps, and numerous badges in gold, red and blue; and the usual gear like underwear; socks; boots; towels (2); shirts (3); ties (3); finally the gas respirator and housewife, a sewing outfit. There was no end to the articles of uniform; it would take a cart to get it back to the mess, the week was spent trying them on, if it didn't fit, it would go back for alteration.

Time was spent ironing, pressing, stitching badges on: gold for best, red for working rig, blue for white uniforms; they all had to be stamped, everything that was blue would have a white name on it, everything that was white would have a blue name on it.

The 'housewife' was a nautical term; it comprised a small blue holdall which contained everything for sewing; there were needles of every size, cottons of white and black, thread and wax, a thimble and scissors, finally, navy-blue wool.

The Chief said, 'As from today, you have one week to get your name on to every article of your kit; this includes your mattress and your blanket. If you are not handy with a needle and thread, now is the time to learn; if you *don't* do it, you'll be in dead trouble, got it?' 'You will start in the Navy "All Correct and Kitted Up"; on Friday you will have a kit inspection and woe betide any man who is not up to standard. On the bulkhead near the door is a picture of a Kit Inspection; that's how I want to see it laid out, blues to the left and whites to the right.'

On the Friday of the second week we were ordered to dress in uniform for the first time, so we dressed in our working 'rig No. 3s' and packed our civilian clothes away.

We fell in in two rows in the mess, while the Chief inspected us;' some men suited uniform, others didn't; some looked as though they had been involved in an accident; one or two looked hopeless, to which he replied, 'Talk about Fred Karno's Navy! I want to see creases in those trousers, so get busy with the old iron and press them, inside out for you in bell-bottoms, and the normal crease for you two, Doe and Dyer, in the Fore and Aft Rig, and put some spit and polish in those shoes, and square your caps off, let's have a bit of nautical shape in them, otherwise, you look like a heap of drunken sailors – what are we then?' 'A heap of drunken sailors, Chief,' we said with one voice!

After much spit and polish and trousers coming off and then on again, brushing each other down and saying, 'How's that, alright?' I said, 'How's this cap, alright?' One bloke said, 'I don't know how you do it, Doe, you're just made for it!' I said, 'I always wore a peaked cap in civvy street. When I was in the Gas Company, they said then I always wore it Navy fashion, besides, I was in the Boys Brigade, used to uniform!'

We all fell in on the ground floor, opposite the covered way, facing the Training Commander's office; it was the ritual to see the T/C before commencing our official training. If anyone is unhappy with the Navy, now was the time to say so, or forever hold his peace. He would be released right away. I don't think there was anyone who was released from our entry.

At 1.15 p.m. we stood in the forecourt facing the Training Commander's office, with our oilskins folded over our left arms. During the dinner hour, it came over the tannoy, 'All the Hands. Do you hear there? Hands will carry oilskins'; and on the noticeboard, 'Hands *will* carry oilskins', and woe betide anyone going out without an oilskin; it meant everybody! If you didn't, you were on a charge!

Suddenly everyone under the covered way quickly stood still. We were quickly brought to attention, the Chief about turned, facing the T/C office, and the Commander approached; he looked every inch a Naval officer, the smartest man I had ever seen, tall, broad, clean cut, very good looking, greying at the temples, creased trousers, polished shoes. Each man that he passed gave him a salute, which he returned like an automaton; he was a man who was highly respected, and was in his office like a shot. Now I know what they mean by saying, 'Gangway for a Naval officer!' He was dynamite.

When I stepped into his office, I took my cap off, held it under my armpit and came to attention. When he lifted his head and looked me straight in the eyes, I looked into cool steel blue eyes. Here, I thought was a magnificent officer; the three rings on the base of his sleeve, denoted that he would go far in the Navy; you would go to 'Hell and back' with him in command!

I told him why I had joined the Navy, that I was very unhappy at home, and went at some length into the reason why; prior to 1930 I was in the National Children's Home and Orphanage from 1922, my father having died in 1918, just three months before I was born. He quietly listened to what I had to say, then he said, 'So many boys from orphanages join the Navy, they seem to prefer the communal life. Do you?' I said, 'Yes, sir, I do, I like the comradeship.' He replied, 'Yes, quite. Have you any relations in the Navy?' 'Well, my father was here at Chatham, working on 'C' Class submarines, my mother lived at nearby Gillingham at the outbreak of the 1914–18 War; he was an aeronautical engineer, and was called back to Coventry to see the Sopwith Pup, which had just gone into production.' The 'Pup' was an earlier type of Spitfire, and she was just as devastating in the First World War.

I went on to explain the conditions under which I had signed, when the recruiting Chief Petty Officer had said that if I signed on now as a cook, I could transfer to a more suitable branch; when a vacancy arose, I could transfer to the Seamen's Branch. To which he replied, 'Yes. Well, we shall have to see about that, I will let you know in due course.'

His name was Commander Ludgrove and he took over the command of the County Class Cruiser *Kent* soon after the interview, which was undergoing a refit at the time. That was December 1937 and I said goodbye to any chance of a transfer to another branch.

Monday morning after breakfast, the Chief came into the mess for the last time; we had our hammocks and our kit fully kitted-up, all done by our own hands, all ready to start the three months training. 'You have finished your preliminary training, so from here, you move your gear into the mess opposite, "2MM". You will be known as "Two Double Monkey, Left Half Duncan Block".

'You will report to Leading Seaman Cock, who will be your

instructor for the duration of your training, which will be just over three months.'

Leading Seaman Cock, was an old sweat who had done at least ten years service and was trained to be an instructor.

We fell in in the yard outside the covered way; it was the first week in January 1938. Having been home on leave over the Christmas period, it was freezing cold, frost was on everything. Leading Seaman Cock arrived, and introduced himself, saying he would be our instructor for the whole of our training. 'You will be known as 159 Class.'

'The first thing to do is draw your gaiters, which you will wear at all times whilst on duty during working hours,' he said. 'Follow me,' and in we went, to the store opposite, and drew a pair of gaiters. 'Every Friday evening, you will come in here, blanco them and hang them up to dry, alright?' Then we went into an adjoining room where we had a lecture on the Navy, ashore and afloat. There were small models of battleships, cruisers and destroyers, the whole fleet at sea, in miniature. I thought, This can go on for as long as he likes, anything is better than being outside on a freezing cold morning like this. Just then the tannoy sounded 'Stand Easy'. It was 10.25 a.m. Anyone who had a fag lit up. If you hadn't got any cigarettes, it was too bad. The Canteen was right across the parade ground and at the other end of the drill shed, too far to get a cup of tea, shame! While we were thinking about tea, the tannoy sounded 'Out pipes, hands carry on with your work.' It was 10.35 a.m. Woe betide anyone who took a puff after that; anyone who had a lighted cigarette put it out, or trod on it; there was the barrack guard at different points, watching and waiting for anyone who was a bit slow in putting out his fag. 'Put that fag out!' he would bellow like a bull.

At 10.35 a.m. we fell in, in twos in the yard, the Leading Hand, as he was known at all times, brought us to attention, and said, 'Right turn, quick march, left wheel' and around the rear of Duncan Block we went, left wheel again, back along Terrace Road, overlooking the parade ground, down the first lot of steps onto the parade ground; there we marched and counter-marched, formed fours for the first time. I knew my drill as the Boys Brigade had taught me all military drill. 'On the left, form line', 'On the right form squads', 'On the left, form file', 'Slow march', 'Forming fours on the march', it all came second nature, I never made a mistake! The Leading Hand approached me and said, 'Where did you learn to drill?' I said, 'In the Boys Brigade. We were taught by army officers.' 'Right, from now on you take the right-hand "Pivot", OK?' he replied. The right-hand 'Pivot' was the man in the front rank on the extreme right, who everyone took their time from, especially when we had to get the line straight, for instance when the instructor says, 'By the right, dress.' I would stand fast, while everyone turned their heads to the right and got their dressing from me.

We marched and counter-marched; we could get lost on this huge parade ground, where the devil is the instructor; we left him behind ages ago, but still we kept marching, past the Swimming Baths, then the Gym, up to the end of the P.G. The terraced road turned left at this point and went over the P.G. Next was the entrance to the Sick Bay. A bitter wind had got up and was blowing down the Medway from Sheerness; it was completely exposed, the flat marshlands of the estuary; you could feel the bitter north easterlies on that northern shore of Kent, and down on the P.G. it blew freezing cold; it was a big P.G., fully exposed. On that first morning, it came pretty rough for some, but not for me, I was used to being out in all weathers, especially during the winter months, with no coat, hat or gloves.

Then a voice rang out. It sounded miles away, '159 Class, will come to a halt,' he bellowed, then, 'HALT! Stand fast that man!' We stood there, shivering, waiting for him to catch us up; when he finally put in an appearance, he said, 'The wind does not blow so hard up this end.' We were past caring – why did we ever join?

'Now we'll do "On the left, form line".' On the march later, it was, 'From the halt to the halt, right form,' and so on. I knew it all, to the chaps from civvy street it was like Chinese; as time went by, they got the hang of it, cold wind, or no cold wind.

12.00. The tannoy sounded, 'Hands to dinner, up spirits'. We turned about, marched towards the steps, on to Terrace Road, up the steps opposite, and fell in in the covered way of Duncan Block, glad to get out of the wind. We dashed up to 2MM where 'Cooks to the Galley' sounded. They came back with dinner, which was shepherds pie. I noticed a large dixie with pea soup in it; the Navy is renowned for its 'Peadoo' and this cold day, it was just right. I finished off with 'Currant Duff' for afters, another Navy speciality!

1.00 p.m. The tannoy sounded, 'Both watches of the hands, fall in, carry oilskins'. The oilskin is canvas-lined; outside it is like black tar, is just as stiff, with no give in it at all, the most uncomfortable coat I ever wore; it cut at your wrists and chin, and would give you a shave any day; it was absolute murder, but it did keep out the wind and the rain.

We fell in outside the covered way, with our nice new oilskins on, done up at the throat; you dare not turn your head, it might give you a nasty shave! I felt all trussed up like a penguin. The cold wind blew down the Medway; the P.G. was fully exposed from the north-east.

We marched off to the Parade Ground, where we were brought to a halt. This particular afternoon we would collect our rifles from the store and get accustomed to handling them. 'Quick march', and off we marched, 'Left, Right, Left, Right', and came out near the dockyard gates, crossed over the road and went into the one-storey building opposite. Inside it were rows of rifles, bayonets and webbing gear.

We were each given a rifle and webbing gear, plus a belt to take your bayonet, and doubled up outside in two ranks. I naturally held my rifle in my right hand and held it at the trail, just off the ground; it was the most sensible thing to do under the circumstances. Some seemed to nurse them to their chests, others looked about them, looking for a solution, and saw the way I held mine. The Leading Hand came out, didn't like what he saw and turned away for a minute. I could see he was fuming; he had never seen anything like it, the air was 'blue'.

'Before you move off like a load of rabble, you will start by putting your rifles on the ground, put your belts on properly, then you can carry your rifles with your right arm, like he is doing.' That's me!

We all followed the teacher, with our rifles tucked into our right side, the butt of the rifle approximately six inches off the ground, turned right and came out on the parade ground again and came to a halt. We let the butt of our rifles touch the ground. The Leading Hand carried a rifle too, for the express purpose of showing us the movements of the rifle. He said, 'The first thing is to slope arms.' He brought his rifle up from his right side, across his chest – with his left arm, as well as his right, put it on his left shoulder, holding it with his left hand, it was at the slope on the left shoulder, always the left, not the right. 'Now, you try it when I say, "Squad, slope arms", I want you to move together, got it?' 'Squad, slope arms.' There was a shuffle, rifles going this way and that, and eventually, when everyone was satisfied that he had sloped arms, they stood stil, which was an understatement – half of the rifles were on the ground; they were afraid to move, they had done it all wrong, much to the annoyance of the Leading Hand, who let forth a string of naval language, the likes of which I had never heard before. Cutting out the swearwords, he said, 'You think you are members of His Majesty's Navy, well you're ******* well not, you're just like a lot of ******* girls at a ******* party, got it?' Then I heard him yell, '****** well, leave them!' Then after a minute's silence, he said, 'Now, you can pick up your rifles, and ****** well, hang onto them. If I see, or hear of another rating dropping his rifle, I'll have him on a 10^A Punishment for one week, got it?' Just then, it started to snow, faster and faster, thicker and thicker, you just couldn't see through it. I heard someone say, 'I feel like ****** Scott of the Antarctic, ****** well stuck out here.' The Leading Hand said, 'Silence in the ranks.' After what seemed like an eternity, he said, 'If we are all at the slope we can march off now.' Into the Drill Shed we went.

'Put your chin stays down, after you come to order arms, that is.' He brought his rifle down to the order. He picked his rifle up again, 'Now, I will show you the rudiments of rifle drill, "Holding the rifle at the trail"; "Changing arms"; "Shoulder arms"; "Present arms"; finally, "Rest on Your Arms Reversed", which is only done at funerals!' Rifle Drill was practised regularly, two or three times a week, for three or four months; it became a part of us; we would carry our rifles at the Passing Out Parade.

Another session of our training during the cold spell in January was 'Boat Pulling' in no. 3 Basin. We were all dolled up in our gaiters, oilskins, and chin stays down; I felt like a blinking penguin. The oilskin was uncomfortable, as I have said, what with the edges of the oilskin cutting into your skin all the time, it used to be so stiff that you couldn't swing your arms when marching either. Bearing this in mind, we marched from the covered way at 8.30 a.m., Duncan Block to the Dockyard, going over the bridge at the end of the parade ground on your left, passing the large Sick Bay on your right, turning to your left at the bottom of the hill, the entrance to the dockyard on your right.

The first ship I remember was the old Monitor, HMS *Marshal Soult*, laying just inside the dockyard on the right, with her broad beam and her huge turret carrying twin 15-inch guns; there wasn't much room for anything else, built purely for bombardment, not for fighting, as such. There was HMS *Dragon* and other 'C' Class cruisers over the far side of No. 3 Basin. We marched on round the basin to where we saw a couple of fifty-foot whaling boats tied up, down on our knees and reached for the rung of the steel ladder that was attached to the side of the basin; when we reached the bottom, we just jumped in the nearest boat. The water was black, you couldn't see anything through it, it was all oil, discharged from every ship in the dockyard. It was often said if you fell in the basin, you would be sent to the bone yard, RN Hospital, Gillingham to be pumped out!

There were about twelve of us in the whaler; when we had finally sorted ourselves out and had decided which way we should be facing, the Leading Hand decided that he was the last man in the boat and stood in the prow of the boat; he had his oilskin on, seaboots that came right up to the thighs, two purser towels tucked into the top of his oilskin, plus a pair of kid gloves on, the only resemblance to us, 159 Class, he had his chin stay down, expecting rough weather, no doubt.

'Right ho, me hearties, let's be having ya, get an oar each,' said 'Captain Bligh'. I grabbed my oar, it was long enough for a short flagpole, put it into the rowlock. 'Right! Altogether,' he shouted. 'Just a minute,' I said, fumbling with this enormous oar to get it into the right place. 'Altogether lads, Two Six,' he shouts. 'Altogether Now!' There was quite a commotion in the boat, a few made a stroke, but the others were making a splash, that's all you could say for it. I caught a crab for a start and so did half a dozen others. 'What's the matter with you, Ted Doe?' That's me! They called me Ted at the outset, Mervyn was hardly the name for a sailor in those days. A vicar, yes. A sailor, no. One of my uncles was a 'Ted' and so it was to this day. I said, 'I can't feel my elbows let alone my hands, they're non-existent anyway.' He replied, 'You'll be alright – just keep your arms pulling on that there oar, and don't put it in deep, turn your oar when coming out of the water, try it – got it?' It was surprisingly easy, I found, but then there were others who caught a crab; it would be a long time before we were fit enough for the boat race! Now we got some kind of rhythm going, 'Two Six, In out, In out!' and then it snowed, visibility was down to zero, we were somewhere out in the middle of the basin, and it snowed, and snowed, and snowed. It came over as dark as night; there were phantom ships crossing our bows. These turned out to be the duty tugs.

We managed to turn the boat round before we nearly collided with a cruiser on the opposite side of the basin, it was HMS *Ajax*. She looked good by what we saw of her, with her 'bottle' necked funnel, which gave her a rakish appearance.

It was like coming in from the South Pole, climbing the vertical ladder that was attached to the side of the basin, circulation had returned to lifeless arms and legs, we fell in on the jetty and marched back to Duncan Block.

The tannoy sounded 'Hands to dinner', the duty cooks went to the galley to fetch our meagre rations which consisted of pea soup (Peadoo!), every day it was Peadoo, it was thick and hot with all sorts of vegetables in it, with the odd slice of onion or bacon for good measure. We helped ourselves to two good soup plates full. During the dinner, nobody mentioned the boat pulling in No. 3 Basin. What we had after the soup, I can't remember, but I do remember what we had for afters, good old jam tart and custard. Nobody cooks it quite like the Navy, because I haven't tasted anything like it for the last fifty years, garnished with lashings of thick custard!

The afternoon was spent doing seamanship and knots, whippings etc. in the lecture room on the ground floor. It was cold down there, no heat on as far as I could see, but anything was better than being in a whaler in No. 3 Basin. The knots which I had learnt in the Scouts came in very useful – at least six knots I had learnt for my Tenderfoot Badge and they gave me a good start. We were all standing in a line, facing a wire hawser which ran from one side of the room to the other, waist high; we stood, each with a piece of rope attached. The instructor would say to all of us, 'Now do me a bowline,' or 'Do me a sheetbend,' or 'Do a sheepshank,' and so on. I was lucky, but not so for many of my mates; he would pass along the line, blasting and carrying on as only an old sailor can, the air 'blue' with his remarks. 'What the f****** hell do you call that? Like a b***** load of "Brown Hatters" the lot of you, what are you?' 'Like a load of "Brown Hatters"' a weak voice would say, between his teeth. *I didn't know what he meant!* Neither did the rest of 159 Class, but a few months in the Navy would soon cure that! The instructor had his hand on my knot, but he was turned away, giving someone a string of abuse. 'You're like a load of girls at a party.' I said, 'What is a Brown Hatter?' My mate said, 'You know, one of *those*.' I said, 'Oh – henparty!' His head quickly turned and we stood eyeball to eyeball, only a few inches apart! I was frozen with fear, but *my knot was right*. 'My God! At last some sort of order prevails,' he shouts. So throughout the afternoon, I did every knot, and splicing or whipping that he called for and one or two others had been Scouts in their younger days, so that eased the language of the instructor. He ended the afternoon with me, asking me what troop I had been in. I told him I was Bulldog Patrol Leader and had been the first in the troop to pass the Second Class Badge, for which I was presented with a trophy from the local Commissioner of Scouts. And later I joined the Boys Brigade because nearly all my school mates were in it.

'So that's where you learnt military drill,' he said. 'Yes, I know all my drill, every Thursday for two hours, we were drilled by an army officer, once upon a time; we carried rifles during the War, of course, before my time.'

Next day, it was practising for the 'Ducksuit Test', every man had to pass it. The original idea was that a man joining his ship for the first time had to swim, fully clothed, round his ship, from port to starboard and back to port again, a complete swim around his ship. The ducksuit comprised his jumper and bell-bottomed trousers, but it was made of very stiff and thick canvas, so in water it restricted you swimming in the normal way; it was diabolical, it was murder!

We had a morning session in the swimming baths which were situated at the end of the parade ground, nearly opposite Duncan Block, before you come to the Sick Bay, which I thought might come in handy in case of a mishap. We came to a halt outside the baths, having marched a roundabout way from Duncan Block opposite, up on Terrace Road. In single file we marched into the swimming baths to be met with duckboards covering a floor of filthy water, where we had to change. Hanging above us were rows of dripping wet ducksuits, all freezing in the sub-zero temperatures, having just been used by an earlier class, all dripping wet. I'm sure I saw icicles hanging from the nearest suit. Good grief, I thought, not these surely. I made my way over to where there was an occasional form and commenced undressing.

'Right, me hearties, let's be having you,' screamed the Leading Hand. 'Get the suit on, directly above you.' I started to say a few choice words to myself, but the words were lost, I was shivering uncontrollably. I was completely naked and made a brave attempt to get my leg into the stiff icy bell-bottoms. I reached for the jumper going over my head, stiff with cold, but the ducksuit was *on*! I couldn't move. 'It will be warmer in the pool,' said the Leading Hand. Other chaps were having the same trouble in various forms as we all waddled out like a load of pregnant ducks to the pool; my jumper was wide enough for three men and fell over my shoulders like a bell tent. I thought, This is going to give me a bit of trouble. I couldn't utter a word, my teeth had stopped talking. 'Come on, look lively!' shouted the Leading Hand, as he half-pushed the remainder of the class into the baths. 'Look lively!' He's got a fat chance of that, I thought, as we lined up on the side at the deep end. There were several instructors in attendance, in case anyone got into difficulties. I couldn't keep still, and my teeth were rattling away, doing a war dance. The water was twice as cold, deep and menacing.

The Swimming Instructor said, 'Right, 159 Class, let's see what you are like at high diving!' Good Lord, I've never been off a high-diving board in my life. Well, I won't let the side down, I thought.

He called out the first man, who went up to the top of the high board and did a beautiful dive. The next went off the top diving board and he also did a super dive, absolutely flawless, and the next, and the next, all dived beautifully, first-class diving. Next, it was my turn. I had not only never high-dived before, but I had only been to a swimming bath twice, once at the Westcliff-on-Sea baths, second, at North Finchley. I could do a few strokes of the breast stroke, but that was the sum total of my swimming. I was keen to learn. My name was called out. I wasn't going to let the side down, and wouldn't funk it – it wasn't in my nature – do or die! I climbed to the top diving board, walked to the end, just tucked my toes over the edge of the board, raised both arms, hands locked together, looked as professional as the others, bent at the knees, sprang and slipped – that was where professionalism ended. I went down alright, but hit the water all wrong, stomach first! Down, down I went; I felt as though I had hit a brick wall; I lost all movement of my arms and legs; my stomach felt it had been ripped open. I realised I was groping on the floor of the baths; within a few seconds I broke surface, but I remembered I had taken a deep breath before I dived – and that's what saved me. They were going frantic on the side of the baths.

A couple of boathooks grabbed my ducksuit by the collar and I was dragged to the side of the baths; I couldn't move; my arms and legs were useless. The instructor was trying to say something to me, shouting down at me, 'Stay put, stay in the water for a while. Try to move your arms and legs.' Which I did and after a few minutes I was swimming about a bit, but feeling very sore around my stomach, then I eased myself up out of the water. I had done no injury to my stomach, but by the colour I had given it a hell of a bruising. After a while I felt myself again, but the bruising and the aching stayed with me for a time.

One of the instructors showed me how to dive off the side, which in actual fact was the correct way to dive off the side of a ship, and how I would dive off the side of the baths, which I practised and practised. I liked swimming so much that I did a lot of voluntary evenings during the three months basic training. I became very proficient at swimming and got to know the instructor very well; he said that I could take my Ducksuit Test any time I wished. I said, 'I will take it when 159 Class take it at the end of the course.'

At about this time I received a letter from my mother thanking me for making an allowance for her, out of my pay, ten shillings per week; my pay was two pounds, four and sixpence a fortnight, so that left me, one pound, four and sixpence for my pocket-money.

The allowance remained that amount all through my service in the Navy, irrespective of my promotion in 1944 to Leading Air Mechanic. I was the only son to have done that, and was the only son to have joined the Regular Forces, pre-war and served until 1946. I was branded the black sheep, because I had cleared off and joined the Navy. I couldn't bear the atmosphere at home and my mother, who was living with Mr Miles, and yet we were all expected to go to Church every Sunday. Some black sheep! I volunteered to give my life for King and Country, have four medals to prove it and would have done if it had been necessary. Don't let anyone have any qualms about that!

We had our first session in the gymnasium next door. I enjoyed the exercises which would, no doubt, get us very fit, doing it every week for three months; we were also encouraged to take up boxing. I had the 'gloves on' with chaps who were the same weight, very often, for three minutes each round for three rounds, until the end of training.

Seamanship Classes were held in the left half, Duncan Block, on the ground floor; we did many hours doing knots and splicing ropes, large and small, which came to me quite easy. We also were shown how the loose ends of rope were dealt with: they were 'cheesed', coiled up, in other words. Loose rope was never allowed on the decks of a warship, it was always 'cheesed'. Also, there were many lectures about the fleet at sea, battle formations, the types of ship which make up the fleet; these lectures went on for great lengths – the difference between a battleship, and battlecruiser, a cruiser and a light cruiser, and so on, until we knew the difference between ships and what their purpose was in wartime. In peacetime, the main purpose was 'Showing the Flag' in all parts of the world. We had the largest navy in the world, several hundred ships, which was increasing every week with new modern ships. The Navy as I saw it was second to none; that's why we spent every day scrubbing wood; anything that was metal was polished to death; if it didn't polish, then we burnished it, or painted it. Everything was kept at a high standard, so much so that the ships used to glisten as they passed at sea; all the bright bits used to shine; if they didn't, there used to be 'hell' to pay from the Admiral; the flagship was so full of 'bull', that it used to float on it! There was one order which used to keep the Navy on its toes, going crackers, or something like that: that was 'Attention for rounds'. I'm sure there was a Duty Officer, a Duty Petty Officer, and a Duty Royal Marine Bugler who used to go through each mess, every day, in each block, then, as they got to the end of the barracks, turned round and came back again, keeping everybody on their toes! God! Attention for rounds, again!

The three-month Training Course consisted of drilling and marching, rifle drill and bayonet drill, ·22 rifle shooting, seamanship, boat pulling, ducksuit test, diving and swimming, gymnasium, gas school at East Camp, the odd kit inspections in the Drill Shed every three weeks, and generally playing silly buggers, marching past on the parade ground every Thursday, and Sunday Divisions; on Thursday we marched past with fixed bayonets, and on Sunday we marched in our No. 1 best uniform; occasionally there was a cameraman on the bridge at the end of the parade ground; the best shots were taken of us from there. At the end of our training there was a special parade of all the classes, and there would be a 'March Past'.

It was the end of January, 1938. We had, in the meantime, some heavy falls of snow, snow showers to contend with on the parade ground; if it wasn't the snow, it was the biting wind that used to blow from the north-east, down the Medway and on to the fully exposed parade ground. We lived in our oilskins, gaiters and boots, with the chin strap down all the time; there were no gloves or scarves. They were never heard of in 'This Man's Navy'. We were never issued with the comforts of home. However, the Leading Hand, who was instructing us, wore kid gloves. Our hands were frozen holding on to the rifle, with the wind blowing so hard, blowing in our ears. I seem to remember, in snatches, him saying something about 'Stand easy', and the other bit I caught was, 'Going to the rifle store to draw our bayonets'. Surely not bayonets in this weather? 'Stand easy' sounded across the windy parade ground just as it started to snow again; it was 10.25 a.m.; 'Out pipes' would sound at 10.35 a.m., ten minutes to get up to the end of the parade ground, and about a hundred men in the queue for a cup of tea. 'Won't make it in time,' so we got some fags out, or 'Ticklers' as we called them, and stood around the wall for our protection, contemplating what it would be like fixing bayonets in this weather, for 159 Class. 'Out pipes' sounded, and we fell in in twos again, and marched the length of the parade ground, turned right across the road, where there were several one-storey buildings; the nearest was the Rifle and Bayonet Store, which we entered. 'Take one bayonet and scabbard each,' said the Leading Hand. Now the pre-war bayonet was like a small sword, sixteen inches long, polished steel – no wonder they glittered when marching with them fixed. We drew a webbing belt each for the scabbard, fitted ourselves out and inserted the bayonet in the scabbard. When fitted out, we fell in outside in twos and marched back the way we had come to the parade ground where we came to the order arms and stood still; it had stopped snowing for a while.

The Leading Hand always walked up and down the front rank, contemplating the next move, eyeing us all one by one, no doubt wondering just what a 'balls up' we were going to make of it. Fixing bayonets was not easy under the circumstances, when you couldn't feel your fingers in the sub-arctic weather. It was going to be tricky, it looked alright on the cinema screens, but this was reality, and it had started to snow again! 'Right! Let's be having you!' the Leading Hand shouted, as if we were miles away. 'When I shout "*Squad will fix bayonets*" the right-hand man [that's me] of the front rank, will smartly take three paces forward. Got it? Place his rifle between his knees and reach to the left for his bayonet hilt,' he went on [that would be me]. 'When I say, "*Squad will fix*", the right-hand man [me again] will draw his bayonet and hold it high, as if reaching for the sky, above his head, the rest of the squad will look to the right, place their rifles between their knees and reach to the left, for their bayonets and draw them, hold them high, and when I shout "*Bayonets*" the squad will bring them down, with an almighty "*Crash*" on the end of their rifles; they should *go* with an almighty "*Click*" when the button on the end of the rifle is fully depressed. Got it? And, when I say, "*Attention*" you take your right hand off the bayonet, grab the rifle and come to attention – the bayonet should be fixed. Got it? Right! Squad will fix bayonets – Squad will fix – Bayonets!' Crash! Clatter! clatter! clatter! These were bayonets hitting the ground followed by the odd, Clatter! Clatter! Talk about a b******. The Leading Hand turned away in disgust and started looking at faraway places!

Most of the squad had numb hands – you couldn't feel the rifle, let alone the spring clip at the end of it.

He said, 'We will practise, practise, practise, fixing bayonets, every day, morning and afternoon, 'til we get it right, there will be no "Stand Easy" for any of us. You will wish you'd never heard of "Fixing Bayonets".' And I never did forget it. When I saw them years after, I thought of 159 Class, practising in the snow, on a day in January 1938, Chatham Parade Ground.

He went on, 'The Navy has been called upon to be a boarding party, or a landing party, in any part of the globe. You can be called upon, irrespective of rank or rating; there are *no* passengers on a warship, just members of her crew. At any time, at all times, every man jack should be ready, whether you be a seaman, stoker, or a cook, you'd do well to remember it.'

That spurred us on to greater things and by the end of the week it went, clickety click! We were doing it faultlessly; it looked good to see a squad 'Fixing Bayonets' absolutely correctly and by the end of three months we passed at a high standard.

We also had ·22 rifle shooting in the evenings; the lower half of the drill shed was only for those who were shooting, nobody else was allowed in. I spent a night, once a week, rifle shooting, and at one time considered going in for the small arms badge as my shooting was above standard; what with my swimming, I kept myself busy.

The days and weeks passed with monotonous regularity; one morning it was boat pulling in the dockyard, cold, but not snowing, p.m. was seamanship in Duncan Block; the next day was in the swimming bath in the morning, p.m. in the gymnasium; next day was rifle drill, p.m. rifle shooting. Every week varied, with a march past with a Marine band on the parade ground every Thursday afternoon, marching with fixed bayonets, and Sunday morning we had Divisions in our No. 1 Dress Uniform and officers wore the cocked hats, epaulettes and swords, in fact, the whole regalia which they wore in pre-war days, never to be seen since. They looked magnificent, with doeskin waistcoats, finished off by a patent-leather belt and gold buckle; the trousers were narrow, with a broad yellow stripe down the seam; the shoes had to be seen to be believed. They were patent leather, high heel, not unlike ladies heels, but were boots which disappeared up under the trousers, finished off with a cocked hat, epaulettes, sword and white gloves; it was too expensive after the War, so it was discontinued.

On Thursday afternoons, everyone who was under training took part in a marching out parade; there were several hundred of us. We used to fall in outside the swimming baths, at the far end of the P.G. with rifles at the slope, sometimes with fixed bayonets. The Royal Marine band was in position at the saluting dais halfway down the P.G. under central steps. There were green marker flags at intervals down the left-hand side, which gave the platoons a guide when giving 'Eyes Left' when passing the saluting dais. The red marker flag was placed ten yards before the canteen wall, which blocked the far end of the parade ground.

The officer who was leading each platoon would look for the red marker, usually after he had given 'Eyes Left' to the commander of the parade, approximately thirty yards before he reached the canteen wall; he then had plenty of time to give the order, 'Change direction right – right form'. It was a case of 'follow my leader'. When the first officer gave the order, the second officer would give the order at the same spot.

There was a wide passage between the canteen and the drill shed, which gave passage to North Road, turning left to St George's Church and the main gate of HMS Pembroke, the Stone Frigate; but occasionally there would be a b******, the order was given too late and a platoon was driven up the canteen wall, or the rear rank would pile into the front, or half of the men would see the danger coming and 'right form' of their own accord, but the second rank didn't and so there was a shining example of how *not* to march in Revue Order on Sundays.

The main parade was Sunday, Sunday Divisions they used to call it; everybody turned out in their No. 1 Best Blue uniforms, no gaiters or belts on Sunday parade. The officers were in their pre-war dress uniforms, cocked hat, epaulettes and swords; they looked superb, not a hair out of place, it was called the 'Revue Order'.

We were inspected over and over again, our uniforms were brushed, our shoes were polished to death; civilians have never seen the Navy getting ready for a parade. We used to spend an hour or two brushing each other down, looking in mirrors, asking a messmate if this, or that was straight, talk about b******; we didn't mention it, but there was pride! Every man jack was proud, but if you asked him, he'd say, 'I've never known such a lot of f****** b****** in all my life,' then look in the large mirror to see if he was alright.

More often than not it was attended by the Commodore of the barracks, but on this occasion it was taken by Admiral Evans, 'Evans of the Broke', who was at the time Commander-in-Chief of Nore Command, a very, very fine man, who was thought the world of in the Navy and in civilian life too; he was a man's man who spent a great deal of his younger days with Captain Scott of the Antarctic, in expeditions to the South Pole.

Divisions were a special parade, all the more so this morning, as Admiral Evans was taking the salute at this morning's parade – we would do him proud this day!

All the men left each block of Duncan, Anson and Nelson, down the steps opposite and down to the parade ground, and arranged themselves according to what Division they belonged to. We in Duncan Block were in the Foretop Division, the next, came the Main-top Division, and so on. We fell in on the P.G. at 9.30 a.m.; the march wouldn't start until 10.30, so we formed up in double ranks, and stood, first at attention, then at ease, then at attention, taking our dressings from the right, satisfied that both our ranks were dead straight; the Officer of the Foretop marched along inspecting us; woe betide if anyone got pulled up for anything; then down the rear of us, he looked and looked and looked. No, he didn't find anything wrong with the front rank, so he did the same with the other rank. No, he didn't find anything wrong, so he came to the front and stood us at ease again.

There must have been hundreds of us on parade, all I could see were men, there were no Wrens in the Navy in those days, just men; our ranks were about thirty or thirty-five, all stacked up against the next lot. There was plenty of room, as Chatham parade ground was long, a terrific length, ideal for a march past of this order; there must have been a thousand Jack Tars on parade.

Over on the right was the drill shed, an enormous shed which they could get the entire parade into if it was wet; next building was the gymnasium; the next was the large swimming baths; before you came to the end of the P.G. then you came to the bridge which took the road from Terrace Road and went down to the main dockyard gate. This went over the end of the P.G. and was an ideal place for the cameramen to be – you get an absolute picture of the parade. Over on the right was a clock tower, halfway along the drill shed roof; this clock used to sound the half hour and the hour with monotonous regularity.

We were brought to attention again – our officer was keeping us wide awake – then at ease, there was a lot of shuffling of feet, then attention again and finally at ease, until some poor bloke in the rear rank couldn't stand it any longer and said, 'For Christ's sake, make up your bloody mind then!' The officer said, 'Silence in the ranks.'

Then the moment had arrived and the marine bugler sounded off; the clock struck 10.30 and we were all brought finally to attention. You could hear a pin drop on the parade ground, every man stood rock still. The C.-in-C., Admiral Evans of the Broke had arrived; he didn't mess about, saw the first rank and continued to inspect us, stopping occasionally to speak to someone he knew, or had served with. There were loads of 'brass knobs' with him, the bugler sounded off again, and then, a voice came from nowhere, loud and clear, 'Parade will march parst in revue order – er – er!' Some toffee-nosed sod, no doubt. Some comic in the rear squealed, 'Taking your time from the dockyard clock, Tick – Tock, Tick – Tock.' The clock was just above us on the drill shed roof; it caused a smile on my face and plenty of others too, no doubt, going by the titter in the ranks. The thought came to my mind, 'Lady Anna will carry the banner!' but a matelot in the rear rank squealed, 'But I carried it last week.' 'You'll carry it this f****** week.'

The officer standing in the front of the platoon drew his sword, the seconds ticked by, then a voice from nowhere bellowed, 'Parade – Quick, M-March!' The Royal Marine band struck up with 'Standard of St George', the Navy's favourite march. The front division moved off, we were next, everything was moving now, all giggling stopped forthwith. 'Foretop Division!' that's us! The officer shouted above the din, 'Quick March!' and we were off, keeping beautiful line abreast, heads held high, chests out, we marched as though we were proud of it, and so we were, every man jack of us, we marched with a swagger. Then came the order from our officer, 'Eyes Left!' and he brought his sword down, so that it was pointing to the ground. Every man, except the pivot man on our left, gave a smart 'Eyes Left!' to the Admiral who was standing on the saluting dais, and then we heard the officer shout, 'Eyes Front!' and we continued marching to the 'Standard of St George'. I thought, Yes, of course, the colours are the 'Standard of St George', the red cross with the white background.

Then the last vital order came, 'Change direction right, Right Form!' Only just in time, another two or three paces and we would have been into the canteen wall. We turned right and continued marching between the canteen and the drill shed, and turned left on to the road which took us to the main gate, on the left there was a driveway which took us to St George's Church, where we came to a halt and fell out, feeling relieved that that was over for another week.

Monday morning came round again and we were in our second month of training. We found ourselves collecting rifles, bayonets and webbing gear with belt. I thought we can't be doing fixing bayonets this time. We marched back to the parade ground – the weather was better than last time, no snow, but there was a cold wind blowing.

We did fixing bayonets and nobody dropped their bayonet this time, so we came to the order arms and stood still; the instructor said we had come to the stage of what a rifle and bayonet was for – bayonet fighting. So the first part of the morning was spent learning the rudiments of the art: 'A short point stationary to the throat, followed by a long point stationary to the stomach. Those words died hard, never to be forgotten, I hoped I would never have to use the bayonet for that. I lost track of all the rudiments of the art, remembering only two that would stand me in good stead if it ever came to it! The rest was like quarter staff, and I learnt it in the Scouts.

And so the weeks went by, but the weather didn't improve. There was boat pulling in atrocious conditions, snowing nearly all day; I thought the weather would improve by now but it's always the same when you are stuck out in a boat; it would be different when we got indoors again. Ducksuit practise again in the cold, where the water was all cold and dirty, but it no longer bothered me, this was what we had to get used to. Once in the water, I was happy and content, although the canvas suits seemed to tear at you; the seams were unbearable to say the least. I was always glad to shed them at the end of the session and hang them up on the lines ready for the next unsuspecting bloke, and the best of British luck to him too!

The rest of the training passed with dull monotony: the gymnasium, seamanship, lectures on the Fleet, ·22 rifle firing in the evenings, but mainly it was marching up and down, backwards and forwards, on the parade ground, sometimes with rifles at the slope, sometimes with fixed bayonets, sometimes none at all, so it was a good time to double, and the Navy does nearly everything at the double! When you have a 'gas masks on', we did it at the double; when the glass visors steamed up, it was better at the double, even if you couldn't see where we were going. Whenever we crossed the parade ground, any hour of the day, any day, Sunday included, double march! One day I was carrying my kit bag down, from Duncan Block, across the P.G. to the drill shed, where I was to have a kit inspection on one of the long tables which were always there for that purpose. The pre-war naval kit bags had to be seen to be believed: they stood five feet tall when fully packed, with heavy rope reinforcing round the bottom, with your name, official number – mine was C/MX55965 – on the bottom between the rope; when it was fully packed it took some lifting, let alone carrying.

It was a long walk with my kit bag over my shoulder; I went down the staircase of Duncan Block, through the covered way, down a whole flight of steps, across Terrace Road to one of three main steps which took you down to the P.G., passing the Naval Police who stood at the top of the three steps at all times, whose duty it was to see everybody was dressed properly and everyone was doubling across the P.G. I was walking across the P.G. I couldn't run with the kit bag on my shoulder as it was too damned heavy, when it seemed all hell had broken loose: whistles blew and there were men shouting. I stopped and looked round to see who was making all the noise, and a petty officer and a seaman were frantically waving their arms and blowing their whistles at me. I stopped and one shouted, 'Double up there!' I pointed to myself and said, 'Who me?' He said, 'Yes, you!' I didn't take kindly to being told I had to double with my enormous kit bag, and walked away again with my kit bag on my shoulder, muttering to myself, 'He can go and get stuffed!' He said, 'What did you say?' I said, 'It's a hell of a way.' He said, 'You should get a handcart and go by road!' When I got up to him, I said, 'Sorry, I have a bad leg,' and started limping. He was being too cocky, with that whistle around his neck, he was only the barrack guard. I said, 'What if there's no handcart?' He said, 'There should be one!' I said, 'Where?' He said, 'This end of the drill shed, near the Kitting Up Store!' I said, 'I'm afraid I'm new here!' 'Well,' he said, 'that's the orders, everybody has to double across the parade ground every minute of the day, and every day of the week!' I said, 'That's news to me – I'll take it back.' He said, 'No! No! don't take it back!' With that, the Petty Officer who was also at the top of the steps, put his head over the top and said, 'What are you having a pow-wow about, put him on a charge!' With that, a heavy-looking bloke doubled over, saw the enormous kitbag and said, 'I will carry it for you, mate, it's easy,' grabbed the kit bag and nearly ran down the steps. I limped after him, caught him at the bottom of the steps. 'Thanks, mate,' I said and there I was holding the kit bag, until the Petty Officer said, 'Leave it here, mate, go and get the handcart!' which he did, doubling over the parade ground and fetched the hand cart by way of the road which ran over the bridge at the end of the P.G. and up to the steps where I waited with my kit bag. Thanking the Petty Officer and the seaman, I lifted the kit bag onto the handcart and returned the way I had to go into the end of the drill shed, where I unloaded my kit on the first available table, laid out my kit, blue articles to the left, with white names on, and white articles to the right with blue names on; everything had to be displayed, everything that was possible had to be tied with tape, with your name showing, approximately nine inches across; it took an hour or two to get it laid out correctly. There was the whole of 159 Class having a kit inspection, it took up all the tables. I found that the sooner you got it laid out the better; as soon as you were ready, the sooner you reported to the Leading Hand who came and checked everything from a list. Provided you laid it out correctly, the sooner it was over, then you had to repack everything in your kit bag again.

The morning came when I had to take the 'Ducksuit Test'. The Instructor said, 'Do you fancy taking the test, Doe?' I said, 'Yes, I'm ready.' So was most of 159 Class. I put on the ducksuit and dived off the deep end. Yes, it restricted by movement, but I was being timed by the instructor. I started with the breaststroke and was well out away from the sides. How many lengths I did, I can't remember, I just kept going until the whistle sounded. At one point, I heard someone shout, 'Swim around for ten minutes!' I knew I was nearing the end; I cannot describe how a ducksuit feels; it's like being in the water with a coat of armour on. However, I passed OK.

Finally the end of the three months basic training was over. Thursday afternoon was the March Past, and how we marched. We carried our rifles at the slope as the sun shone on the first day of spring.

On the Friday afternoon we had a group photograph in our No. 3s, our working rig, on the bowling green next to Duncan Block; then we left for a 'Friday While', a long weekend leave, from Friday 'til Monday morning, in the Navy!

On Monday morning I fell in, in the yard opposite the covered way, at Duncan Block. We were then told by Leading Seaman Cock that our basic training was over – he was leaving to take another class. We two, Dyer and myself, would report to the Cookery School at Anson Block; the remainder, who were stokers, would report to the Dockyard for their stokers' training.

My heart sank, the day I had been dreading had at last arrived. I immediately requested to see Commander Ludgrove but was told that he had left and was now in command of HMS *Kent*. I had made out a request form to see the Divisional Officer, and saw him the next morning at 'Requestment'. He listened to what I had to say, but then blocked my request, saying, 'Do you realise that it costs thousands of pounds to train you?' I said, 'I would have to be trained no matter what branch I was in!' He retorted by saying, 'What did you say?' His face was livid. I said, 'They told me that I could always transfer! He was not telling me the truth, sir, was he?' The Divisional Officer said, 'But there are no vacancies.' I said, 'How do we know there are no vacancies?' 'Now, now.' said the Divisional Officer, 'There's no need for remarks like that. My advice to you, Doe, is to get on with it; we often have to do a job that we do not like.' I said, 'Yes, sir, but as soon as I hear of a vacancy, I will request a transfer right away, because I do not feel I can do justice to a job that my heart is not in.' The D/Officer was getting a little annoyed at my insistence – he knew I was right, that an injustice had been done. 'We will take a note of your case, it will be looked into, alright?' He turned away from me and had a word with the Chief Petty Officer. The next thing I knew was that the CPO suddenly shouted, 'Held in abeyance, about turn, Quick March!' and I was out of the door.

I knew I was up against the Service. The establishment will not move. But I was just as determined. I went on a 'Friday While', a long weekend leave, came back to barracks 'three days adrift' and was marched round to the Officer of the Day at the main gate. I was ordered 'Off Cap.' It

My first uniform – the Author in 1938.

meant that I was a 'defaulter'; he listened to what I had to say and said, 'Commander's Report.' The next morning at 9.00 a.m., I fell in with all the other defaulters, then I heard someone shout, 'Assistant Cook Doe.' I doubled up to the Commander, 'Off Caps' and a CPO read out the charge: 'Assistant Cook Doe, was absent without leave, namely, from so and so, until so and so, on Thursday!' The Commander turned to the D/Officer, and he muttered something about an injustice, blah, blah! He turned to me and said, 'Your Training Commander spoke highly of you, you've done very well so far – why don't you stick it out for a while, you may find that you like being a cook.' So I was let off with a caution. You may find that you like being a cook – never!

Next day I reported to the Cookery School. I found the Chief PO easy to get on with which gave me a quick start which made me eager to learn. As I put on an apron, it felt foreign to me, wearing No. 6 uniform, all in white, complete in a cook's hat, and an apron on. I thought, This is not for me, I'm an engineer by trade.

However, the Chief made me very welcome, which helped. He had the class round an open cupboard showing us all the spices they used in naval cookery. Later we were shown how to make 'clear soup' and every kind of soup, and as the weeks passed, we cooked every vegetable, every kind of fish, fish cakes, every kind of joint, from beef steak and kidney pies, from currant duff/steamed pudding to Queen of Puddings, the Navy's favourite soup 'Peadoo' (Pea Soup) to fruitcake, iced cakes, how to do icing and Swiss roll. For sixteen weeks we slaved at the Cookery School, until the day came for us to pass the cookery examinations.

At 4.30 *a.m.* I had to report to the Cookery School alone and light the fires to heat the ovens, with no help of any kind. I had to do a seven-course dinner for at least a dozen officers, which had to be ready, served up at 12.00 o'clock sharp. A special table was laid for twelve officers, with best silver and napkins, each place had full cutlery for a seven-course dinner. Cleanliness and smartness were paramount, a steward stood by, the chief stood to one side, just in case I got into difficulties, a challenge to me who hated cookery! Everything was served straight from the range on silver dishes, cookery at its best.

I served the soup, fish, joint, with three vegetables, sweet, savoury, cake, absolutely bang-on. It was perfect to me! I felt proud as I stood by, while the officers ate a hearty meal. One after another made his assessment which was passed on to the Paymaster Commander, who made his final judgement. From where I stood near the range, I noticed him nodding his approval. I had passed 'Satisfactory', which was not high, but high enough for me to pass for 'Officers Cook', which was higher than ship's cooking for the lower deck for the men. I would go to the wardroom galley. When I saw my certificate, it was marked with a V.G. (very good), which would mean 'O.C.' on my badge.

Next was five weeks' bakery at the Bakery School, situated on the ground floor of Anson Block, below the Cookery School. They had large electric ovens, and the standard was cleanliness to a very high standard. Once there, about a dozen cooks, all as new to the job as I was; the chief was a first-class man, who was easy to get on with; we just used to muck in, mixing the flour, with yeast and salt, the same amount in the mornings and again in the afternoons for every type of loaf and rolls by the hundred, put into long, spotlessly clean 'proving bins', covered over with spotlessly clean cloths, until the yeast had made it rise and it had been 'proved'. The dough was cut up into hundreds of lumps and put on the scales to weigh 1 lb for a full tin loaf, 1/2 lb for a small tin loaf, then it was kneaded by all the hands, standing around a big table with a pound of dough in each hand. There were two of the chaps greasing all the tins; we would do about 500 loaves in the morning, and about 500 in the afternoon. This was the same every day and we made the bread for the whole barracks, the wardroom too. Passing the baking examination seemed a foregone conclusion, and we passed.

After five weeks it was over, I changed my mess from 2NN in Duncan Block, to right half, Nelson Block, next to the wardroom. I reported to the chef, a chief petty officer, who was a damn nice bloke. I got on well with him, he got the best out of me; cookery wasn't so bad after all; it has its advantages and we worked like a well-oiled clock. I turned-to to any job that wanted doing, I found myself basting roast potatoes, seeing to all the veg on the range, in no time at all becoming the veg cook. I was left to it, the Chief had a word with someone, I took a delight in being given some responsibility and went to town doing my own thing. The Chief had a word with me one morning, 'And how do you like to be in charge of the entire veg, Doe?' I said, 'Yes, fine thanks, Chief.' 'Right, as from today, it's yours. Veg Cook! OK' he said. I stood at the oil-fired range all day, seeing this and that was done, and got ready preparing the veg, creaming the mashed potatoes on the Hobart electric mixer, being here, there and everywhere. The heat from the oil-fired heaters was unbearable at first, but after a while, I got used to it scorching my face; time passed quickly; there was not time for 'Stand easy' or a cup of coffee; there wasn't time for it. I know why we were called 'galley slaves'!

I don't know whether it was working in the heat in the galley but I suddenly got bad throats, so I reported to the Sick Bay where the Surgeon Lieutenant examined my throat. He said, 'How old are you?' I replied 'Twenty, sir!' He said, 'Your tonsils are septic; they must come out immediately; they're poisoning your whole system; you usually have them out when you are young; it's a bit risky at your age!' I said, 'I was supposed to have had my tonsils out when I was seven at the orphanage. I went to Chester Infirmary.' He said, 'Well, they must have only cut them; no wonder your glands have been swollen all these years!' My mother again.

I was sent to the hospital at Dartford, in Kent, and had my tonsils out. I had a rough time of it. The Sister said, 'We had a rough time with you, you nearly kicked the bucket! Coming out of the anaesthetic, you nearly choked to death. If the nurse hadn't stayed with you, I don't know what would have happened. The surgeon said, 'It was a bit risky.' Once it was over, I stayed at the hospital for three weeks. Upon returning to HMS Pembroke, the RN Barracks, I was put on light duties for a while before returning to the Wardroom Galley.

In September 1938 there was the Munich Crisis. The Navy was quick off the mark. Reservists were being called up to the colours by the ten thousand, the barracks was crowded, ships that had laid idle since I had joined were suddenly manned and put to sea, as part of the Reserve Fleet.

The naval barracks, once built at the turn of the century to hold 5,000, was suddenly overcrowded, thousands of reservists were called up, the number increased to 15,000 and increasing, it was queues for everything, for dinners, for your pay, to going on leave – it was hell being in barracks. There were huge lorries coming through the main gates at all times, carrying vast supplies of ammunition for the ships and anti-aircraft batteries which sprang up in the dockyard, and our own ack-ack battery which was situated between left half, Duncan Block and the Gunnery School.

Ships were leaving the dockyard from time to time, putting to sea for what we used to call 'a shakedown cruise'! New ships arrived, the brand-new HMS *Southampton* and the *Sheffield*, the original 'Shiny Sheffield', City Class cruisers, come to join the 1st Cruiser Squadron; more would soon follow, thirteen at least. What were those things at the masthead? Radar, in 1938!

The Tribal Class destroyers, larger and more heavily armed destroyers arrived followed by the J-boats, also larger and faster destroyers, HMS *Jervis*, *Juno*, *Jasper* and *Javelin*, *Jackal* and others, then the M-boats, HMS *Milne*, *Marne*, *Meteor*, *Matchless* and *Mashona* and countless others, the H-boats *Hardy*, *Hotspur*, *Hyperion*, *Havoc* and others.

The C-Class light cruisers having been laid up for many months in No. 2 and No. 3 Basins, built between the wars, suddenly got up steam, one after another of them, left the outer basin and entered the River

Medway to proceed upstream, to zig zag , up and round the bends in the river to Sheerness to join the other of their class at Portland. Their names were HMS *Coventry*, *Curlew*, *Caledon*, *Carlisle*, *Colombo*, *Cairo* and others.

I left HMS *Dragon* after being drafted to her, and returned through the main gate of the Dockyard to barracks again, which was all one, dockyard and barracks. The queues had subsided a bit, with all the ships which left, and the Navy had put to sea alright; the Fleet was assembling at Portland, Cromarty Firth and at Scapa Flow; we would be ready, come what may. All the battleships would be leaving at Sheerness; the battleship, HMS *Royal Sovereign*, 'The Tiddly Quid' they always called her, was a Sovereign, and the name 'Tiddly' meant smart in the Navy. Several battleships were at Portsmouth and Devonport, and they would be making for Portland Assembly Base to await instructions.

I went into the drill shed where the Drafting Office was and looked at the boards on the walls: hundreds of names under the names of ships; there were the names of my mates: Ron of East Barnet drafted to HMS *Royal Oak*, Arthur, who joined up with me, drafted to HMS *Resolution*, Les was drafted to HMS *Juno*, and so on, all good mates who had trained together. I looked at the boards but there was no sign of my name; perhaps it was delayed owing to having my tonsils out. It was October 1938 so there was plenty of time yet for a draft. I was still on light duties so I waited, dying to get to sea, returning to normal duties in the Wardroom Galley.

To us in the Navy it was the real thing; war seemed imminent; in civilian life it became known as the 'Phoney War'; civilians at home thought it wouldn't happen.

HMS *Cumberland*, a County Class cruiser, had recently returned from being the flagship of the China Station, and after doing two and a half years commission, went straight into dry dock for a refit. There were ten County Class, of 10,000 tons, the odd one, HMS *Shropshire* was lent to Australia, and became HMAS *Australia*, otherwise there would have been eleven County Class: HMS *Cumberland*, *Berwick*, *Norfolk*, *Suffolk*, *Kent*, *Sussex*, *Dorsetshire*, *Devonshire*, *Cornwall* and *London*.

In the spring of 1939, I saw my name on the noticeboard of the drill shed in a draft to HMS *Cumberland*. I reported to the drafting office in the drill shed; before leaving barracks, I had a kit inspection, to see if I had everything, then I got a small handcart to move my gear to the dockyard. I marched a hundred yards or so and found myself at the gates; the sentry asked for my draft chit, which said, 'One Rating, Officers' Assistant Cook, M. Doe, HMS *Cumberland*'. 'She's on the right, No. 3 Basin,' he said. I knew where she was, I had seen her towering above the buildings, opposite Duncan Block, her paint gleaming after her refit; she looked a beauty.

As I approached I could see the improvements they had made to her: she had a cutaway stern; a hangar that housed two aircraft; four single AA guns were now twin 4.5", making eight; two sets of multiple AA guns, four barrels each; armour plating on her sides, above the waterline, several inches thick; and other improvements which I didn't see at the time, like the catapult for launching the aircraft and the cranes for picking up the aircraft, one to port, one to starboard. Well, with the added weight, she must have been in the region of 12,000 tons. I had heard that she was 13,000 tons!

I learnt that the Captain was a well-seasoned skipper, Captain Fallowfield, and that the *Cumberland* was leaving in a day or two, first to call at Sheerness at the top of the Medway and collect ammunition, then to join the Home Fleet at Portland as a member of the 2nd Cruiser Squadron.

As I climbed the gangway, I thought how lovely she looked, that she was going to be a happy ship. In fact, she turned out to be 'A very happy ship!'

I reported to the Royal Marine who stood at the top of the gangway, showed him my draft 'chit', then went and collected the remainder of my gear. He told me where to go aft, to report to the Chief in the officers' galley, under the hangar. I reported to the Chief Petty Officer Cook and about six other chefs, who were busy in the galleys, and he told me where to go for a locker in which to stow my gear. It was one deck below in the locker flats; the cooks' mess was on the starboard side, in which I stowed my hammock in the place provided.

I then went for'ard to report to the Master-at-Arms, who is in charge of the rank and file, and who I came to know as Nobby Clark. He was the senior Chief Petty Officer on the ship, and was in charge of everybody and everything.

On returning aft towards the officers' galley, I noticed how immaculate the whole ship was, inside and outside; the paintwork was of a very high standard, an eggshell blue; you could see your face in it; everything that was metal was polished to death: brass, copper or plain steel. I reported back to the Chief who took me through the galleys. There was the main Wardroom Galley, the Gun Room Galley, the WOs' Galley, the Captain's Galley and the Electric Bakery that worked independently from the galleys. They were small but compact, big enough for two or three to work in, and spotlessly clean; all the metal shone as did the rest of the ship. The white-tiled deck was washed down after every meal and was left spotless at the end of our duty each day. I thought, Standards are very high!

The Chief said, 'Did you report to the MAA Office?' I said, 'Yes, Chief.' He said, 'That's OK then, you'll get your Action Station from him in a day or two.' I was introduced to my watch, to a petty officer and a leading cook, then to the opposite watch – the Chief, of course, a second leading cook and my opposite number, another assistant cook. He and I would share the work during the day; I would be the assistant cook of the Port Watch. We carried at all times a duty card, blue for starboard, red for port, with your name, rating, official number, religion and Action Station on. We all turned to in the Wardroom Galley, the only galley in operation for breakfast. The only galley that was independent of us was the Captain's Galley; there was a petty officer cook and a leading cook did their stint every day.

Breakfasts consisted of fried cruets, or toast, buttered egg, fried egg, or boiled egg, sausages, bacon, tomatoes and beans, coffee or tea. The first duty I had to do was to 'flash up' the oil ranges which were very efficient. The burner, which was on a swivel, was turned into the firebox. Just below the burner there were two taps, one for air, one for oil. As soon as the air tap was turned on, the nozzle on the burner started spinning; as soon as you turned the burner into the firebox, you, only then, turned on the oil. Then there was an almighty roar and the automatic ignition did the rest. That roar continued the whole time, which made normal conversation impossible, and you had to shout in each other's ear. Relief came at about 1.15 p.m. every day 'til 4.00 p.m. when it all started again for dinner in the evening.

There was a nine-inch slit at the side of the burner for the purpose of seeing it was alright, but it was wise to keep your head away from the 'periscope' as it was called, as flame was known to flash out from time to time. Within minutes the hotplate was red-hot and the temperature in the galley increased rapidly.

We turned-to, doing any job that wanted doing, but, more often than not, the Chief detailed you off. Every day was a laugh, I was happy with the crew, all of them.

At 9.00 a.m. we had our breakfast, having been on duty since 5.00 a.m., and that was only the breakfast stint!

Then we tackled lunch, laughing and joking most of the time. Most of my day was spent in the sink, dishing up, which was endless, then the spuds to peel; we all took a hand in that. The lunch was prepared and cooked; at 1.15 p.m. we shut off the oil-fired ranges and had our lunch, after which all the washing up was done. All work surfaces and the large table were washed down. Finally the deck, right through the galleys, was scrubbed. It looked beautiful with the white tiles; these were in normal conditions, but it wouldn't be so wonderful in rough weather!

We were all off-duty 'til 4.00 p.m., when the duty watch turned to in the galley to cook dinner for 8.00 p.m.

I decided a walk out in the fresh air on the upper deck was called for and was joined by my Leading Hand. We walked down the port side as far as the fo'c'sle and back up the starboard side, continued this little jaunt for a while, then went below for a shower.

When 4.00 p.m. came round, the Port Watch was the duty watch, which was me! A petty officer was in charge, leading cook and myself. I made a cup of coffee for the three of us, and flashed up the oil-fired ranges. The hotplates glowed red-hot in a few minutes. I thought, This would be dangerous in rough weather! For safety sake, there was a steel safety bar, six inches high, which ran right around the range, to stop anyone falling onto it, and prevent a ten-gallon pot from coming off, or, worse still, a large vat of boiling oil.

We pressed on with the dinner which would be for 8.00 p.m. which went on 'til 9.00. We finally had our dinner, shut down the oil-fired range, dished up, washed down the working surfaces, finally, the deck, and went below to sling our hammocks for the night.

At 5.00 a.m. I jumped out of my hammock, no Reveille – they don't 'call the hands' until 5.45 a.m., dressed, lashed up my hammock and stowed it in the place provided, had a wash and reported to the galley. Everyone else was on duty, but nobody said anything like 'You're late!' It was very tactful of them, a case of getting the breakfast underway. I could see that *no* coffee had been made, so I got a ten-gallon potfull of water and put it on the range, brought it to the boil, then added a tin of powdered coffee, then took it off immediately and let it cool down. When it was cooler, I strained it through a hair sieve, then returned it to the range let it get hot again and let it simmer – *never* let coffee boil a second time, it turns bitter. I then made six cups of coffee; one, I gave to the Chief, five for the rest of us; the breakfast proceeded just the same, but a mug of coffee was very welcome by all. I turned-to frying some of the 150 cruets for the buttered egg that my Leading Cook was busy making alongside me at the range. Before I knew it, the stewards came up to collect the fried breakfast which came out of the heating chests, served up on silver dishes; the coffee was served up in silver jugs. The range was turned off at 9.00 a.m., so we had breakfast on the large table, and who was adrift this morning? We had a laugh!

The lunch proceeded according to plan; during the morning we heard the main engines start up; we had slipped our moorings and were getting underway. Each galley had a scuttle that you could look out of so you had a clear view of anything going on outside; we were level with the upper deck. As I looked out, we had left No. 3 Basin and were going through the outer lock; the Royal Marine band that was on the jetty struck up with 'Rule Britannia' and then we were out in the River Medway, pointing upstream in the direction of Sheerness, but there were many bends of the river we had to negotiate first. I withdrew from the scuttle and continued dishing up the dirties.

We dropped anchor at Sheerness and proceeded to ammunition ship. Next day, we came out of the Medway, facing Southend for a while before turning to starboard and down the Channel to Portland.

During the afternoon, when we were off duty, the Master-at-Arms came up to see me, to give me my 'Action Station.' We became very good friends as time passed, but this day I was new to the ship and he was the MAA. He said, 'You're new aboard this ship, right?' I said, 'Yes, Master!' He said, 'Come with me.' We stepped out of the galley on to the upper deck, looked at the hangar which was above our four galleys and the bakery and he pointed to a small ladder, which went up the rear of the hangar to a searchlight battery, ·5" guns and the mainmast which came through several decks, through the rear of the 'Gun Room Galley' and up beyond the rear of the hangar. He said, 'Right, follow me.' Up the ladder we went and stood on top of the hangar, where we faced the searchlight battery. Just a little way away were the ·5" anti-aircraft guns. He looked up the mainmast, which seemed to go up to the clouds, then said, 'When Action Stations sounds off, you get up there as fast as Christ will let you!' We looked up the mast, which was all polished oak, the base of which was approximately 2'6" in diameter, the top of which was swaying gently in the wind. I was sure it was a hundred feet high at least. I felt a lump come into my throat, although I was never afraid of heights – it was the top swaying to and fro! 'There's a single rope ladder there, you see, which takes you up, right to the top of the mast. When you get up there, there is a small platform, do you see it?' said the MAA. I looked and looked until I felt dizzy. I said, 'Yes, I think so, Master.' He went on, 'Well, there is one.' I knew I was having my leg well and truly pulled! He continued, 'There is a telephone up there, and it will be your job to scan the horizon 180° aft, from port to starboard.' He put out his left arm, then his right, 'If you see anything, no matter how small, grab the telephone, and report it to the bridge, don't forget, no matter how small – got it?' I brought my eyes down from the top of the mast. God, I thought, it looks as high as Everest. I looked him in the eye, sort of dizzy like; he said, 'You alright?' I said, 'I'm OK.' He said, 'Only they've got to have someone reliable, that's why I chose you.' With that I stuck my chest out a bit and said, 'Right ho, Master, you can count on me,' and we climbed down and went into the galley. Before he left, he gave me a good pat on the back, and said, 'I knew I could rely on you, Doe.' Every time I saw him, I said, 'You can count on me,' and every time I came out of the galley, I glanced up at the great big mast, looking for the small platform. I couldn't see it and nearly had kittens. Was he pulling my leg? I wouldn't funk it, I'd go up that mast if it killed me!

We arrived at Portland late in the afternoon; the harbour was enormous, full of warships – the Home Fleet was in. HMS *Hood, Repulse, Nelson, Rodney*, and nearly all the 'R' class battleships, the *Royal Sovereign, Royal Oak, Resolution, Ramilles*, and *Revenge*, they were all here, except the battle cruiser, *Renown*, which was having a refit at Portsmouth. There were no 'Q.E.' class battleships present, they were with the Mediterranean Fleet, all five of them.

Of the cruisers – there were too many to count – I did notice the *Southampton* was anchored a little way off; the destroyers, just blended into flotillas here there and everywhere; there seemed to be hundreds of them.

Next day, I got my 'Action Station', handed to me by the Chief, a small card, a bit longer than a cigarette card, red in colour. Inside was my name and official number, which was C/MX55965, my religion, C. of E., and my 'Action Station'. The MAA was pulling my leg and every time I passed him between decks, I always said, 'You can count on me Master.' I wasn't going to let him get away with it! We had a good laugh in the galley when I told them. Anyway, the 'Station Card', as it was known, was your identification card, you lived with it and only gave it up when you went ashore. I was a member of the port watch, red in colour; my action station was 8" forward magazine, cordite handling room, situated three decks down, serving 'A' and 'B' Turrets, four 8" guns.

I soon discovered there were *no* passengers on a warship, only ratings, everyone was detailed for his action station, irrespective of his rank or rating. For normal cruising you worked in your normal part of the ship; mine was the galley. For 'Action Stations', everyone had to be 'closed up' in two or three minutes, the sooner the better for the ship, which became a fortress, not a soul to be seen on the upper deck, as always, hurtling through the water, reaching top speed as soon as possible; there was this urgency in the ship and in the men. I had to run like hell from the galley which was right aft near the stern, the full length of the ship; the quickest way on the County Class cruisers was straight along the upper deck! I had a free run right up past the bridge, to 'A' and 'B' Turrets, right up front, near the fo'c'sle, down through a hatch, between 'A' and 'B', down through the shell handling room, discarding my belt with keys attached as nothing metal should be carried into the magazine. I wore white gym shoes at all times for this reason; so did everyone else; we all wore gym shoes whilst on board. Shoes were *never* worn. Within a minute, I was down between the 9" solid hatch to the 8" forward magazine.

In the forenoon next day, we weighed anchor, and steamed out of Portland Harbour, followed by the cruiser *Southampton*, for exercises in the Channel, practising launching aircraft and recovery. We carried two 'Walrus' amphibious flying boats, each one in the hangar above our galleys and the bakery, and one already sitting on the catapult, waiting to be launched, outside the front of the hangar.

We spent the forenoon just dashing about with the *Southampton*. Every time I looked out of the scuttle, she was still trying to recover the aircraft, then it was our turn and the catapult was swung outboard to port. The pilot, Lieutenant Skidorsky (Polish) got in the Walrus and started up the engine, then, 'Bang', the aircraft shot off, from port to starboard and she was airborne. She made two circuits of the ship, the ship slewed round at about 90°, smoothed the water in our wake, and the Walrus landed quite easily on the smooth water. We used this method of landing the aircraft every time, the ship slewing hard to port or starboard, about 90° did the trick; we never had any trouble, then the port or starboard crane lowered her a hook, picked the aircraft up bodily and was lowered back on her catapult; it was easy as that.

The aircraft, a Walrus amphibian, was used by all ships; it was easily adaptable, a small flying boat, a single engine, 'pusher' type. There was one other, similar to the Walrus, a Sea Otter, which was the same, only the engine was reversed, it was a 'puller' engine. They carried three men and it could land on an airfield as well as the sea, the wheels being retractable. It carried a machine-gun in the nose and, I think, it carried one aft. There was one other type of aircraft which was carried by battleships and cruisers, that was the Sea Fox, but they were soon replaced by the Walrus as the permanent reconnaissance aircraft.

Next day, we went out of Portland harbour with HMS *Nelson* and *Rodney*, two of our most powerful battleships, considered to be the 'big ships' with nine 16" guns on the fo'c'sle alone, in three turrets; the two battleships were identical, except the *Rodney* had a slight difference with the top of her mainmast. Before the naval treaty in 1927, the two battleships were being built larger to about 50,000 tons, with probably more 16" guns on the stern, but owing to the naval treaty, which Germany, France, Italy, USA and Japan, as well as Great Britain, agreed, the maximum weight for capital ships was 35,000 tons, but we already had ships that exceeded that weight, so did the Germans and the Japanese.

The big ships were at sea, followed by HMS *Cumberland* and *Southampton*; we were off to do a big 'shoot'. We took up in line ahead, broken only by the Aldis lamp flashing from the bridge of the *Nelson*. Our Aldis lamp replied in morse code, probably telling us to close up.

After about an hour's steaming, somewhere in the wastes of the Channel, probably somewhere west of Land's End, we met our target ship, HMS *Centurion*, escorted by the destroyer HMS *Shikari*. Both ships were painted bright yellow from stem to stern. HMS *Centurion*

HMS Cumberland, *County Class cruiser, Portland, June 1939.*

was a First World War battleship, which fought at Jutland in 1916; now she was used as a target, painted all over bright yellow, full of cork, with not a man aboard her; she was radio-controlled from her attendant destroyer, the *Shikari* which was also painted yellow. Both disappeared over the horizon to get into position as the target at twelve miles range.

The *Nelson* had fired at a target at twelve miles range, with her triple 16" turrets a year or two previously, and scored six out of six direct hits; it remained to be seen today what her score would be!

The *Nelson*, as a result of her accurate gunnery pre-war, was presented with a cockerel, a dummy, which she used to fly from her mainmast – she was the 'Cock O' the North'. The second time she was noted for her accurate gunnery was at D-Day when she wiped out German tanks 8 miles away at Caen!

'Action Stations' sounded off over the tannoy loudspeaker; a young Marine bugler was in no doubt, blowing his guts out, it seemed so loud and quick! There was this sense of urgency about it, a reminder of what the call to battle would sound like. We were going to fire our main big armament of eight 8" guns, A and B turrets forward, and X and Y turrets aft, just outside the officers' galleys; they were manned by Royal Marines, X and Y, while A and B were manned by seamen.

The chief petty officers of the galleys fore and aft stayed put in each of the galleys, forward and aft, making hundreds of corned beef sandwiches for the entire crew, officers and men alike; they would be at Action Stations throughout the day, and this is how things would be like, on the real day – there are *no* passengers on board HM ships!

As the first two notes sounded, I knew! I dropped everything and tore along the upper deck from right aft, just forward of X and Y turrets. Hell's bells! I thought, This is it!

I shot down the hatch between A and B turrets, right forward, down through the Shell Handling Room, discarding my belt with key chain attached, through the nine-inch solid hatch of the magazine, down the slender vertical ladder, where the Petty Officer waited for the last man to arrive. I got a nod of approval from him; I had made it in less than a minute and a half! When the last man arrived, it took two men to close the hatch; although it was weighted and sprung, it took two men all their time to close it, then there was silence. That was the only way in and the only way out. We put on our anti-flash gear, consisting of a large white balaclava helmet and long gauntlet gloves, and stood by the loading positions which consisted of two loading positions, A turret with four men, and four men serving B turret, making it eight men for loading and the Petty Officer stood by the vertical ladder. In the centre we stood, two of us, with an eighteen-inch charge of cordite in both hands, waiting for the bell to ring, then Slam! the first charge was sent through the hatch in the bulkhead, followed by the second charge that the other bloke had. We pulled a handle, and it disappeared on a conveyor belt up to the Shell Handling Room above us, and so the process was repeated, but did it? The bell sounded at the other end, they put their charges through and there we stood waiting! Four charges went through, two for each turret, four guns, that's fair enough!

There, hundreds of yellow cases stood down on the racks, with four charges in each case, broken only by a gap just wide enough for a man to pass – we couldn't see the other chaps for cases.

And so the waiting continued. We hadn't opened fire as we would have heard the guns go off, and felt the vibration.

After you have been in the magazine for an hour or so, it gives you a slight headache; you realise it gives off a sort of aroma, 'cordite gas'; the headache increases – it did with me anyway, no air, just cordite gas.

Half an hour passed and still the guns had not fired. We relaxed, put the third charge ready in case the bell should ring and sat down on the steel deck. Nobody had spoken since we closed up, then I noticed there wasn't an air shaft in the magazine; there were several things which looked like sprays, every few feet, up against the deckhead (high). I asked the Petty Officer what they were for, he said, 'For flooding the magazine, in case we are hit, or on fire!' Charming, I thought. I was exactly twenty years old and saw no fear in anything!

He stood there, holding on to the vertical ladder which was secured to the deckhead above, and to the deck below. He was keeping an eye on us all, I realized after a while, looking upwards towards the hatch, listening for any news.

After two hours I wanted to pass water so I said to the Petty Officer, 'Any chance of going up top to the heads?' He said, 'Not a chance.' So I waited for another half an hour and tried again. 'I'll have to go – I'll do it in my pants!' I said. 'Oh, alright, but make it snappy, nobody is allowed to leave their action station and nobody better see you!' he said. We opened the hatch, and I slipped quietly out of the Shell Handling Room, and quietly opened the hatch between the two 8" turrets. I was out on the upper deck right near the fo'c'sle, breathing fresh air again.

A Turret was flush on the deck to my left, B Turret was to my right, higher, on top of the superstructure, with the heads underneath. I dashed for the door, which was closed during the 'shoot', and wrenched the handles on the watertight door.

I took a quick look around, there wasn't a soul anywhere to be seen. I did notice the guns of A and B turrets were facing outboard, in a position to open fire. The guns of the *Nelson* and *Rodney* were also facing outboard, ready to fire a broadside. I couldn't see the target ship, *Centurion*, she was too far over the horizon. I dashed into the heads, did my business and made for the watertight door, just below B Turret, when there was an almighty explosion, or so it seemed. It went, a great thundering 'BLAM', I went backwards from the door and hit my head on the bulkhead a few feet to the rear. I sat on the deck with a jolt, I couldn't hear anything, and from my eyes, all I could see was smoke and flames. A and B 8" turrets had opened fire! But I never heard the 'fire gongs', which normally sound prior to the guns firing. There should have been a 'Ding Ding!' every time a gun is about to open fire, but I never heard it from inside the heads.

I wonder if I could make for the hatch between A and B turrets before they fired again. I couldn't hear the fire gong this time anyway. I shot out of the heads like a bat out of hell, dived down the hatch between the turrets, pulling the clamps over the hatch and went through the Shell Handling Room like a man possessed. I couldn't hear anything, my vision was blurred for quite a few minutes. I thumped on the hatch to the magazine where the Petty Officer was waiting for me.

He said, 'Where were you when the guns opened fire?' I put my hands to my ears, expressing that I could not hear exactly what he said, all I could hear was a ringing, with bells from some church. My eyes could see nothing but huge sheets of flame. He gestured to me to sit down.

After a while my faculties returned so the Petty Officer tried again, 'Where were you when A and B turrets opened fire?' he said, 'Just coming out of the door to the heads,' I replied. 'Didn't you listen for the fire gong?' he said. 'I never heard the fire gong,' I replied, 'I was in the heads!' 'That must have been a rude awakening! Are you alright?' he concluded. I said, 'Yes, OK now,' but I was telling an untruth. I felt that my ears wouldn't be right for months, all I could see was the explosion at the door of the heads.

The guns fired several rounds after that, which kept us busy during the afternoon. They sounded the 'Secure' and we made a dash for the ladder. As we came up from the magazine I heard the pipe 'Hands to tea.' I collected my money belt from the Shell Handling Room and made my way aft to my galley where the Chief had a good cup of coffee for us, and lashings of corned beef sandwiches.

We stayed at Portland for a few days, doing exercises with ships of the Fleet. One day I had an hour or two ashore in Weymouth; it was quite a ride in the liberty boat, with fifty or sixty other sailors tossing about in a small boat, especially when going through the breakwater of Portland Harbour to the open sea. It was always rough due to the cross-currents at that point.

Then, on a beautiful Sunday morning in June 1939, the people of Portland and Weymouth had a sight they would never, ever see again: the Home Fleet, as it was called before the War, was putting to sea, 250 ships raised steam. The Royal Navy was putting to sea, to show the people of this island home of ours the Imperial might that we possessed, our National Heritage! And so, through the breakwater they came. I have a photograph to this day; HMS *Hood* was leading, taking her rightful place at the head of the Fleet, followed by the *Repulse*,

Nelson, Rodney, followed by the 'R' battleships, the *Royal Sovereign, Royal Oak, Resolution, Ramilles, Revenge*. We slipped quickly, to take up station on the port side, as a member of the 2nd Cruiser Squadron. The *Southampton, Newcastle* and the *Sheffield* among others of the 1st Cruiser Squadron were taking up station on the starboard side, so the pattern of the Fleet gradually emerged, followed by at least a dozen light cruisers, the *Dragon, Delhi, Dunedin, Dauntless*, and others.

As the Fleet formed up in line ahead, making their way up towards Lulworth Cove, off the port side, flotilla upon flotilla of destroyers which had been waiting in the nearby Roads off Weymouth Bay, unable to get into Portland Harbour, took up station on the port and starboard sides of the Fleet, forming a protective screen right around, as far as the eye could see; it was line upon line of warships. Sixty or 70 destroyers joined farther up the Channel; the Tribal Class destroyers were leading, new ships, bigger than their counterparts, followed by the J class, the M class, the F class, and the H class, these last two flotillas were older destroyers. There were *nine* destroyers to a flotilla, so it gives you some idea the size of the Home Fleet, the largest fleet in the world.

It took the best of the forenoon for all the ships to leave and to form up. As we went up the Channel, there were the aircraft carriers too, which formed up in the rear of the Fleet, but as I was in the galley that morning, I was fully occupied with the midday lunch and was only able to snatch a glimpse of what was going on. Now and again, our galleys were on the upper deck, so we saw everything from day to day.

At 1.30 p.m. on Sunday, when we had shut off the range, we had a chance to go out and have a look around, and what a sight to behold, a sight that I will never, ever, forget, not in anybody's lifetime. As far as the eye could see, whether you looked port or starboard, forward or astern, there were warships in line ahead, keeping perfect formation, like soldiers on a parade ground, the battleships, all nine of them, keeping exactly behind each other, following each other's wake, in the centre of the Fleet, with us, the *Cumberland*, and the rest of the 2nd Cruiser Squadron in line ahead. On the battleships' port side, the *Southampton* was the leading cruiser; on the battleships' starboard side, also keeping perfect formation, was the 1st Cruiser Squadron.

I thought, There's a hell of a lot of 'watchkeepers', men whose job it was, on the bridge of every warship, to keep the ships in perfect formation. I took a look up towards our bridge; I bet there were a lot of men on their toes, watching everybody else, not daring to put a foot wrong.

This then, was Britain's Imperial Might! The very sight of it made you feel proud to be a member that glorious Sunday morning in June 1939. Suddenly, the Chief was at my elbow, and he said the same words, 'God, it makes you feel proud, doesn't it?' I said, 'Yes, it certainly does, Chief.' It made a shiver run down my back in awe. It would never get together again, in one huge fleet.

We steamed in this formation through the straits of Dover, up the North Sea. Eventually off Invergordon, we broke up; the *Hood* went on ahead, one group carried on to Scapa Flow; we followed the *Hood* with other cruisers, three of the 'R' class battleships also followed us into Invergordon. We were taking up war stations. Of the destroyers, some went to Rosyth and the Firth of Forth, the remainder went on to Scapa Flow, some went on patrol.

The last but one exercise was about to take place. The next morning we left to do another 'shoot' and spent the forenoon steaming round and round the target ship at ten miles range. The 'R' Class battleships were out there, blazing away at the target; it would be our turn next, when suddenly there was a change of plan. The Aldis lamp was flashing from the bridge of the *Southampton*, and went on flashing for quite a few minutes, then the *Southampton* and the *Sheffield* left the shoot and dashed off in the direction of Denmark. At the time I gave it no thought, but it wasn't long before a Secure was given over the tannoy and all the hands went to Defence Stations, which meant that most of us went about our normal duties, mine being the galley.

The *Cumberland* and the *Edinburgh* left the shoot four hours later, and headed in the same direction as the other two cruisers. I didn't know it at the time but the *Southampton* and the *Sheffield* had gone as far over the other side of the North Sea to the German coast as it was possible to get. The plan was to act as German warships breaking out from Kiel, hug the Norwegian coast until they were up by the Shetlands, then race to get between Shetland and Faeroes 'gap'. Once through, they would get into the Atlantic and create havoc in the shipping lanes, and even into the South Atlantic, which they did.

What we didn't know at the time was that the whole of the Home Fleet would be there to stop us and the Coastal Command flying boats. Would we get through?

We went as far as possible, to get near to Kiel, and passed German patrol boats; you could cut the air with a knife; a large German schooner, with three masts, came too close to us for comfort, but by then, the first two cruisers had left four hours previously, it was time for us to go, four hours later.

The speed was increased and in line ahead, we went. Soon we were doing in the region of 30 knots; that was the first inkling of the *Cumberland*'s speed, she could go. Later, we learnt that the *Southampton* and *Sheffield* had got through unseen. It wasn't possible but we learnt why later. The FOG came down, we had to reduce speed to a crawl, and so we pressed on through thick fog, and got through both times; not a ship did we see. We learnt later that we passed the *Nelson* by three miles.

After that fiasco we returned to Scapa Flow and laid at anchor for a few days. War with Germany was imminent, we finally left the Flow on 24 August 1939 and proceeded down the west coast of Scotland, through the Irish Sea, round Land's End and into Plymouth, where we immediately ran into dry dock, had our bottom scraped and painted, and had quite a few stores loaded aboard, among them tropical gear for every man jack aboard and lime juice. We knew we were on our way to the Tropics. We were allowed one run ashore and had to be back aboard at 10.30 p.m. I just had time to send a telegram to my mother, it read, 'I am leaving for Foreign Waters – will write soon – Love – Your Son – Mervyn'.

My one grievance was: no leave before we left. Normally every HM ship has twenty-one days *before* it leaves. We had none! Just twelve hours to send a telegram home. I was twenty-one years of age.

We left Plymouth the next morning, 31 August 1939, and sailed due south, in the Navy's lingo, 'With utmost dispatch'! First stop, Freetown, West Africa, for refuelling. War had been declared on 3 September 1939 on our way to Freetown. There was 'Hands to darken ship' every night at sunset, not a light to show; watertight doors were closed and all portholes and scuttles too, so it was my job, when both watches fell in at sunset every night, to nip out of the galley door and close every scuttle round the galleys. So when 'Hands to darken ship' sounded, we were in an oven, not a door or porthole open. The galley was ventilated so that 'forced air' came out of little openings in the fanshaft, but with two or three galleys with their oil-fired ranges going and the hotplates white hot, we had a foretaste of what it would be like every night in the galley in the Tropics. The ship, every day during daylight hours, took a zig-zag course: a turn to port, so many degrees, a turn to starboard, so many degrees. It kept this up, all day long, every day, only a few minutes at a time; after a while, you never noticed it; it was an anti U-boat manoeuvre, to put a U-boat off his stroke having a cruiser changing course continually.

We were on a war footing now that war had been declared. 'Action Stations' were called for, half an hour *before dawn* every morning, other than that, it was called for any time during the day, if circumstances called for it; otherwise we were at 'Defence Stations' throughout the day, which allowed me and the others to carry on normal routine, but we were ready at any time.

So we were zig-zagging under a cloudless sky, with the sun scorching down on anyone who had to be on the bridge, or on the upper deck. The sea was changing from the familiar green, to cobalt blue of the Tropics; at night the sea was alive with phosphorescence, particularly in the bow wave; the bows were cutting through millions of stars, as I used to sit, off watch, fascinated by the display at night.

Next morning, we were told over the tannoy, 'Tropical rig will be worn by all the hands, sun helmets to be worn on the upper deck, lime juice to be issued to all hands, that is all!' 'That is all,' I said. 'He said enough.'

We made our stop at Freetown, where I peered out of the scuttle to see a lot of natives sitting outside their mud huts, complete with goats and chickens. I didn't like what I saw of Freetown. Refuelled, we were off again for Rio de Janeiro; on 11 September we sighted an unidentified aircraft off the Cape Verde Islands; knowing that it was a seaplane, it must be from an enemy ship. We immediately signalled C.-in-C., Freetown, 'Sighted unidentified aircraft – west of the Cape Verde Islands – a seaplane, possibly from an enemy capital ship – request reinforcements – Action Stations.' 'Action Stations' sounded and as I raced along the upper deck I saw the ship was racing for full speed. *We were converging on an enemy battleship!*

The German aircraft spotted us as quickly as we spotted him, because he disappeared over the horizon; we were following at our best speed; we searched and searched with our own aircraft in every direction. The cruiser HMS *Neptune* and two destroyers arrived and took up the search; we all gave up after two days. We knew it would be one of the German pocket battleships, either the *Graf Spee* or the *Scheer*. The third pocket battleship we knew was in home waters at the time. It so happened it *was* the *Graf Spee* which was in the South Atlantic; if we had only caught her as early as September 1939, it would have saved a lot of ships being sunk, and would have been the battle of the Cape Verde Islands, instead of the Plate.

We resumed our way to Rio. Lower deck was cleared and we assembled in the large locker room, those who were off duty at the time, that is. A large map of the South Atlantic had been erected, the first thing I noticed was that it was all in squares. The Navigating Officer pointed out that we were on our way to reinforce the South Atlantic Squadron, it was believed that enemy raiders were in the vicinity, and we were to patrol set squares with the members of the squadron, namely HMS *Ajax* (Flagship), *Achilles* and *Exeter*. Each would have a square to patrol for six weeks, then we would change over, taking it in turns to go down to the Falkland Islands for repair, or for boiler cleaning. At once, one could see that there was not enough HM ships to patrol three million square miles of ocean, taking into consideration that one of the most important trade routes passes through the area: the meat ships pass on their way from Buenos Aires and Montevideo. Ninety per cent of our meat came from this area. One of my mates from the orphanage at Frodsham, Cheshire, served on board the *Highland Monarch*. She was only one of her class, a regular meat ship and passenger ship; there was the *Highland Chieftain*, *Highland Princess*, *Highland Hope* and *Highland Monarch* and others; we knew that we had to keep this route open at all costs.

A fortnight later we arrived at Rio – what a beautiful harbour it was. We dropped anchor for the night and slipped the following morning, early, for the River Plate and Montevideo. We arrived at night, so we stooged about outside till the morning.

The galleys had become very hot in the last few days, 140°F after crossing the Line (crossing the line of the Equator); at night, when it was 'Hands to darken ship', every door and scuttle closed, with only a drop of air coming from the fanshafts, it was absolute murder; no wonder they called the galleys 'Dante's Inferno' or 'Hell's Kitchen'. We, in the galley, used to wear the briefest of clothing, tropical shorts, turned up in the legs as far as possible, so high, that it would be indecent to have them further up; no shirt, stripped to the waist; everyone who had been in the galleys after sunset, would soon strip off! All I had on was a large handkerchief round my neck to catch the sweat, which ran from my head, down my neck, stopped at the navel, then ran, down my chest, and my back, and ended up squelching in my white gym shoes, just like paddling – they used to be washed in water every night and left to dry in the galleys for the morning. Before getting into our hammocks at night, which were on the upper deck, we were working in temperatures in excess of 140°F! No exaggeration. The ranges were shut off as soon as possible, or do all the cooking on one range instead of three – that depended on what we had to cook. We used to change our tropical shorts at least three times daily!

We sighted the *Ajax* at first light, and no doubt the Commodore, Henry Harwood, in command of the South Atlantic Squadron, had been informed about our brush with the pocket battleship, *Graf Spee*, off Cape Verde Islands, as we broke W/T silence, asking the C.-in-C. for reinforcements. It's the only time W/T silence is broken, in emergency, or better still, when action is imminent, but what we did not know at the time, was that the *Graf Spee* and the *Cumberland* were on a converging course with each other, in other words, both ships were coming towards each other at a combined speed of 40+ knots, under fifty miles apart, oblivious of each other. Radar had not been fitted to every warship in 1939. It was only a signal from the German spotter aircraft that there was a 'British Heavy Cruiser coming towards you' that made her turn about and get out of it, which she did. Phew, that was a near one!

Later in the day, we steamed into Montevideo, which was some way down the River Plate, or Plata. The mouth of the river was in the region of 120 miles across – the only way we could tell, was that the colour of the water changed from blue to a muddy colour, typical of rivers the world over.

We tied up alongside the outer harbour. Leave ashore was given to both watches; I went ashore with my old pal, Ron, from the Royal Marines to see what 'Monte' was like. The people were very friendly, very pro-British, but we had only a few hours ashore; we were treated to drinks, but time was limited.

Refuelling took place while we were there, also, a lot of stores were loaded on the ship. Next day, we left Montevideo and took up a patrol of the area, while *Ajax* took it in turn to go down to the Falklands for a self-refit. The *Achilles* would be the next one to go, and then the *Exeter* before we would go; that would be the first week in December. The Falklands brought back memories of the past, the First World War! Would the *Graf Spee* seek revenge for the Battle of the Falklands when the battle cruiser *Invincible*, under the command of Admiral Sturdee, delivered a crushing defeat upon the German force of ships, headed by Admiral Graf Spee on the *Scharnhorst*, sinking all but one, the light cruiser *Emden*, which got away. Would she, the *Graf Spee*, come to seek revenge for the ships which were sunk, and for the loss of Admiral Graf Spee. The whole time we were down there, we wondered whether she, the *Graf Spee*, and possibly her sistership, the *Scheer*, would come and seek their revenge for the Battle of the Falklands, 1914.

It was now, only September, the War had only just started, but at sea things were moving fast: the *Graf Spee* was already here in the South Atlantic, so was her sistership, the *Scheer*, two German pocket battleships, several armed merchant ships and a host of U-boats. We had the *Shropshire* at the Cape, and the *Neptune* at Freetown; the only battleship was the *Renown* which was nearly 2,000 miles away to the north.

So we had a fair old time ahead of us, with three million square miles of ocean to patrol. The two Leander Class cruisers, *Ajax* and *Achilles*, 6,000 tons each, were more like large destroyers, while the York Class cruiser, the *Exeter*, 8,000 tons was not exactly the last word in cruiser design, with only six 8" guns, and no armour; and we, the *Cumberland*, a County Class cruiser, 12,000 tons to date, eight 8" guns and armoured above the water line, in my opinion, had the luxury of a large hangar on the stern of the ship, which would make 'one hell of a target', but as the *Norfolk* and the *Suffolk* would show against the *Bismarck*, the speed of the County Class would be superior in battle, and the use of a smoke screen, the other thing, that would reduce their ungainly size. In theory, their three funnels and a large hangar would appear to be a drawback, but in practice, would be a challenge to any superior enemy force, and not an 'old lumbering County Class' as one survivor of the *Exeter* put it. Not so. A happy ship is an efficient ship and the *Cumberland* was both – she would have shown you.

We continued patrolling for six weeks in the Plate area and went north to Santos; *Exeter* would patrol the Plate, *Achilles* the Rio area; six weeks later, the *Achilles* went down to the Falklands, and so on; HM ships were stretched to the limit. When the *Exeter* returned from the Falklands after a further six weeks, we joined together in a 'Throw-Off Shoot', firing sub-calibre 8" live shells in the wake of the other, not close, a few hundred yards. After we had been doing this for about an hour or so, the weather changed for the worst; by midday, we were nearly standing on our heads. We were preparing lunch. I looked out of the scuttle, a heavy sea was moving quicker than we were going, a mountainous sea which kept racing at us, hitting the port quarter of the ship, making the bow lurch up in the air. One minute you couldn't see any sea at all, just sky, the sea was down there in a great big valley, then the sea came rushing up till you couldn't see any sky at all. This happened every few minutes with regular monotony; one good look astern was enough, the sea wasn't in waves, it was like mountains, seventy-foot waves, no exaggeration! We wouldn't survive the next one, but somehow we did; we were like toys in comparison.

The oil fuel ranges were roaring away, all three of them, the noise deafening; you couldn't make yourself heard, so we switched off two ranges, did all the dinners in one galley, and moved everything into the large wardroom galley. There were several ten-gallon pots on the hotplate, a bit overcrowded; in spite of getting a splash of red hot soup down you when you were thrown against the range, thank heavens for the guard rail! Soup eventually splashed on to the white-tiled deck, which soon became like a skating rink, no matter how many dry cloths we put down. Soon, there was as much soup on the deck as there was in the pots; we skated back and forth. The temperature was 140°F!

There was a crate of eggs standing in a corner, but not for long though. Normally it would be alright, but it was on the move; it got on the part that was all slippery and away it went! I shouted, 'Look out!' to my opposite number who was busy at the sink with his back to us; he just jumped with both feet into the sink of greasy water with his gym shoes on. A petty officer made a dive for the crate of eggs, the deck of the galley came up at an alarming angle, anything and everything broke free, he hit the bulkhead on the far side where I had been looking out of the scuttle at the rough sea a few minutes before, and carried on, head first into the crate of eggs, petty officer's cap and all! He got up covered in raw egg. I looked at the scuttle: just above it, it was all sea, couldn't see the sky!

The heavy table at the other end of the galley, usually secured to the other end, decided to come adrift with all the food on it, being prepared by other members of the galley. We all tried to hold it back but this was not possible with all the amount of soup that was on the deck. We slithered all over the place, so the table went towards the bulkhead; we just couldn't hold it. Meanwhile, the angle of the deck went the other way, the table rushed back at us! Looking on helplessly, the Chief took command in the ensuing chaos. 'Right! Shut down! Abandon the galley. Someone will get killed at this rate.' My Leading Cook was hanging on to the range, which was white hot, managed to shut it off as the table went hurtling past him. As the noise died down, the air and oil switched off, a petty officer managed to get both pots of the offending soup out of the galley, and stand down in the sink of the WOs' and Gunroom galleys, so at least the officers got soup for lunch, and lashings of 'Herrings in tomatoes'. The good old 'Herrings In' was a 'stand by' for all the officers. 'Send for the shipwrights to come and fix the table before it smashes itself into firewood!' said the Chief, which they did. The rest of us turned-to and cleared up the galley, picked up the spuds, which continued to run back and forth over the deck, and got the tiled deck dry again.

Soup was on the menu that day for lunch. We switched on the oil-fuel range once again, and turned-to to get the evening dinner, what was left of it. The deck continued coming up at an alarming angle, I could hear someone shouting, 'For God's sake dip your f****** funnels in, why don't you?' The steward braved coming up to see how lunch was getting on but was met with a string of abusive language and disappeared quicker than he came up. He said, 'You want to see the *Exeter*,' but was met with a string of obscenities as long as your arm. Feeling a little flush faced, he said, 'I'll see you later.' He passed me on my way back from the heads and repeated it, 'You want to see the *Exeter*.' I replied, 'No thanks, it's been a f****** holiday for us in the galley, you stupid b******! Get stuffed!'

At 1.15 p.m., lunch over, we went on the upper deck to see for ourselves. The *Exeter* was half a mile away, off the port bow, half submerged all the time; one minute all the bows and her 8" turrets disappeared, right up to her bridge, at the same time the whole stern came out of the water, the four screws, rudder and her keel where the 'Plimsoll line' is, above that it is painted battleship grey, but below the

Plimsoll line it is red. I wouldn't have believed it, but to see the keel! The next, the bows came up with tons of water falling away, and pointed skywards, turrets as well, with the whole of her stern section disappearing in the mountainous seas. As the day wore on, the seas moderated, but it was rough while it lasted. I was never, ever, seasick, no matter how rough it was, never even thought about it.

We left the *Exeter* patrolling off Montevideo, went south for a while. It was the first week of December 1939. Many ships were being sunk; we got a 'Mayday' signal, 'Am being attacked by a pocket battleship', then the message ceased. Sometimes they gave us the *Graf Spee*, sometimes it was the *Scheer*, but most ships were being sunk before they could signal.

The Commodore, Henry Harwood, knew that the enemy would try Montevideo sooner or later, so he concentrated all ships to this area. We met *Ajax* on her way back from the Falklands and intercepted a German supply ship, the SS *Ussukama*. She scuttled herself just before we opened fire and they abandoned ship when we got in close. The Captain and crew were taken prisoner, so we left *Ajax* and took the prisoners down to the Falklands. The date was 9 December 1939 and we had them interred at the Falklands. So we had just started a self-refit, the boilers were the first thing that wanted attention. The ERAs had just started on the first two out of four boilers on 13 December when W/T silence was broken by the *Exeter*; it ran: 'I have sighted the German pocket battleship *Graf Spee* . . . am going into engage her.' Then we had a further signal from *Ajax*, it ran: 'I have sighted the German pocket battleship *Graf Spee*.' *Ajax* and *Achilles* were going in to engage her. Poor devils, they'll get blown out of the water. Don't stand a chance, they're just like puppies going up against a wolf. This is the *Cumberland*'s version of the Plate.

'Action Stations' sounded immediately, the *Cumberland* weighed anchor, and raced out of the harbour at her best speed, on two boilers. They worked frantically on the other two to bring them into play. I was already at my post in the forward 8" Cordite Handling Room. All I could hear was the terrible scream of the engines, a very high-pitched whistle, struggling for speed.

What I write now was relayed from the Captain's Chief Steward after I got to the scene. He said, 'The Captain, W.H.G. Fallowfield, rang the engine room soon after leaving Stanley Harbour at the Falklands, and said "How are the other two boilers?" He was told from the engine room, "They are coming into play now, sir!" The Captain replied, "Then, give me everything you've got, Chief!" To which the Chief said, "She is doing in excess of her designed speed of 31.8 knots now, sir." The Captain called the engine room again, "Can't you give me more speed? I must have every ounce of speed you can give me." The speed increased to 33 knots and more. The engine room rang the bridge, in sheer desperation the Chief said, "If she keeps up this speed, she'll blow up." Captain said, "No matter, I have got to have all the speed you can give me. We must get there to save the tiny cruisers."' Then we ran into thick fog, for 500 miles, but the *Cumberland* raced on, blow up or not, the engines screamed their defiance, the speed was kept up, no matter if we couldn't see where we were going, hour after hour. It was suicide but we raced on!

We made it to the Plate, a distance of 1,200 miles in 34 hours, a record, mostly in dense fog. We caught up with the *Ajax* and *Achilles* at the mouth of the Plate – both looked worse for wear but they had forced the *Graf Spee* to take refuge in Montevideo and it was a miracle they were still afloat. The *Exeter* retired, badly damaged, having put up a terrific fight; she took the brunt of the battle which was fought at high speed throughout the day. The *Graf Spee* thought they were destroyers, they looked so small; she tried and tried to shake them off, but in the words of Captain Landsdorf, 'They kept coming at me, like destroyers!' The *Exeter* retired to the Falklands on the orders of Commodore Henry Harwood, who asked, 'Can you get to the Falklands?' to which Captain 'Hooky' Bell replied, 'I could make Plymouth if ordered!' to which the Commodore replied, '*God Speed.*'

Ajax signalled *Cumberland*, 'How did you manage to get here so quickly?' to which we replied, 'ANTICIPATION.' That was Thursday, 14 December 1939; upon arrival we immediately left the *Ajax* and *Achilles* at the mouth of the river and went down towards Montevideo where the *Graf Spee* was lying at the outer harbour, facing us and the open sea. We got close enough to see the Germans going about their duties; she had sixty hits, among them the galleys were destroyed, there was no fresh water, several of her 6" guns were knocked out, her aircraft was destroyed and her hull amidships was like a pepperpot, there were so many holes in her.

A Uruguayan gunboat came out to us, saying, 'You are breaking

International Law coming inside territorial waters.' The only thing to say, I said, 'Balls!' We didn't reply. We knew about territorial waters, and were in no mood to haggle over 'International Law', with the enemy within striking distance. We just wanted a show of strength; we were a heavy cruiser, more capable of deciding the result of a battle. We politely withdrew upstream, joined the other two light cruisers and waited for her to come out.

So Thursday came and went, so did Friday and Saturday, she had to come out on Sunday as that was the deadline, otherwise she would be interred by the Uruguayan authorities; we were keen to have a go at her. There were only three ships waiting at the mouth of the river. Contrary to belief at the time, there were no battleships or cruisers reinforcing us, just the *Ajax*, the *Achilles* and *Cumberland*. The first two ships were short of ammunition, having fought a running battle all day on Wednesday. Only the *Cumberland* had a full outfit of ammunition, so it was going to be up to us to stop her breaking out from Montevideo!

On the Sunday evening, I was sitting on the upper deck, very handy for getting to my Action Stations, writing a letter to my mother, just in case, saying the usual things, like: 'This is what I joined the Navy for' and 'If anything should happen to me – I had done my duty.' I gave my letter to my mate Ron, and he had given me his. I wished him the best of luck and we shook hands. At 2000 hrs (8 p.m.) the sun was setting, the sky was a huge red glow, when 'Action Stations' sounded. I did not feel nervous at all, it seemed another 'Action Stations' on just another day, it was routine; here we go again.

The *Graf Spee* had left harbour, and was coming up the river. An eyewitness said that all three ships turned to meet her, increased speed, with the *Cumberland* second in line ahead, next to the Flagship, *Ajax*, which catapulted her aircraft and sent a signal of battle flags up her mast. As I ran for'ard along the upper deck to my Action Station, I thought I saw Nelson's famous signal, 'England Expects!' For a second there was a surge in my blood. It was not to be, it was only a 'mirage'.

As the sun set over Montevideo, we approached the *Graf Spee*. Gunfire was not necessary as the sky was red with explosions and the noise was deafening, coming from her – she was scuttling herself, just three miles upstream, right in the middle of shipping lanes; she was completely on fire from stem to stern!

We sounded the 'Secure' and were able to see for ourselves the

The Graf Spee *shortly after being scuttled.*

destruction of the *Graf Spee*. She was, by the time we got close to her, settling in the mud, nearly up to her upper deck, and stayed in that position till she was moved several months later. We circled round her till 2.00 a.m. Monday morning, the only noise to be heard above the explosions was the ship's company of all three ships who had come on the upper deck, and were cheering each other hoarse and from Commodore, now Rear Admiral, Henry Harwood, Knight Commander of the Order of the Bath. Then came the signal 'Many a life has been saved this day.'

When I got back to my galley from Action Stations, the two Chiefs were mixing the Christmas Pudding in a huge bin. Bottle after bottle of 'plonk' was going in. 'It's going to have everything,' said the Chief. 'The Skipper and his entourage are coming to stir the pudding tonight!' It was 'Hands to darken ship' at 2000 hrs, 8 p.m. The one door and every scuttle was closed, three ranges were going full blast, the temperature was up to 130°F and rising, the noise was deafening! The Skipper, Commander, 1st Lieutenant and an assortment of officers piled into the galley. Within one minute the handkerchiefs were out, wiping sweated brows. The officer next to me stuck his mouth into my ear and bellowed, 'Is it always as b***** hot as this?' I bellowed back into his, 'Always! Come back in an hour's time, it will be in excess of 140°F, if we are b***** lucky!' He made a hasty retreat.

The whole of the ship's company danced the Conga round the ship on Christmas Day, and we retraced the 1,200 miles back to the Falklands at a much slower pace; the War had been on only three months.

The *Exeter* was in a hell of a mess, down by the bows, but seaworthy in spite of her damage, which was above waterline. They were working round the clock, every day, before she was in a fair seaworthy condition, ready to come home for Christmas 1939, which she did, home to a rousing homecoming in Plymouth. All the ships came home, *Achilles* to New Zealand, to a 'Victory March' in London for the *Ajax* and the *Exeter.*

We spent Christmas 1939 at the Falklands, having a self-refit. The second week of January 1940 saw us taking on board the Captain and crew of the S.S. *Ussukama*, the German vessel which scuttled herself. We were taking them eventually to Cape Town to be interred there.

But before that, we made a routine call to South Georgia Island, then steamed south in the direction of Antarctica, the whaling fleets had had a bit of trouble with enemy supply ships taking the oil, so we stooged round in Antarctica for a while, seeing nothing but icebergs and penguins. We left to make another call at Tristan da Cunha, halfway between Cape Horn and Cape Town; the English settlers there were waiting for essential supplies and the Royal Navy made periodical calls at these islands. Having made our 'drop' at Tristan, we pressed on to St Helena, before sailing on to the Cape and Simonstown, where we ran into the dry dock to have a complete refit. Our prisoners were handed over to the South African Defence Force, destined for the Transvaal, up-country.

Captain Fallowfield awarded both watches of the hands seven days leave each watch. My mate, Ron of the Royal Marines, and I, had a wonderful leave. We stayed at the Union Jack Club, just under Table Mountain, with the people of Cape Town, who couldn't do enough for us. We were there at the end of January 1940 when the weather was at its best, mid-summer. Gifts of fruit by the crate-load were sent to the ship, plus cigarettes and Castle beer, finally a small carcass of a young springbok was brought aboard to cook for the officers. We had to keep it strung up for several weeks; when it smells high it's time to cook it, a rare delicacy, like a young reindeer.

We took advantage of the time of year to climb Table Mountain, and what a beautiful sight it was at the top. The people were wonderful, the climate ideal, but all good things must come to an end. I loved Cape Town and so did everyone else.

As we left Simonstown after our refit, the Royal Marine band struck up with 'Wish me luck as you wave me goodbye', the song everybody was singing at the time.

In addition to having the boilers due for overhaul, we had an anti-magnetic mine device fitted. We could have done with radar, but that would have to wait until we got back to the UK. When that would be, heaven knows!

Round the Cape we went into the Indian Ocean, came up against the 'Cape Rollers' and were soon burying our nose under. My duty that morning was to fetch a couple of 1 cwt. sacks of spuds from the H.A. gun deck, a tricky job at the best of times, but that morning, I didn't relish it. About fifty yards for'ard, I had to climb a thin steel ladder, not uncommon aboard ships, about a foot wide, nearly vertical, just a steel ladder with no handrail, up on to the twin 4" AA guns. Between the two twin guns, there was armour protection made up of two spud lockers, extra protection for the gun crews. I unlocked the lockers, and took out two 1 cwt. sacks of spuds, put the first bag across the back of my neck, the easiest way to carry such sacks, and proceeded past the gun crews and their leg-pulling, towards the top of the ladder which, from the top, looks dangerously close to the side of the ship. I thought, as I looked down the vertical ladder, that if I slipped, I would be over the side as easy as wink. With that, the ship heaved right over on her starboard side, the sack slipped from my shoulder, hit the guard-rail which runs around the upper deck, and burst; half of them went over the side, the other half scattered in all directions on the upper deck. I went back to the spud locker, picked up another sack, put it across the back of my neck and proceeded past the gun crews, amid laughter and leg-pulling! 'I'll make it this time, do you want a bet?' This time, I let go of the bag halfway down the ladder – waited till the ship came back on an even keel, then let it go! I nipped down the ladder after it, but it burst as it hit the deck, just as I had hold of it, and I held it from spilling all over the deck. I half dragged it back to the galley, whereupon the Chief said, 'Had a bit of trouble this morning, Ted?' 'You can say that again, Chief!' He laughed, so did the others. 'It will be your job tomorrow,' I said.

After a day of patrolling, we came back to Table Bay and saw the biggest assembly of ships ever to anchor in the bay. There was the *Queen Mary, Mauritania, Aquitania, Empress of Britain, Empress of Canada, Empress of Japan,* and the Royal Mail liner *Andes,* carrying the whole of the Expeditionary Force of Australia and New Zealand, better known as the 'Anzacs' – 90,000 men, nurses and their equipment. They had gone ashore into Cape Town, and had caused a lot of trouble; all the public houses had to close. We sent ninety Royal Marines to the *Queen Mary,* the ringleaders were soon arrested and that put an end to the trouble. We left the Marines on board till we reached Freetown, West Africa.

The night before we left Cape Town, we heard a message from Lord Haw-Haw, of German radio, who said, 'There is a large convoy leaving Cape Town, it will *not* reach the UK – it will be destroyed by our surface ships, U-boats and aircraft.' Talk about a 'welcome committee'. Charming!

We left Table Bay with lumps in our throats, would we ever see dear old Cape Town again? These ships and men were going to be our baby all the way to Greenock, UK. We led the convoy, the *Queen Mary* was on our stern, steaming very slowly, with the cream of the Mercantile Marine following, one by one, in our wake, till they formed up in two columns, then increased speed to 25 knots; the 'Old Girl' was good at increasing speed, the familiar whistle of her engines would be with us until we reached the UK. This was the best speed for the convoy, anti U-boat speed. They could all do it except the *Aquitania;* she had a job to keep up with us, but she had to; it was a case of survival.

There was only one other ship with us to Freetown, HMAS *Australia,* a County Class cruiser like ourselves, formerly HMS *Shropshire,* lent to Australia for the duration; she took up a position astern of the convoy. We arrived at Freetown and refuelled; the *Australia* left us and headed back down south to the Cape, and on to Australia.

It was up to us on our own, HMS *Cumberland* to race through the danger zone, against surface ships, U-boats and enemy aircraft. It had been decided to take a wide arc, out into the North Atlantic, right over to the west, then turn in, our only chance of survival!

One ship was having trouble keeping up to 25 knots because of her age, the old *Aquitania;* one minute it was, 'Can you keep up?' next it

HMS Hood *– a beautiful lady.*

was, 'Stop making smoke!' Poor old girl, she was doing her best. I'm sure that she knew that if she couldn't make the 25 knots, she would be a sitting duck for the U-boats, who were assembling for the kill. The most she could make was 23 knots.

The *Cumberland* remained at the head of the convoy, making light work of 25 knots, but keeping a lookout for trouble. So far, so good, the U-boats couldn't get us at this speed.

We had at last got as far as the Azores – no enemy ships, no U-boats, too far over for enemy aircraft. Contrary to some people's belief, which I have read in a popular book on the Navy, we escorted the largest convoy to date, *alone*! Only the cruiser *Australia* came with us as far as Freetown.

As we neared Home Waters, HMS *Hood*, *Sheffield* and the old aircraft carrier, *Argus*, came out to meet us. The *Hood* went to the head of the convoy; the *Sheffield* bagged a U-boat just before we met her. We had other alarms before we'd got round Ireland, before seeing our ships with all the troops aboard, safely in the Firth of Clyde, to Greenock, as safe as houses with no loss of ships. We saw all our ships berth, and steamed down the line amid a terrific roar from the Anzacs, who flooded the decks of every ship, cheering us all the way down the Clyde, as a mark of appreciation that we had escorted them all the way from Cape Town, without loss!

We entered Liverpool Bay and finally went into dry dock at Cammel Lairds, Birkenhead. There was another County Class cruiser, the *Berwick*, in the next basin. The battleship, *Prince of Wales*, was on the far side of the basin, fitting out, near completion, also the light cruiser, *Dido*, was nearing completion. The submarine, *Thetis*, renamed *Thunderbolt*, was being overhauled after her accident in Liverpool Bay.

The *Cumberland* had a new captain come aboard, Captain the Honourable Guy Russell, nephew of Sir Samuel Hoare, six feet tall, very broad, good-looking, with a prominent chin, steel-blue eyes, every inch a captain!

He gave us four days leave, each watch. I went home to East Barnet to see my mother for a couple of days. I learnt during my leave that I had never been christened and that my mother had made an appointment with the then minister to have me christened in uniform. I insisted that I took the first name of my father, Spencer, and so it was done, my mother's conscience was clear; couldn't bother to have me christened in Leamington Spa, where I was born.

I returned only to find Liverpool had been bombed, the whole of the shopping area had been flattened, the dry dock was flooded again so that we could bring our twin 4.5" Anti-Aircraft guns to bear during the night.

Next morning, we steamed up the Mersey and left Liverpool behind, turned to port, and went down the Irish Sea – we were off to the Tropics again and Freetown. The galley grew red-hot once more – and 'Hands to darken ship' was piped; it was nearly unbearable with three oil-fired ranges going. We soon got used to going to Action Stations half an hour before the dawn, every morning, month in, month out, to be on duty in the galley till 9.00 p.m., with the doors and scuttles closed and the ranges roaring away. The hotplates were always red-hot and you had to shout at each other to make yourself understood.

One door used to be opened with a curtain across it which the stewards used, transporting the dinner, on silver dishes, to the pantry below. The outer door to the upper deck was shut until after Action Stations, when the 'Secure' was sounded. The only air we had to breathe (it was up to 140°F again) was forced through a fanshaft, through small brass openings every few feet, it was suffocating. 'What are you? Galley Slaves? What are you? You'll have to speak up, I can't hear!' I used to sleep on the upper deck, the only time I could breathe.

Something was brewing in Freetown which was classed as the White

Man's Grave. There were two battleships, several cruisers, destroyers, transports full of troops, two Free French destroyers and a lot of coming and going in the harbour!

I met the mate who I had joined up with in 1937 in Freetown, where we all had sun helmets on because of the heat. I came towards him and said, 'Oh! Doctor Livingstone, I presume!' He said, 'What are you on then, Stanley?' 'The *Cumberland*,' I said. 'I'm on the Reso [the *Resolution*] – it appears we are on the same show – Dakar!' he said. 'Then, all the best, old mate,' I concluded, and we shook hands. His name was Arthur, of New Barnet, Herts., we went to the same school, joined the Boys Brigade and joined the Royal Navy.

We were sent to patrol off Dakar, Senegal, West Africa, two or three hundred miles north of Freetown. At the time it was Vichy French, pro-German, and they were suspect! One day, we sighted three French cruisers, 10,000 tons each. They had got through Gibraltar, just after the sinking of the French Fleet at Oran. They were making for the Cameroons, a French possession, further south. We intercepted them and asked them politely to join us on the side of the Free French – they didn't answer our signal, instead they increased speed away from us. We knew then that they were Vichy so we increased speed up to 30 knots and went after them! The Captain gave them one warning, 'Stop! Heave to! or we shall open fire!' They knew that our Skipper meant business! They heaved to, turned about and we escorted them into Dakar.

Half an hour later our spotting aircraft sighted an unidentified merchant ship making for Dakar. We intercepted her and told them we were sending a search party aboard her. The search party were clambering aboard one side, only to find the crew abandoning ship on the other. The search party found that explosive charges were due to go off, so they quickly got off and returned to the ship – we had a good view from our galleys, being off watch!

The *Cumberland* immediately withdrew to a safe distance, and opened fire at point blank range. She went down before the charges went off, when there was an almighty explosion.

The crew, all Vichy French, had sorted themselves out, in the meantime, in four lifeboats, tied together, towed by a motorboat. They crossed our bows, making remarks in French, and signs with their fingers, which only meant one thing, continuing their abuse. The

Skipper, I knew he wouldn't take that lying down. From the bridge he shouted, 'Open Fire!' The ·5" machine-guns, which were situated on top of the hangar, opened fire on the lifeboats! I saw the whole thing from A to Z, from outside the galley. I was off duty in the afternoon, saw the ship sunk by gunfire and the abuse they were giving us, and I was present when the officer said, 'Don't fire at the boats, only alongside them!' The Vichy French panicked and dived over the side, right into the line of fire. The result was that they didn't surface, and lost quite a number of them. If only they had stayed where they were, in the boats! It was only a three-second burst; there were heads bobbing up out of the water for several minutes; some bodies were recovered. Once more we gave them the order, in French, to come aft, alongside the after gangway. They were reluctant at first, but eventually they came; there was murder in their eyes as they passed me outside the galley, which was aft; they continued their abuse, but this turned to a mumble at the sight of the Royal Marines who came with their rifles and fixed bayonets, and made them move quickly, down below, kept under armed guard, till we got rid of them at Freetown.

Next morning we refuelled, we left with the two battleships, *Resolution* and *Barham*, the cruisers, *Devonshire*, *Dragon*, and *Ark Royal*, and ourselves, *Cumberland*, several Free French destroyers and British destroyers, two transport ships, each with 2,000 Royal Marines, and 2,000 Free French troops. I thought, this is going to be a big show, first of its kind in this war, coming at the end of Dunkirk. It was going to be a show of strength: General De Gaulle and Admiral J. Cunningham were aboard the *Barham*.

We arrived off Dakar in dense fog, and waited till the morning. In the meantime, General De Gaulle went ashcre in a motorboat. They fired at him from the shore batteries and he had to withdraw or be sunk; they were firing big guns at him. They shot down a Swordfish aircraft, which had taken off from the aircraft carrier, *Ark Royal*, which had just arrived on the scene that evening. We should have waited for visibility to improve but somebody had itchy feet, and that was General De Gaulle! The fog came down and obliterated us all.

Dakar was the capital port of the state of Senegal, West Africa, a French possession. It had been receiving a great deal of arms and tanks for North Africa. The ship that we sunk a day or two before had armoured vehicles on the decks.

The *Cumberland* was ordered to go in before dawn broke the following morning, on our own, without any support, *not* to 'Fire' until we got the order. We went to Action Stations at the usual time, half an hour before dawn and that is where my version of it ends. 'Action Stations' sounded on the bugle – and I was off as fast as I could go to the for'ard magazine.

My mate, Ron, who was on the port 4·5" gun battery, out in the open on the H.A. gun duck, gave me the account of what happened when I came up from the magazine, and what happened, happened fast!

At 5.00 a.m. or thereabouts, we approached the harbour, or so we thought, because there was thick fog everywhere; we knew that on both sides of the port, there was a heavy gun battery, 8" or 10" guns. There was also another on an island, well fortified, that we knew! There were the largest battleship the French had, just completed, the *Richelieu*, three cruisers, destroyers, and submarines in there, that we knew! We knew there were Germans and Vichy French (pro-Germans) also.

There was a deadly hush as we steamed slowly into the harbour, nothing stirred; we slowly turned about; we put our stern on the harbour and on our way out, all hell was let loose – the shore batteries opened fire, at point blank range, but they couldn't see us because of the fog, although they knew we were there, somewhere. The shells were falling thick and fast all around us; we couldn't reply as we were awaiting the order! Some of the shells were coming from the *Richelieu* by the size of the splashes; it was difficult to see anything, the fire was ferocious; they couldn't see us, but they were having a good try. My mate, Ron, of the Royal Marines, said, 'They should have sunk us, it was heavy and accurate.' But they didn't. Where was the order to 'Fire!'

We swung first to port, then to starboard, to try and shake them off – where was the b***** order? We were getting our skates on. They'd hit us sooner or later.

Everything was chaotic! The Free French Forces would not land, the gunfire should have been coming from the battleships as covering fire, *not* from the Vichy forces ashore! The Marines made a bold attempt to land, but withdrew, with terrible losses. It was suicide! So they all withdrew, French and Royal Marines. The whole operation, it seemed, was abandoned!

We were having a charmed life, being peppered by shells, large and very large; all the way round us, they were landing. Then amid all the noise, they *hit us* on the starboard side, above the armour plating, below the galley, two decks down, in the main switchboard. All power ceased for a second, we couldn't fire a shot. Twelve men died. I knew them well including the officer, Sub Lieutenant Dowthwaite, who was in charge of the main switchboard.

The shells were 10" and 14" armour-piercing, delayed action. We found the shell head which gave us the size of the shell from the French battleship *Richelieu*. It had penetrated the side of the ship, destroyed the Marines band room, and exploded in the main switchboard room. Twelve men died instantly. It also damaged the 4·5" anti-aircraft magazine which was flooded forthwith; one shell head came up through the deck into the locker flat. Two men, who were sitting on the deck doing Fire Party, didn't know what had hit them. The shell head took one's head clean off, and buried it in the locker next to mine, the other chap just survived. That's how we knew what size the shell was, it was printed on the shell head.

When a petty officer, who was the P/O of my watch and on the first aid party, got around to opening the locker, with the remains of a shipmate's skull in it, for burial purposes, he nearly collapsed.

All the power ceased, the main 8" gun turrets wouldn't work, neither did anything else, let alone the lighting; we were for a minute or two a sitting duck, until they switched on to auxiliary power, which was the same as before, except it ran on a separate circuit for 'Emergency Only'.

We were back in business and knew only too well where the gun batteries were as we could see where the flashes were coming from; if only we got the order to 'Open Fire'. We never did know whether the battleships opened fire or not; there was nothing else for it so we withdrew, lucky that it was only one hit; it could have been worse, but there's one thing I do know amid all the noise and confusion, that a Vichy submarine, whilst returning from patrol, sized up the situation and attacked the ship nearest to her from seaward, the battleship *Resolution*, with torpedoes and blew a hole in her side, twenty foot square. I thought of my mate, a stoker on the *Resolution*.

We all finally withdrew, but not before the destroyers depth-charged the Vichy submarine and brought her to the surface, the crew surrendered and were put aboard the *Cumberland*.

The 'Secure' had sounded when we ceased firing at the shore batteries, which were all 10" guns, we found that out later. I went up on deck to get some fresh air; it was then that I learned what happened and saw the damage, they were still heaving 4·5" shells over the side – a close run thing. We could have all been blown to bits. It was one hell of a b******, the Dakar Operation!

I went inside. All our end of the ship was full of smoke, with water everywhere. 'They had to flood the magazine amidships, otherwise, we'd all have gone up,' said a seaman who was trying to get some order down in the locker flats. 'But what's that awful smell?' I said, viewing what was left of my locker. 'They were boiled alive, or electrocuted, in there; that's all that is left of them!' The bodies had been removed, all twelve of our mates. The smell hung around for weeks.

The two Chiefs were issuing 'Corned Dog' sandwiches; they had been busy making during the action off Dakar, while the remainder of us were at Action Stations. My chief, who saw me coming into the galley, said, 'You alright, Ted?' I said, 'Yes, thanks, Chief. Got a blinding headache with all that cordite I've been breathing, though.'

Just then, we arrived in Bathurst, a bit of a place in Gambia, further along the coast, where we held the funeral of our dead shipmates; they were laid out on the quarterdeck, with the Union Jacks over them. We slowly steamed down the river which was at the side of Bathurst; they cleared the lower deck, which meant that 'All the hands' mustered aft, and we held a burial service, then we returned to Freetown.

The whole fleet had returned; the *Resolution* came in with a couple of tugs, making four knots, with a hell of a list on her. She was patched up to make the long voyage to the USA where she was refitted and made 100 per cent seaworthy again. She left with a destroyer escort; my mate Arthur was alright.

We disposed of the Vichy French prisoners with a marine escort in boats to the shore. Every one of them had on a submarine jersey with the Cross of Lorraine on the front; as they passed the galley, there was a look of hatred in their eyes; the feeling was mutual – the double cross!

After a day or two we left Freetown for the last time, I am glad to say, licking our wounds. We could manage on auxiliary power indefinitely, until we got back to Simonstown Naval Base, where we did the necessary repairs, then it was off across the South Atlantic to the River Plate again. We met the cruiser *Hawkins*, and later the cruiser *Enterprise*; then went on patrol east of the Plate. We had one scare – there was reported to be a raider in the vicinity, and the *Enterprise* joined with us for a concentrated search. After three days we resumed our normal patrol. HMS *Cumberland*, was made the flagship of the South Atlantic Squadron. She covered 206,000 miles at sea since she was commissioned in the spring of 1939, 100,000 miles in nine months and did 112 days at sea out of 118 without sighting land. I think we held the record for doing 1,200 miles in 34 hours, going to the River Plate on 13 December 1939.

I have only mentioned the high spots on the *Cumberland*; during the two years I served aboard her, there were many more. There were many, many weeks patrolling at four knots, over and over the South Atlantic, not going anywhere, just having to be out there.

Other times, the seas were tremendous, south of the Cape, down to the Roaring Forties, i.e. on the way to Australia; you hadn't been to sea unless you had been down there. All around the Cape the seas were rough.

We had been in and out of Simonstown so often that they unofficially adopted the *Cumberland*.

I had by now been in the Navy three years. They were at this time building dozens and dozens of destroyers and needed men with three years service, so I volunteered, receiving a draft back to the UK via the *Enterprise*. I got held up in the *Enterprise* for two months hunting for the raider, but I did get to the Cape eventually, caught the Canadian Pacific liner, the *Duchess of Athol*, at Cape Town, and we sailed alone, without any escort, to Freetown, went through the Danger Zone, eventually arriving at Gladstone Dock, Liverpool, where we had a job getting into the dock owing to the enormous cranes sticking out of the water, the aftermath of the blitz on Liverpool. We caught a series of trains from Lime Street to Chatham, Kent. Once there, I reported to RN Barracks, HMS Pembroke, where I had a meal, wash and brush up and slung my hammock in the 'Tunnel' for one night.

The following morning I was given nineteen days foreign service leave. I went home to East Barnet, where the locals looked on me as a bit of a 'hero'. My mother carried on as usual and didn't at any time ask where I had been, or what I had done, so I didn't say anything at all. I was glad to be going back to barracks, and that was something with all the overcrowding.

RN Barracks, HMS Pembroke, is situated at the foot of a hill which goes back towards Gillingham and becomes 'The Great Lines' and can

The Author on leave after the Dakar operation, 1941. Operation Menace.

be seen for miles; where the hill hits the barracks, it runs along the rear left half and right half of Duncan Block, L.H. and R.H. of Anson Block and L.H. and R.H. of Nelson, finding level ground at the Military Road which skirts the dockyard and the River Medway.

So when you come out of the rear of each block, you face a roadway which runs the entire length of the barracks, and on the other side of the roadway, which is a large hill, there are three huge steel doors, one for each block. These are the entrances to the 'Tunnel', which houses the entire personnel of the barracks at night – everyone slept down there, officers included; the only personnel in the barracks at night were the anti-aircraft, firewatchers and the auxiliary services. This 'Tunnel' is a massive air-raid shelter, made up of concrete tunnels, like the Underground, running for miles, deep down, under the 'Great Lines'.

How far it went, I never did know; I didn't have time to explore it. One thing I did know was that if the barracks was completely blitzed or destroyed or bombed out the barracks would continue to function from the 'Tunnel' as every office was down there. It could sleep everyone in barracks, and that stood at 23,000 men in 1941; the 'Tunnel' was the last thing in air-raid shelters in more ways than one.

The only thing wrong with it was the damp – with no ventilation, there was the sweat of thousands of men, who slept down the middle on benches, head to toe. Overhead, they slept in the orthodox way 'slung' on both sides of every tunnel; you just could not move for bodies, right, left and overhead. It became most unhealthy; men volunteered by the hundreds for sea; they preferred to be sunk at sea than sleeping on top of one another. The buzz went round that there would be an epidemic at Chatham.

Sooner or later, I got a break from sleeping in the 'Tunnel' and was detailed for fire-watching; we took pot luck in Nelson Block. We had a chap who was always boasting how fit he was – he would take on anybody. He would jump up, grab the bar above the hammocks and do physical jerks on the bar, then would stand in front of you and take deep breaths. He would say, 'There you are, you too can have a body like mine.' I thought, I have heard this before, we'll see how tough he is tonight when Jerry (Germans) comes over. As sure as eggs, the tannoy would say, 'Air Raid Warning, Red.' You'd hear the bombers in the distance then the tannoy would say, 'Air Raid Warning, Purple.' When they were overhead. There was that whistling sound, then 'Crump' 'Crump!' Somebody's got it. I reached for my tin hat (steel helmet) and was just going to get under the nearest table when I thought, 'Where is my opposite number?' He's under the table, sweat pouring off him – you'd think his last hour had come, his lips were quivering. He said, 'Do you think they'll hit us, do you, Ted?' I said, 'If your name's on the bomb, there's not much you can do about it!' Suddenly there was an almighty 'Blam!' and the whole building shook. They hit the toilets in between left half and right half, Anson Block, one rating was killed. They were bombing indiscriminately, looking for HMS *Ajax*, which had returned home.

'Anyway, you have your steel helmet there with you,' I went on. With that remark, he put his tin hat on; next time I looked at him, he was curled up like a baby under the table, asleep. I heard no more whimpering from 'a very fit young man', and give him a shake when it was over.

The next morning, there was very heavy cloud over the dockyard and the surrounding area. I was going across the parade ground when two enemy bombers just came out of the clouds, dropped their bombs in the dockyard and were off again. The *Ajax* had been removed after the previous raid, so they hit only a small merchant ship.

A week or so after, I happened to go for a shower in the washplace on the ground floor, and who do you think was in the next cubicle? None other than, 'You too can have a body like mine.' I took one look at him, all thirteen stone, massive arms and legs, but his head looked as though it had shrunk into his shoulders, no neck. And you know what they say about men with no necks? I looked down and there was the tiniest 'Little Willy' you ever did see! I said, 'You might be a man, but you couldn't do a woman much good, with that tiny little willy!'

Christmas 1941 came and went. In February, we had a lot of snow everywhere. I went home for a 'Friday While', a long weekend to civilians. While I was home, I started having headaches; as the day wore on, it got worse, so I went to bed. My mother called the doctor who lived a few doors away; his name was Dr Lang, who said, 'Oh! just a touch of the flu.' Next morning I was nearly unconscious; the doctor was called again and said, 'It's meningitis!' They whisked me off to the Wellhouse Hospital, now Barnet General; the snow was thick on the ground, the temperature freezing. The ambulance was held up for at least an hour and we waited outside the Isolation Block, with the doors of the ambulance wide open; my mother was beside herself with worry. She had already lost my father and my eldest brother and was panic-stricken.

I came to as Dr Segar was in the act of giving me a lumbar puncture. He was renowned for his expertise, everyone in the district knew of him and his brilliance as a surgeon. I was in good hands; he went in the first time with the needle. There were two other men with meningitis, but I was the only one who survived. There were no drugs in those days – Penicillin had not been invented. There were only the M & B tablets, or in liquid form, which I had.

The Sister said, 'You were lucky to have Dr Segar; he went in the first time through your spine; it was absolutely brilliant.' She went on to say what my illness was. 'It is cerebral spinal meningitis, that you have.'

I was in hospital several weeks, and was paid a visit by a specialist and his entourage of students, who stripped me of everything. I lay on my back while they stuck pins in me all over. 'Can you feel that?' one said. 'No,' I said. 'Can you feel this then?' and he continued to prick my legs front and back. 'No, not a thing.' I was made to get out of bed to see if I could walk, but I couldn't. I said, 'I can't feel your hands on my right leg at all, it's dead, and my right buttock also.' With that, they turned me over on my stomach. I was enjoying this, and they proceeded to attack me with an assortment of pins and needles. 'No, I can't feel a thing.' They retired to a corner in a huddle, and the only thing that I could hear was a 'No, no, no.' They thanked me very much and disappeared.

The Sister came over to me again and said, 'The Doctor has said you are to be discharged from the Royal Navy.' I said, 'You can't do that, you can't discharge me; just phone Chatham, you'll see.'

The Navy were quick off the mark and said I was to return to the Royal Naval Hospital forthwith. They would be sending an ambulance for me.

After much haggling, it was agreed that I had to have convalescence for two months; if I was stronger then, OK. But if not, an extra month's convalescence. I had had a very near thing, couldn't walk and a long journey at this stage wouldn't be very beneficial, so the Navy relented. This was Dr Segar's intervention, no doubt.

I was put into hospital blue, pale blue serge suit, white shirt and red tie. The only thing Navy that I wore was my peaked cap; I felt like a Christmas cracker.

North Mimms Park was my destination, and what a beautiful mansion it was. The only patients there were several hundred wounded, survivors from Dunkirk. I was the only sailor there and didn't those squaddies (soldiers) make a fuss of having the Navy with them. They said they were proud of having the Navy with them.

After a few weeks I was able to walk with a stick; my right leg was numb from the buttock downwards. There was no physiotherapy in those days, it was a case of trying yourself to get well, regular exercise, with plenty of rest.

The weeks passed. One day, a naval ambulance called to pick me up and take me back to the RN Hospital – 'Boneyard', as it is often referred to – at Gillingham, Kent.

The next morning I went before the Surgeon Lieutenant who was a consultant. There were no physiotherapists in those days and it was his job to get me better. In a queer sort of way, the first thing he said to me was, 'What's bothering you, hm?' a gross understatement of facts, I thought, a typical naval officer's remark. I said, 'Just what it says on my case papers before you, sir.' He quickly looked up at me saying, 'Alright, alright, there's no need for that sort of remark!' I saw his eyes narrow (first round to me, I thought). 'Well, what's the trouble?' he said. 'I have a job to walk; after having cerebral spinal meningitis, my right leg is numb from the buttocks down,' I said. 'Well, you're on our feet now, aren't you, you'll be alright!' he said (second round to him). 'I can't walk very far, I certainly can't run, if that's what you mean,' I said (game, set and match to me). With that remark, he gave up and rang the bell; the door opened and a sick berth attendant came through. The Surgeon Lieutenant said, 'I want a green card for light duties and I'll sign it.' With that our meeting was at an end; so much for being discharged from the Navy!

I was returned to barracks and the next day I reported to the AODD's office on the ground floor of Duncan Block. I was given a job with the Accounts Officer, Divisional Duties, who was in charge of all miscellaneous branches, such as cooks, stewards, writers, supply departments. I was in this job for a few months and never went back to the wardroom galley. Firstly, I could never stand up to the job; I felt as though I had become a Writer, typing and seeing to documentation, requestment and defaulters; it suited me fine, my right leg was improving, sitting down all day, learning to type as well.

I had to check all the Admiralty Fleet Orders – AFOs – which used to come to our office, every month or so; they had to be gone over before being given to the Accounts Officer, who was a Paymaster Lieutenant. One day I was browsing through the latest edition of AFOs, when I saw and repeated aloud to all in the office an order it ran: 'The Admiralty will accept any General Service Rating [that's me!] into the Fleet Air Arm – all past service will count – for seven years Active Service, five years on the Reserve' – Bla, bla, bla.

My time had come. What I had always wanted. Hip, hip, hooray! What I had wanted in 1937!

I immediately made out a request to see the Commander, through the Divisional Officer, to transfer to the Fleet Air Arm. It was granted. I had won, after five years. It's where I wanted to be in the first place.

I had a medical – my right leg was improving month by month. The medical officer didn't mention it, neither did I.

My uniform was changed, I had a kit inspection, all the clerical work was done, my pay book was altered, my official number was changed from C/MX55965 to SS/FX2108 – I was now in the FAA. I did the 'Leaving Barracks' routine, which took three days to complete, believe it or not; it usually took four days, but the preliminaries had been done.

I tagged on to the end of another party who were doing the LB routine, went round hour after hour to all the different departments, getting a letter stamped at every one of them. We were just marching, four of us, past the Gunnery School and were confronted by a 'Chief Gunner's Mate' who said, 'What are all *we*?' emphasis on the word '*we*'. They always say in the Navy, 'What are all *we*?' '*We* are just going up to the Gas School, *we're* on LB routine,' I said, and produced the letter with the stamps on it. 'So, you're the *just* party as well, *just* going here, *just* going there!' he said sarcastically. 'Get stuffed,' I said under my breath!

We reported finally to the Drafting Office in the morning, where I received a slip of paper addressed to HMS Gosling, near Warrington, Cheshire, with a railway warrant and meal vouchers. The kit bag and hammock were already on the van; as we passed through the main gate of HMS Pembroke, I put two fingers up in a victory salute and shouted to the sentry on the gate, 'You can st*** the b******!' I wouldn't see Chatham again, thank God!

I arrived at HMS Gosling I, near Warrington, Cheshire, in the afternoon. It was about two miles up the Leigh Road, past Padgate, an RAF Camp and Risley, which is now a prison. Gosling was about 500 yards farther on; turning left down a country lane, there were three other camps, Gosling II, III and IV in the area. It looked a mixed bag of huts. I went up to the sentry on the gate and showed him my documents; he showed me a hut and the Regulating Office where I reported to the Chief Petty Officer and got settled in.

I reported to the Training Commander in the morning, who informed me that Gosling was only a Basic Training Camp. I said, 'It was a waste of time being sent here. How long will I have to wait before I can start my technical training, I have done superior training before the war?' to which he replied, 'Quite.' He had my service documents in his hands; browsing through them, he said, 'I see you're General Service, a Regular.' I said, 'Yes, sir, 1937, I joined.' He replied, 'So I see. You have been on active service, too.' I kept quiet; the less I said about that the better. He probably hadn't seen a warship, let alone been at sea!

He seemed to ignore my last remark by saying, 'We can't arrange the technical course straight away, you understand. You'll have to go to see the psychologist, she will see which branch of the FAA you're most suited to!' She? She?

The Wren officer was a most attractive lady and I got on well with her. After about half an hour of tests, she gave me her conclusion: 'I recommend you for Radar and Electrical Mechanic, the highest that I can recommend you for.' 'Thank you, Ma'am,' I said, 'but I'm not interested in Radar or Electrical.' She asked, 'Which branch do you prefer?' I replied, 'My father was an aeronautical engineer. I would rather like to follow in his footsteps, on engines.' She replied, 'Engines it will be then! I recommend you for Engine Mechanic, Air – is that right?' I said, 'Yes, thank you very much, ma'am.'

I spent the next two weeks going up to the Seeland Course, just outside Chester; it was then all fields. We were dumped on top of a railway embankment and had to make our way down, with kit bag and gas mask, to the camp which was some way over the fields. It was a small arms and rifle range; we fired the ·303 rifle, revolver, Sten automatic and machine-gun, followed by the hand grenade. I was in my element. I'll always remember being down at the firing point with a ·303 service rifle, spending what seemed like hours flat on your stomach, firing at a target, with a hell of a wind blowing in your face; it seemed like a thousand yards away; I couldn't see it half the time as my eyes were full of tears, which made the target difficult to see.

A fortnight later I was drafted to RAF Hednesford, on Cannock Chase, near Rugely, Staffordshire, where I did my technical training on aero engines. There are two types: in line and radial. Rolls Royce and DH Gypsy Majors have their cylinders in a line, Bristol engines and the majority of American, are radial, having their cylinders in the form of a circle. I had instruction on the Rolls Royce, Eagle, Kestrel, and the Merlin; the Griffin came later on in the War, and I had instruction on it in 1945, also on Bristol, Pegasus, Hercules and others like Pratt and Whitney, and Wasp (American).

Of propellers, mainly De Havilland and variable pitch were used. Rotal propellers came into the War later.

Components were used by makers according to the aircraft; there were hundreds of components, hundreds of them.

We drew hundreds of systems – there were the basics like fuel, oil and cooling systems. There were also the carburettor fuel system, like the Claudel-Hobson, other oil pressure systems for the DH variable pitch propellers, and so on.

Then there was the Supercharger, fitted mainly on the rear of Roll Royce engines, from the Merlin to the Griffin, for extra speed; and there was the automatic boost control. When the pilot brought that into operation, it gave him an extra 50 m.p.h. for only three minutes, only to be used in an *emergency* in combat!

The course lasted several months, with different types of aircraft to begin with, such as the DH Tiger Moth, then the Hawker aircraft of pre-war days which I used to see at the Hendon Air Pageant, they used to call it in the 1930s. When I was only fourteen years of age, the Hawker, Demon, the Hart and Hind they were all powered by the Rolls Royce Kestrel engines. Finally the *last* biplane, the Hawker Fury, capable of 260 m.p.h.; then came the first Hawker Hurricane, a monoplane. There was the old Bristol Bulldog, a biplane, the only one from Bristol's. There were heaps of aircraft, so many that I lost count of them, but I do remember the Hamden bomber, Airspeed Oxford, the Avro Anson, and Lysander. The Lysander was the first aeroplane that I climbed into on the course, and I had to start the engine and run her up. To feel the aircraft come alive with your hands was quite unnerving the first time. Then there were the Gloster Gladiators and the Gauntlets too.

On completion of the course, I was drafted to 776 Squadron, HMS Blackcap, Speke Airport, Liverpool, a training squadron. They were happy days, the happiest days of my entire life – I was working on aircraft as my father had done. We had American Chesapeakes, Blenheim Bombers, Boulton Paul Defiants, Blackburn Skuas, Rocs, and finally early mark Hurricanes. As the aircraft became obsolete, they were flown away by women pilots of the ATA (Air Transport Auxiliary) for scrap.

There were two very large hangars, one each side of the control tower, taken over by Lockheed American Aircraft Company, all to do with the Lend-Lease business. At 8.00 a.m. and 8.00 p.m. every day, a huge convoy of fifty aircraft used to arrive with a military escort, with motorcycles front and rear, from the docks, from ships of a convoy; the huge doors would be opened and in would go fifty Mustang fighters, with all the brown adhesive tape that the aircraft used to be covered with for their journey over the Atlantic removed and cleaned down, the propellers and the wings fitted, then thoroughly checked over, then pushed out of the rear doors on to a large concrete apron, put in lines, the tail wheel fastened to a large ring in the concrete, brakes applied 'hard on', and for the next hour or so, we would have to put up with fifty Mustangs, each having their engines ground tested; then they would be pushed over to the centre of the field, to await air testing. In the meantime the huge front doors were standing open, awaiting another fifty Mustangs, which had just arrived in a convoy from the docks at Liverpool. As soon as they had disposed of the first batch of Mustangs, in went the second, the doors closed until 8.00 p.m., then another convoy would arrive, the doors opened, the whole thing was repeated. The staff, mostly women, were working a shift system round the clock; aircraft were being turned out twice a day, at 8.00 a.m. and 8.00 p.m.; it was production on a grand scale.

One week they turned out Mustang fighters, the next week it would be Thunderbolt fighters, and the week after it would be P38 Lightning fighters; after that, it would be Hellcats and Wildcat fighters and so on, the best aircraft that America could produce, and their pilots were superb too.

Twice a week they were brought over in B17 Flying Fortresses, or Liberator bombers, fifty or so pilots; they would test fly the Mustangs, then fly them back to Burtonwood, which was in the vicinity of Wigan, an enormous disposal base for the American Air Force.

There was one aircraft that used to attract my attention every time I went past it called the Bell Aerocobra, a fighter, not dissimilar to the Spitfire or the Hurricane. A very neat little aircraft, it had an engine in the rear fuselage, behind the cockpit. The propeller was in the front, as is normal, connected by a long crankshaft under the pilot's seat to the engine in the rear, a distance of at least five feet. Just imagine a long shaft, spinning at speed under your feet; it must have created an enormous amount of 'torque' loading. However, it was withdrawn after a while, the long shaft used to snap at high speed; the pilot was killed on each occasion.

It was while we had Skuas that my first flight took place, after my

Blackburn Skua.

mate and I had fitted a new accelerator delayed action pump to the engine of a Skua. We ground tested the engine and called for a pilot to test fly it. First, may I say that the Skua was a dive bomber, designed as such by Blackburn Aircraft Company, and was the first aircraft in the War to shoot down an enemy aircraft. It was a good aircraft in its day, at the moment it was used as a target drone-towing aircraft for the Queen Charlotte Gunnery School, on the beach, at Ainsdale, near Southport, Lancashire.

Most of the FAA aircraft were two-seaters. A matter that we, as air mechanics, took for granted, was to go up on air test, and the pilots looked for one of us to go up too. We thought nothing of it. The pilot was named the 'Mad Middy'. He had been a midshipman and was recently promoted to sub lieutenant. We never had a parachute on any flight.

It was a beautiful morning, without a cloud in the sky; there was no wind, everything was still, visibility was extreme, just the perfect day. We took off in the direction of the Mersey, being situated next to the river, and headed for the Wirral, and the River Dee, in the direction of Chester.

I had on my helmet a Gosport type of speaker, but no parachute! The pilot was in touch with me from the front the whole time; there was an instrument panel in front of me and the pilot said, 'I'll nurse it, the engine, for about ten minutes, or so, and then take her up to 12,000 feet!' I said, 'OK.' I could see we were already climbing by the altimeter, then I looked out, and we were over the River Dee, at the estuary; we were going round and round and climbing, continuing like this for about ten minutes, until we reached 12,000 feet. Satisfied that the engine was alright, without any warning he put the nose down into a vertical dive; he could have said, 'Watch out, here we go!' or 'I'm just going to put her into a dive, to see if she's OK,' but no! I looked at the altimeter, the engine was racing so fast, that she was screaming, I thought, 'This is what she was built for.' Everything was happening so quickly, down, down we went, in the direction of the River Dee estuary; it was very wide at this point, I remember. We are going to have a watery grave. We are going straight in. I didn't black out, and I wasn't nervous at all. I would have been all for it under normal conditions. Down, down, down, we fell out of the sky. I kept looking at the altimeter. 6,000 feet. 5,000 feet. I disconnected my Gosport helmet, unstrapped myself and looked up to the cockpit canopy, ready to open it. I reached for the catch above my head. The altimeter was down to less than a thousand feet and still in a near vertical dive. I thought, 'Here we go then!' I just had a brief glance at the water coming up at us. At the very last minute, *he pulled her out of her dive*. The very *last second*, he left it, because if we'd stopped to say 'Hello' we would have been in the 'drink' (the sea)!

I said in my statement for the court martial that in my opinion, we pulled out of the dive at less than 100 feet because the altimeter had stopped registering – it doesn't register under 50 feet!!

In the meantime, we raced across the coast, Chester was to our left and I could see the Welsh Mountains to our right. We were tearing along like a 'bat out of hell' at less than 50 feet. He was the Mad Middy alright! Towards the Cheshire Plain, we skimmed over the tops of trees, every time with a 'clank' or a 'bonk', where we had given the trees a good trimming. It all happened so quickly, first it was one thing, then another, at no time did the pilot regain height, he seemed to enjoy low flying. One thing I did know was that sooner or later we'd have a prang. Something would happen! We saw cows in a field and came so close, they just scattered. That's put them off milking, I thought. Then he swung the aircraft over, went between two trees on one wing, continually side-slipping between trees, until he saw a man riding a bicycle away from us, down a country lane. We were still at around 50 feet, the pilot straightened the aircraft so we were dead behind him, so low that we could have given the poor bloke a haircut. He turned round with all the noise and I saw for a brief second the look of panic on the man's face, to see a Skua coming at him at zero feet. I looked backwards over the tail: his bicycle was doing a figure of eight, he had disappeared, and so had we. We were creating havoc in a few minutes; something was bound to happen, and it did!

We came to a hill; it wouldn't have made any difference if we had been flying at a normal height, but he thought he would follow the contour of the hill by rising over the summit and slipping down the other side at zero feet. As we came over the summit, there running parallel with the hill, was a line of pylons, electricity power, directly barring our path! The pilot had one second's decision, whether to go under, or whether to just go over the top.

They were pylons carrying eight cables. In one second, we hit them and there was an almighty flash and a bang, or both together; it was blinding. It lit the whole plane and the area; it is a job to describe what happened! I remember the Skua hit the cables like an arrow and we shot up in the air for about 200 feet or more, just like being released from a bow.

We had broken five out of eight cables and cut all the electricity for North Wales! I knew instinctively that we were an all-metal aircraft, but we were not electrocuted. We were *still just* flying in one piece! The engine was behaving normally, but what was that scraping sound? It could have been anything. The instruments were reading as usual, the oil pressure, engine temperature, there was no 'magneto drop', the revs were more or less the same, only the altimeter was not working as normal, which was understandable, considering we were at zero feet. The aircraft went out of control after shooting up in the air; we nearly went into a loop initially, the pilot had his hands full bringing the aircraft back on to an even keel again.

I plugged my Gosport helmet in again, having disconnected it during the dive; I wondered whether he was alright. He must have heard me plugging in as he quickly said, 'You alright back there?' He seemed as bright as ever. I replied, 'Yeah, I'm OK.' He said, 'Can you see any damage from where you are?' I replied, 'Not a thing, only the Perspex cockpit overhead looks a bit battered, but seems to be in one piece!' The pilot said, 'That's more than I can say for mine!' The aircraft was now flying straight; she seemed to wobble now and again; something was definitely wrong but we kept up in the air anyway.

We were, in the meantime, crossing over the Wirral which divides the Dee from the Mersey, then over the River Mersey, and finally we were at Speke. Just over the side of the river making our final approach to land, two green lights should come on on the dashboard, to say that both wheels should be down and locked, but only one green light came on! The pilot landed to the left of the tarmac runway, on to the grass and we waited for the aircraft to lose speed; one of the 'Oleo' legs would collapse and over we would go. Over we went!

We were down. I had pulled the cockpit hood back soon after the impact in case of fire and was first out of the Skua. I said nothing to the pilot, just walked around the aircraft, examining it: the cockpit Perspex hood in front of the pilot, and the wings were damaged, the propeller had several yards of copper cable about 1" thick wrapped round the propeller and the reduction gear, just in front of the cylinders; the engine cowlings were nearly hanging off, some cable had gone inside the engine and the radio aerial had been cut off just above my head; what with the Oleo leg collapsing, which we couldn't see, she was a write-off! She would stay where she is, only fit to be put on a lorry and towed away for scrap.

I ignored the pilot and made for the Squadron Office, in no mood to speak to anyone except the Commander. I let the Fire Brigade look after the aircraft and the crowd that had gathered.

I knew I would be expected to make a written statement, which I did, and awaited the court martial, which followed in a few weeks. It was a very serious matter and I realized I was the key witness, the only witness. One thing, which stood out in my mind: I was lucky to survive an impact with high-tension power cables in an all-metal aircraft!

In the meantime, complaints from the Electricity Board, police, farmers, the hospitals and all sorts of business people in the area grew out of all proportion. The cows didn't milk, the farmer who came off his bike was claiming for this and that, some wife had had a baby, she was so frightened with the noise, and so on. One farmer said, 'Haven't you got something better to do than just joy riding around the countryside in an aeroplane?'

The court martial was held and I was the key witness. I stood before the Court; the prosecuting officer said to me, 'Do you know what this is?' He put an altimeter in my hand. I said, 'Yes, sir, it's an altimeter!' He went on, 'You said in your statement that "the altimeter had gone off the clock." What do you mean by that?' 'I meant that the needle was at zero, stopped registering, it doesn't register under fifty feet!' The prosecuting officer said, 'Do you mean to say, you were flying at under fifty feet?' I said, 'Yes, sir, definitely, definitely.' I said it all! The Court was adjourned; when we returned, the 'sword' on the table was pointing towards the accused, *Guilty!* He was cashiered from the Navy, lost all pay, pensions, etc. etc. He never apologized to me, justice was done.

A few weeks later, the Chief Petty Officer on parade asked if anyone knew anything about Coffman Percussion Cartridge Starters. I said, 'Yes, I do, Chief'. They are the usual starters we always used in the Navy; our aircraft did not start on a battery, as they did in the RAF. So from then onwards, I worked overhauling Coffman starters in my own little workshop for the whole squadron. I came to be known as the 'Coffman Starter King'.

One morning the Chief said to me, 'You are to report to the C.-in-C.'s flight, over the other side of the field.' I reported to the Leading Air Mechanic, George, who became known as the Chief. He said, 'You are a general service rating, not an HO [Hostilities Only], aren't you?' I said, 'Yes, I trained at Chatham before the War.' He said, 'Well, you have been chosen for this job as you are a regular. I don't have to tell you how to go on, or what rig of the day you should be in, do I?' I said, 'No.' He went on, 'You are now on the staff of the C.-in-C. Western Approaches, Admiral Sir Max Horton, D.S.O., who is at Derby House, Royal Liver Buildings, Liverpool. It is our job to see that his aircraft is always on top line; you will be the mechanic to look after the two DH Gypsy Major engines and hold yourself ready to see the aircraft off, or when she comes in; keep yourself ready in the rig of the day, as you might have to fly with him, and take your tool box. OK? Then I'll leave you to it, Ted.' And fly with him I did, often!

The aircraft was a De Havilland Dominie 7508; it had two Gypsy Major inverted engines, carried eight passengers, and had painted on the side the Admiral's flag. Every morning, I would check it over and ground test the engines, what we used to call a DI (Daily Inspection), then sign for the aircraft in the Form 700, a sort of log book which had all the details of the aircraft, the type, engines and fuel, etc.

First thing in the morning, the pilot used to arrive. He was a lieutenant RN, in other words he was a regular; he was in charge of the C.-in-C.'s flight, and whether the C.-in-C.'s aircraft would be required today, or where we would be flying to. If there was to be no flight, the aircraft was ready for him to take her up on air test, and up I would go. If the aircraft flew, I would fly, because nobody else would be allowed to touch it, it was my baby.

I used to see Sir Max quite often, and went on several flights with him to the Isle of Man, Northern Ireland and other air bases in Scotland. One base we went to, they had Barracudas; I heard it said that they lost a couple of dozen of them in one month – their tails came off in a dive!

The Dominie was a good aircraft, very reliable; I never had any faults with it. There were times when I thought we would never get over a mountain or two in Scotland as she seemed not to have enough power, but she used to make it every time.

Later, we had a new addition, an Armstrong Whitley bomber. It was known as the 'Flying Coffin', they lost so many with the RAF. This was to be my baby, as well as the Dominie.

My first and only impression was that it was underpowered; it had two Rolls Royce Merlin Xs and was a huge aircraft, nearly as big as a Lancaster, which had four Merlin XXIIs.

I had another air mechanic to help me because the Whitley was supposed to have a fuel problem. We spent hours checking it and had the cowlings off on both engines, checked the tanks, but the supply to carburettors seemed alright. We never found the fuel problem, put the cowlings back on again, gave each engine a run up; the port engine was OK but the starboard engine I thought was suspect. It had quite a mag drop: the magneto was not functioning properly, so we cleaned the contact breaker points, and changed the plugs – still, a little drop in revs. I asked for an air test, so our pilot of the C.-in-C.'s flight decided to test the Whitley, and I went up with him without parachutes!

We taxied up to the end of the runway and stood there with engines running waiting to take off. I was sitting in the co-pilot's seat, next to the pilot, looking out of the window at the starboard engine, when I shouted, 'Throttle back!' at the pilot, which he did, 'What's up?' he shouted. 'There's coolant pouring out of the filler cap!' He said, 'If I throttle back, do you think you could fix it?' I said, 'OK, I'll tell the tower to hold it a minute.' I went to the after hatch with a filler cap key, which I always kept on my person, went underneath the aircraft, engines still running, climbed on the wing and on to the engine nacelle, got one leg on one side and one the other, as though I was riding it, and edged my way forward until I was within a foot of a revolving propeller. The filler cap was right on the leading edge of the engine cowling, less than a foot from the propeller; even with the engine at slow revs, it was a hell of a draught, like a huge fan! I placed the key on the filler cap and gave it a good old wrench, surprised how little it moved, so I gave it another wrench and it stopped leaking. I gave the pilot the thumbs up signal and make my way backwards the way I had come, and said, 'That's OK now, sir,' as I climbed aboard.

I sat next to the pilot as we took off in the Whitley; over the Mersey River, the starboard engine started to splutter; I looked at the rev counter on the dashboard as it fell. The engine was losing power – they used to go over on their backs if one engine failed! I looked at the pilot, his right hand was already on the trimming wheel, ready to trim the aircraft, in case she suddenly turned over on her back. He looked quite unconcerned as he looked at me. 'I'll see if we can make a circuit and land,' he said. 'Yes, if it doesn't pack up first,' I said. We landed in one piece.

We went straight over to the Engineering Officer, gave our report on the state of the Whitley bomber. It was urgently required for a special flight, and they couldn't use the Dominie, so I could choose which mechanic I wanted. I chose Don who had helped me check the Whitley – it meant an engine change.

The hangar was cleared of every aircraft, and with a tractor and a few mechanics, we pushed the Whitley in, with only about a foot to spare. We got the tail up in the rigging position and made the engine change, refilled with oil and coolant, towed it out, filled up with 100 per cent octane petrol, ground-tested it several times, signed the Form 700 for the aircraft, and had it air-tested, going up with it – it was OK!

We flew to Northern Ireland on naval business – I went on every trip – and there was a terrific gale blowing all day. We made heavy weather of it, but both engines behaved normally. I saw a submarine on the surface being thrown about; I couldn't understand why she should be on the surface – I thought it would be better to submerge, less buffeting about. The sea was very rough.

We did our business at Belfast, and on our way back as we crossed the cliffs the Whitley dropped like a stone. I suddenly found it difficult to get my breath; it was just about to pancake on the water, when the pilot gave both engines full throttle. There was a surge of power from the Rolls Royce Merlins and the aircraft just recovered herself before hitting the water. Oh, my God. That was a near thing! Thank God for Rolls Royce Merlins. I was pleased with them, I thought we were in the 'drink' that time. The pilot said, 'I wonder if we will make it back to Speke, perhaps we had better land where we can!' I said, 'We'll be alright with my engines!' He replied, 'They are famous last words, we'll be alright!!' We laughed!

It was so rough, the weather in the Irish Sea; we were being buffeted about like a feather. We made landfall near Blackpool, Kirkham, I think it was. We landed and stood still for a minute to get a breather, to get our breath back. A despatch rider came up as we stopped, and said, 'It's too rough for you to take off, better you stay here for the night.' 'OK,' we said. We looked around, but there didn't seem to be any buildings or any sign of life. The pilot said, 'I don't fancy staying in this outlandish spot, do you?' I said, 'No, I don't.' It suddenly grew dark, and there was a force ten gale blowing; the pilot opened both throttles, there was a roar from both my Merlins, and we 'batted' down the runway. The control tower, which was situated halfway down the runway, fired two red Very lights at us, then another two, telling us not to take off. By then, we were airborne! The pilot said, 'I didn't see any red lights, did you?' I replied, 'What red lights were they?' We laughed all the way back to Speke Airport, a bit dishevelled, but hungry.

In 1944, I was asked to go to Newcastle as one of the Bolton Paul Defiants of No. 766 (Training) Squadron had made a forced landing at an MU base there, RAF Houston. I was to take an air mechanic with me, tool kit, train warrant, meal vouchers, and do an engine change, the existing engine being faulty.

We arrived at Houston the next day; the Defiant was already in the hangar. We removed the propeller, fuel, oil, and coolant, took out the faulty engine, put in the new engine, the propeller, oil, fuel, and coolant in the second day, much to the amusement of the flight mechanics of the RAF. A flight sergeant came over to us and said, 'Who gave you the authority to run up this engine? Only a pilot in the RAF is allowed to do it.' I said, 'With due respect, Flight Sergeant, we are *not* in the Air Force, we are in the Royal Navy. We are the Senior Service, and Admiralty Fleet Orders say that I am fully qualified to run up and test an aircraft engine.' When the noise had abated, I looked for the Flight Sergeant – he was nowhere to be seen. I then taxied the aircraft up to where I found it! We phoned the control tower and said, 'The Defiant is now serviceable' and told them where the pilot could pick it up. 'We are returning to Speke forthwith.'

I continued to go on flights with the Dominie to various bases of the Fleet Air Arm, sometimes with Admiral Sir Max Horton, but more often than not, to test the aircraft after a service.

One day I was called to the Commander's office, and was asked if I would consider putting in for Leading Air Mechanic (I was fully capable of being a LAM) as the Engineering Officer had given me 'Superior' in my character assessment. I said, 'Yes, thank you, sir.' I took the necessary Educational Test, Proficiency and Trade Test at Speke, passing each with a 'Very Good' assessment.

Later, 776 Squadron moved to HMS *Ringtail*, Woodvale, near Southport, Lancs, where I received my promotion to leading air mechanic. To anyone else, it means very little, but to me, who had quite a bad start in the Navy, who twice turned down promotion to Leading Cook, Officers, when I was aboard the County Class cruiser HMS *Cumberland*, in the South Atlantic. I had made it at last! It had been a rough passage!

The C.-in-C.'s Flight also moved to Woodvale where I continued to service the Dominie 7508, and other aircraft. I knew that with promotion, there always comes a draft, the two always go together.

It was June 1945, VE Day, the war with Germany was now over, but that didn't mean very much to the Royal Navy and the Fleet Air Arm. The war out in the Pacific was being waged with a fanatical fury: the

Japs were fighting for every inch of ground. The Royal Navy were heavily committed, aircraft carriers were suddenly the capital warship out in the Pacific.

I was drafted to a foreign drafting base, HMS Waxwing, near Dunfermline, Scotland, there to await an aircraft carrier, HMS *Colossus*, which was fitting out at Cammel Lairds Shipyard, Birkenhead. It was destined for Trincomalee RN Base, Ceylon; this would be my new ship; when fitting out was completed, I would join her.

The Americans dropped the atomic bombs on Nagasaki and Hiroshima. The destruction was complete and nothing was left of each city. The Japanese had no alternative but to surrender. VJ Day was celebrated.

And so my draft to HMS *Colossus* and the Pacific Fleet was cancelled. A week or two later I was drafted to HMS Merlin, Donibristle, on the shores of the Firth of Forth, close to the Forth Bridge, facing in the direction of Edinburgh.

There I found myself in charge of a squadron of mainly Fairey Fireflies and Corsair fighters; there was no officer in charge, no Chief or Petty Officer; I was the only NCO.

I marched the men down to the squadron in the morning, sorted out the aircraft that needed daily inspections, saw that the Form 700s were duly signed per aircraft per day. There was no tea break; the nearest NAAFI was nearly a mile. I marched the men back to dinner at 12.00 noon and there I drew my tot of rum; I hadn't drunk it before, but I felt as though I needed it in view of the conditions: *no* Stand Easy, *no* tea break! It was winter in Scotland and the snow was about a foot deep. I had my tot of rum, by golly, every day. 'Up Spirits' never better! Brrrr!

I marched the men back again at 4.00 p.m. for tea, and so that was the routine each day; there seemed an anti-climax now the war in Europe and the Far East was over. Men were leaving the Navy, demobbed, now that hostilities had ceased; they were, what we always referred to as HOs, hostilities only. What of me, a regular?

When I signed the new contract in Chatham Barracks for the Fleet Air Arm, it laid down one stipulation: I signed for seven years Active Service, five years on the Reserve! All past service counted. I had over run my time by twelve months. I was free, due for immediate demobilisation if I wanted it. I should have stayed on.

I went to the General Office and said to the Chief Writer, 'I am due to be demobilised.' He said, 'Oh, no, you're not.' I came back to him, and said, 'Oh, yes, I am!' He said, 'You have another four years to do yet.' I said, 'If you look up my service documents, you will see there was one stipulation, "all past service counted". I signed on for seven and five and I have done eight years! The contract initially, in 1937, was for a cook, the contract then, twelve years Active Service, eight years on the Reserve is now void. Look up Admiralty Fleet Orders 1941; I think you'll find I am correct.' He found it correct and demobilisation was applied for.

When I was down on the squadron that day, I saw the pilot who I had served under on the C.-in-C.'s Station Flight, who was flying the Admiral, Sir Max Horton, to Northern Ireland that day, to accept the surrender of the U-boats and their crews. When I told him I was applying for demobilisation, he said, 'You're making a big mistake, Doe, leaving the service now. You would do well to stay here as you are, there is no telling what might happen.' He was trying to tell me something, but at the time I couldn't see it! Before I left Donibristle, he was promoted to Captain, and was made Commander of HMS Merlin, RNAS Donibristle, Fife, Scotland. I know now what he was trying to tell me: if I had stayed where I was, promotion for me, a regular with eight years service, would be rapid; a petty officer perhaps, or later, a chief petty officer. I knew I was destined for promotion, we had done a lot of flying together and been in a few scrapes together too. I was demobbed in 1946, then my troubles began in earnest. What a mistake I made!

I returned home to 7 Brookside North, East Barnet, Hertfordshire, only to find that the atmosphere there had not changed one bit; all of my brothers had married during the War and had left home.

Mr Miles had got himself a job, as a night booking clerk, at the Union Jack Club in London; my mother was left on her own most evenings and nights – I had walked into a trap.

I received a letter from Cape Town, South Africa, from a girlfriend I had known while I was out there. It was addressed to me, HMS *Cumberland*, c/o G.P.O. London – would I like to live out there? SA had good prospects for a young man; housing was not a problem and she had her own house in a nice neighbourhood. I thought about it for some time, but I couldn't leave dear old England.

In 1950 I got married, which caused a terrible row with my mother

The Author in Clacton-on-Sea, 1951.

and Mr Miles. To cut a long story short, I left the house for good. We stayed with my brother in Clacton-on-Sea, Essex, until we found a furnished flat. There was very little work there, so we moved back to Bush Hill Park, Enfield, Middlesex. Our first daughter was born there, then we found nobody wanted children. We moved yet again to Westcliff-on-Sea, Essex. A Jewish lady accepted us, complete with our daughter, in an upstairs flat. A little later, a second daughter was born in 1955, at Rochford Hospital – we had to find better accommodation, so we found an old house which was nearly falling to pieces.

With the help of the owner and the offer to do all exterior and interior decorating myself, we managed to get the house liveable. A third child was born, a son, in 1960, at Westcliff-on-Sea.

In 1964 we were on a week's holiday at Scratby on the Norfolk coast; while there, we visited Norwich and the surrounding area. We saw a house that we liked and put a deposit down on it; that was St Williams Way, Thorpe, Norwich, Norfolk.

We spent many happy years there, and were blessed with three lovely children, who have grown up and done well in their education and in their respective fields, and left home eventually.

I suffered with pains in my back from time to time; suddenly it grew worse, until I couldn't walk very well. The doctor sent me to see a specialist who said, 'Do you know you have one leg shorter than the other?' I replied, 'Yes, I know, I broke my right leg playing football when I was twelve, in the orphanage.' He said, 'You can see by the X-ray, you have worn out the joints in the lower part of the spine; the discs are worn out – every time you walk, the right leg goes down, hence the spine is jerked over to the right.'

I was admitted to the Norfolk and Norwich Hospital, where I had a mylogram, an injection of a blue fluid into the spine, which makes you violently sick half an hour afterwards.

A few days later, I had a laminectomy operation. I was sent home by ambulance and laid flat on my back on a bed-settee, downstairs, where I remained until the following day. The ambulance called three times a week to take me for pool therapy – a nice hot swimming pool did wonders for my back. After weeks of pool therapy, I gradually got better.

One day, I was at the hospital having therapy, when I was told that a specialist wanted to see me. I was told that my wife, Mary, had terminal cancer. I said, 'Does this mean that I will lose my wife?' His reply was, 'I'm afraid so.' I said, 'How long has she got?' he paused, then said, 'A year, perhaps longer.' I came out of the hospital, numb, feeling as though I had been pole-axed; my whole life fell apart. That year, or so, passed too quickly.

On 4 February 1980 Mary died peacefully in her armchair, near the window in the front room, downstairs.

I had to get away from Norwich – far too many memories; I was alone. I went down to Ipswich in Suffolk, which was really like home to me. I saw my Auntie Eva, who was the eldest of my grandfather's children. Of three sons and five daughters, the only living survivor, she was very pleased to see me; she lived alone too; her last words to me were, 'Be proud of your name Doe. It is a well-known name in Suffolk; your ancestor was Robert le Doe, 1188, Suffolk!' I now have a coat of arms to that effect. Within a few weeks, she was dead! I packed up my furniture, put it into storage, sold the house, moved from East Anglia and came down to Southsea in Hampshire.

There I met my second wife, Cynthia; we were married in a register office and later in church for a Church Blessing on 24 November 1980.

I had to have something to do, so I bought a bungalow in Polegate near Eastbourne, which needed complete renovation of the entire property. After four years, I was still at it, and I had nearly finished it, when my arm gave me stabs of pain.

To cut a long story short, I sold the bungalow and moved back to Southsea, where I settled in a one-bedroomed flat, where I am now.

In 1986, I woke up shivering from head to toe, a doctor was called, he examined me, asking questions on what I had been doing and gave me something which stopped the shivering. Later I had a stroke. I remember in snatches being driven at high speed at night to somewhere, presumably to a hospital, then nothing. I could hear voices, one was my wife, then nothing! Apparently, they took me to the Queen Alexandra's Hospital, which was two miles out of Southsea; they couldn't take me in but gave me temporary emergency treatment, and sent me back to St Mary's Hospital. All I remember was being driven at speed, which seemed to go on and on. Then there was nothing. I must have been unconscious and feel that I must have died for a short while, then nothing, or I must have just faded away. The next thing I remember was of floating through a very large window which was *closed* at the time . . . through the glass I went . . . upwards . . . over the graveyard which is opposite St Mary's Hospital. It was a dark moonlit night . . . there was a very hard frost . . . all the gravestones stood out in the frosty air . . . and yet I never felt the cold! Up, up I went, to the east, the earth . . . it started to appear in shades of blue and white . . . it looked beautiful.

I travelled upwards like this for a considerable time . . . upwards, ever upwards . . . the earth was growing smaller . . . the sky was very dark . . . broken only by the stars which had grown larger . . . they ceased to twinkle now . . . one star grew bigger than all the others . . . the star in the east, in the Bible, it referred to the star in the East, 'when baby Jesus was born' . . . it grew larger and larger as I approached . . . it held my

Armistice Day, 1996 – after my stroke.

gaze . . . it became a brilliant light . . . so bright that I had to put my hand up to my eyes . . . it was dazzling. Suddenly . . . the light opened, there seemed to be a hollow in the centre of the star . . . you could see inside it . . . then something happened . . . suddenly, I saw someone standing in the opening . . . it's . . . it's God! His arms were outstretched . . . He was just as the Bible portrays . . . just as I imagine Him . . . I couldn't take my eyes off Him . . . it is! Yes! Yes! It's God! He slowly came forward, just a yard or two . . . He was looking down on me . . . I went down on one knee and buried my face in my hands . . . the tears just ran down my face . . . uncontrollably!

After a few minutes, I looked up into His face . . . He was waiting for me to recover myself. I cannot describe how He looked, it seemed so peaceful, He seemed to know just how I felt. I said, 'Father! Father!' I seemed spellbound, I just couldn't take my eyes off him . . . then he spoke; in a quiet controlled voice, he said, 'Go back, my son, go back.' I was struck dumb, then I said, 'Yes, Father.' I nodded and slowly withdrew, I didn't look back. I slowly descended the way I had come . . .

The Author at York Minster.

eventually, I looked back, the star was just as bright . . . of Him, there was no sign . . . I knew He was there. I think I wasn't ready to go to heaven – not just yet!

Down, down I went. I thought of my wife and my children, had they found me dead? Were they arranging my funeral?

I took one last look at the stars twinkling again . . . of God, there was no sign . . . I knew He would always be up there! It was no dream, I was not conscious to the outside world.

I regained consciousness in a ward, unable to speak, unable to say anything other than a 'Yeth', whatever that meant! My voice, my memory and all my faculties had gone. Patients in the neighbouring beds were busy talking to one another, but I couldn't join in. I couldn't use my right arm, it had no feeling in it at all. I know that I had seen God, definitely!

After a few days I got up, much to the surprise of all the nurses. I dragged my right leg and went to the toilet, looked at myself in the mirror. I couldn't recognize myself: the whole of the right side of my face was distorted. I tried to straighten my face to put it back where it should be, but couldn't. I found it twice as difficult getting back to bed.

And so in this condition I returned home. After a year or two, I got some normality back: I have my memory, I can talk, but cannot converse with anyone for long. I can write, but not for long, my writing hand suddenly goes berserk and ceases to write. I can walk only a little way before I stop and sit. I have had three or four falls, one seriously.

I have a superb wife in Cynthia; she has helped me in every way; she got me to read every day to her; in that way I learnt how to converse with her, then my memory returned.

I can now remember Leamington Spa, Warwickshire; I can remember back to the age of three, being in a crêche just round the corner from 30 Grove Street. It is now demolished; it was behind the Methodist Chapel in Dale Road. The nurse was always singing the song of the day:

> Oh! the sun shines bright on Charlie Chaplin,
> His boots are a crackling,
> His little 'knicker bockers' they need mending,
> Before they send him to the Dardanelles!

That was the hit song in 1921. Not a bad memory for one who had a bad stroke – it was a rough passage, though. And of 'God, the Father' I shall always remember for the rest of my life! I have seen the Father. I am blessed – blessed are those who have not seen, but believe.